Anne Grenfell
Dr. Wilfred Grenfell
Father Isaac Jogues

The Wild Frontier

The Wild

Let us probe the silent places,
let us seek what luck betide us;
Let us journey to a lonely land I know.
There's a whisper in the night-wind,
there's a star agleam to guide us
And the Wild is calling, calling ... let us go.

–Robert W. Service

More tales from
The Remarkable Past

Frontier

By Pierre Berton

McClelland and Stewart

The Canadian Publishers
McClelland and Stewart Limited
25 Hollinger Road, Toronto

Endpapers by Tom McNeely
Maps by Jack McMaster

CANADIAN CATALOGUING IN PUBLICATION DATA

Berton, Pierre, 1920-
The wild frontier

Bibliography: p.
Includes index.
ISBN 0-7710-1360-4

1. Canada – History. 2. Canada – Biography.
I. Title.

FC163.B47 971 C78-001300-X
F1008.B47

Printed and bound in Canada

BOOKS BY PIERRE BERTON

The Royal Family
The Mysterious North
Klondike
Just Add Water and Stir
Adventures of a Columnist
Fast, Fast, Fast Relief
The Big Sell
The Comfortable Pew
The Cool, Crazy, Committed World of the Sixties
The Smug Minority
The National Dream
The Last Spike
Drifting Home
Hollywood's Canada
My Country
The Dionne Years
The Wild Frontier

PICTURE BOOKS
The New City (with Henri Rossier)
Remember Yesterday
The Great Railway

ANTHOLOGIES
Great Canadians
Pierre & Janet Berton's Canadian Food Guide
Historic Headlines

FOR YOUNGER READERS
The Golden Trail
The Secret World of Og

CONTENTS

Maps

Drawn by Jack McMaster

The Wild Frontier

PREFACE

The legacy of the frontier

We are all creatures of the wilderness, children of the frontier, even though the frontier has been pushed back into the mists of the North, even though the wilderness has given way to concrete. Wild and mysterious, savage and forbidding, this is the cyclorama against which the drama of our past has been staged; for better and for worse it has helped to fashion us into our distinctive Canadian mould.

The fabric of our heritage is woven from a tangled skein: from phrases about God's Country, the Shining Mountains, the Spell of the Yukon, the Great Lone Land . . . from the magic of Jefferys's pen illuminating half a hundred school texts with faithful renderings of Ojibway canoes, Red River carts, York boats and *travois*, not to mention Governor Simpson, Radishes and Gooseberries, and all those *coureurs de bois* . . . from folk songs rendered at Grade Eight pageants: Row, Brothers Row, the Stream Runs Fast and *The Song My Paddle Sings* (someone's vision of E. Pauline Johnson in braids and buckskin); and familiar ballads recited in church basements and male smokers ("There are strange things done 'neath the midnight sun . . . ") . . . out of boys' stories about Ungava Bob and the White Beaver; *Lost in the Barrens*; visions of Susanna Moodie and Catharine Parr Traill roughing it in the bush; films about Nanook and Grey Owl, the Loon's Necklace and the City of Gold; novels about Tay John's genesis and Big Bear's temptations; broadcasts about John Hornby's death on the tundra and Gabriel Dumont's triumphs on the plains; ghost stories of wendigoes, *loups garous*, and the Silent Hunter, the Walker of the Snows who leaves no footprints on the frosted trail . . . out of silk screen renderings of A. Y. Jackson lakes and Lawren Harris icebergs; Hegg photographs of Sheep Camp and the Chilkoot Pass; and all that institutional calendar art by Kelly, Woods, and Innes (Fraser challenging the black canyon for the Bank of Commerce; Champlain arriving in Huronia for Confederation Life) . . . out of seasonal festivals – Klondike Days, Buffalo Days, Frontier Days; out of surnames fuzzily recalled – Selkirk, Dollard, Tecumseh, Jolliet, Lacombe – and place names, long gone, half-remembered: Seven Oaks, Stadacona, Frog Lake, Fort Carlton . . . and out of other place names made newly familiar – Barkerville, Sainte-Marie, Fort Garry, Batoche – restored and revitalized, their artifacts reassembled down to the last forge and wool-carder, the rifle pits carefully outlined, the lawns manicured, the logs scrubbed for those who wish to experience vicariously the frontier life, living the history without the hardship. All this and more: a pastiche of childhood memories of canoe trips down frothing rivers, paddles rising in approximate unison on the approximate trail of the voyageurs . . . of faces caught and lost in the flare of the campfire, staring round-eyed into the murk of the encroaching firs in whose dark recesses one can almost feel the past . . . and of summers at the cottage by the lake where in the dark of the night or the mists of the morning one can still hear, as those who came before have heard, the mocking laughter of the loon, skipping like a pebble across the shrouded waters. It is a cry that never fails to send a shiver down the spine, for this is the authentic sound of the wilderness, sinister yet hypnotic; we hear it and reflect, sensing at that moment (even as the outboards whine) the solitude and the pain of the frontier – romance mingled with despair. If others see us as a sober people it is at least partly because the wild has made us so.

It is all ours, the bad and the good, this savage, noble, inspiring, shameful, unique heritage. We share it – Maritimers and Albertans, British Columbians and Quebeckers, Yukoners and Newfoundlanders. In spite of what Hollywood has tried to tell us, our frontier resembles no other. The American historian Frederick Jackson Turner may have been right when he argued, in a widely discussed theory, that his country's democracy sprang out of the frontier experience, developing from a constant series of adaptations to new environments. It is not true of Canada. The reader will note the word "paternal" cropping up from time to time in the pages that follow; it is a very Canadian word. From the New France of Isaac Jogues, the martyred Jesuit, to the Klondike of Sam Steele, the Mounted Policeman, the Canadian frontier has been controlled and ordered by a fatherly authoritarianism with the reins of power tightly held by absentee landlords – the monarchs of France and England and their deputies; the governors of the Hudson's Bay Company in London; the merchants of St. John's; and a pantheon of Ottawa panjandrums in the Ministry of the Interior, the Indian department, and the Mounted Police – a cohort of appointed officials who have always known what is best for people and places beyond their ken, just as the Jesuits of Jogues's day thought they knew what was best for the Hurons. The colonial attitude extends into our own time. The Yukon and the Northwest Territories continue to be controlled by civil servants who act as surrogates for those interests that have always seen them as ripe for plunder.

This attitude goes a long way back – to the days of John Jewitt and the sea otter trade, to the great gold rushes to the Fraser, Cariboo, and Klondike. The wilderness was to be "tamed" which meant that it was to be exploited by outsiders. Cariboo Cameron was only one of many who found treasure in British Columbia but squandered it elsewhere.

Similarly, the great plains of the North West were settled as part of a National Policy that saw them merely as providing raw resources to feed the East. It was not that Ottawa did not care; but it cared the way the Jesuits cared about the Hurons, with good intentions and a singular blindness. It created a mounted constabulary to save the Indians from the Americans. It was implicit that the Force was also expected to save the invading white settlers (many of whom were Americans) from the Indians. Keeping the peace meant keeping the natives quiet.

Thus did the nation acquire its indestructible frontier myth. It is based, of course, on historic truth, much of it admirable; every Canadian feels a tremor of pride when he reads the tales of the Silent Force. The Musical Ride is our Wild West Show, beautifully groomed and disciplined in the Canadian manner: no whooping Indians nor sharp-shooting Annie Oakleys, only the calm, measured movements of the men in scarlet, cantering symbolically across the coulée-riven prairie, never turning a hair of their close-cropped heads when disaster threatens or evil stands unmasked, bringing law, order, and stability to the unruly frontier.

But this is not the whole truth. The Mounted Police are living testimony to a firm Canadian conviction, nurtured on the frontier, that Father Knows Best. It is the same conviction that made the majority cry "Trust Trudeau!" when in October, 1970, the midnight knock on the door roused from their sleep some hundreds of innocents who were thrown into prison and denied *habeas corpus* for breaking a law that had not been invoked when they went to bed. When order is threatened in Canada, what price freedom?

The Mounted Police kept the Indians in check with talk of a Great White Parent across the sea, but the truth is that *they* were the real parents, stern yet forgiving, of all the supposedly errant frontier children, white and Indian alike. That is the way Canadians wanted it and still want it. Not for them the rough, haphazard, and often flawed democracy of the American frontier. They have much preferred the efficiency of a Sam Steele. Our frontier was as safe as the Anglican Church, if a little circumscribed. What did it matter if the police hauled in Freda Maloof, the Turkish Whirlwind, for performing a hootchie-kootchie dance in a Dawson theatre, or threatened to deport an irreverent vaudevillean for making fun of the Queen? This is not a country in which civil libertarians have flourished. The police made the frontier safe, if not for democracy, at least from dissent – and dissent, on the edge of civilization, could be both violent and bloody. That, at least, we have been spared.

Historically, the Force has always made the law fit the circumstances. There is nothing new about steaming open the mail. It happened in 1895 to the unfortunate Corporal Dickson, confined to prison for allowing Almighty Voice, his Cree prisoner, to escape. Dickson discovered that thirty of his personal letters had been opened by his superior officer, Moffat. He laid a charge against him under the Post Office Act but got nowhere because Moffat was able to prove that he had opened the mail on orders from his superiors. The police attitude was, so what?

Canadian frontier policy has required big government. Its double purpose, west of the Shield, was to save the country from falling into the hands of the Americans and to save the frontiersmen from themselves. The Canadian Radio-Television and Telecommunications Commission, the Federal Transport Board, the Family Allowance Act, and universal medicare are links in a chain that stretches back to James Douglas's Cariboo Road and Sam Steele's law, made up on the banks of the White Horse Rapids, which dictated that nobody would be allowed to drown himself. All are part of what might be called, with neither pride nor cynicism, the Canadian Way.

That Way springs out of the environment. The Precambrian

desert that unites so much of the country visually (making the golf course at Yellowknife look very much like the cottage country of Muskoka) has also confined us. The American frontier was pushed steadily westward, but the Precambrian presence blocked a similar kind of movement to our own North West. Canada was static at a time when America was kinetic. As this book demonstrates, the frontier attracts unusual men and women – dreamers and mystics like Cariboo Cameron; adventurous schoolboys of Grenfell's mould; romantics such as Hubbard and Wallace; men of action like Steele; zealots like Jogues; and resourceful youngsters like Jewitt. How many entrepreneurs left Canada for the United States because their western frontier was barred to them? (We know that a tavern keeper named Cody from Toronto Township was one; his son became Buffalo Bill.) This, too, has had its effect on the kind of people we are.

Because of the Shield, Canadian expansion lagged a generation behind that of the United States. The Americans had built three rail lines to the Pacific before we finally bridged the Precambrian barrier. While the Canadian entrepreneurs of the early twentieth century were still obsessed with the idea of railways, their American counterparts had already ventured into the field of automobiles and aircraft. The gap has not been closed, and that, too, is a legacy of our geography.

For most of us, the frontier lies far enough in the past and far enough from our own experience to be romantic. The bank calendars, the Service poems, the Hollywood films, the boys' books, the Jefferys drawings have all emphasized the adventure and the glamour. We see the frontier in terms of scenery – the plumed mountains piled like sugar in the sky; the toothpaste glaciers squeezing down to mint-green waters; the tinsel cataracts garlanding the scarps; the Tom Thomson lakes, ragged in the wind; the Emily Carr rain forests, eerily viridian. We forget that all this tourist brochure magic once represented an appalling series of obstacles to those who first encountered them. We tend to overlook the pain of exploration. The country was opened up at dreadful cost. Most frontier adventures are also chronicles of human misery, and those that follow are no exception.

Our barriers have been largely environmental; in the United States they have also been human. Canadian frontier literature deals with starvation, loneliness, long portages, crushing packloads, exhausting climbs, the tracking of canoes, and the natural hazards of the trail. The Americans write more often in terms of violence – of scalpings, arrows in the chest, cabins in flames, war drums and smoke signals, and the massacre of wagon trains.

We rarely fought the Indians; we used them – not because our forbears were less cruel or less violent but because the nature of the Canadian frontier dictated it. Canada was a land of fur-bearing animals; the Indians were the key to that trade. John Jewitt's captor, Chief Maquinna of the Nootka, could massacre a shipload of sailors and escape punishment because trade was more important than revenge. The French sent Father Jogues as plenipotentiary to the Iroquois because they wanted to trade in peace. The Hurons suffered the presence of the Jesuits for exactly the same reason.

The Americans did not have the same needs. For them, the Indians were merely in the way – an obstacle to be removed. We can therefore thank the Canadian environment for the Canadian tradition of non-violence, at least as regards the native peoples. Once the furs were gone, of course, we neglected the Indians as badly as anyone else. The conditions in the 1890s on the reserve that nurtured Almighty Voice were as squalid as those of the fellahin of Egypt, but not worse than this writer has observed on the shores of Great Slave Lake in the modern North.

The frontier presents another question. Why the attraction? What impels solid citizens to leave the comfort of their hearths to travel to a lonely and inhospitable realm? One reason is ignorance; the hardships are not envisaged by those who long for the wilderness or, if perceived, perceived only as challenges. Is it not axiomatic that the further away and the more inaccessible the frontier, the more attractive it seems? Familiarity with the wild can breed caution. Grenfell, the missionary doctor, discovered that. He could not lure Canadians to Labrador; it was too close for comfort. His young workers came from the sophisticated colleges of the Ivy League, his medical personnel from England, Australia, and the United States. To most of the people described in these pages, the frontier was an eternity away; Jogues came from France, Grenfell and Jewitt from England, the Hubbards from New York. Cameron's frontier was almost ten thousand miles by land and water from Glengarry County; Steele's lay beyond the forbidding rampart of the Shield. To each, the wilderness was alluring in its mystery; they knew little about the conditions they would face, nor did they want to know. Each gave his own reasons for leaving home to tempt the unknown: Grenfell and Jogues to save souls and bodies; Steele to carve out a career; Hubbard to write articles; his wife to complete her husband's work; Jewitt and Cameron to make fortunes from trade or treasure. Were these the only reasons, or were they plausible excuses, acceptable to friends, relatives, neighbours, and society at large? The evidence suggests that all of these quite extraordinary if humanly imperfect individuals set off with mixed motives, and some that had little to do with ambition, wealth, or even evangelism. They went because they could not resist the irresistible; because they belonged to that breed which cannot endure the humdrum; because they wished to test themselves, body and soul, even at the peril of their lives; and because, within themselves, there were their own frontiers, and these too, must be attacked and conquered.

ONE

The slavery of John Jewitt

Vancouver Island: 1803

"*. . . Behind the village – mysterious and gloomy – rose the green wall of the forest into whose dark recesses the Indians rarely ventured. Who knew what demons lurked among those creeping mosses, what spirits were concealed in that infinity of waist-high bracken? Above the tangle of salal and grape, above the webwork of rotting logs, above the grotesque shapes of plate-sized fungi rose the great trees – the monstrous cedars, the towering firs – blotting out the sun and cloaking the forest in perpetual twilight. The Indians preferred the wide beaches, the open ocean to this ghost world . . .*"

John Jewitt, the armourer, was cleaning muskets at his bench in the steerage of the trading ship *Boston* when he became aware of a commotion on the deck above – a running and a thumping, the sound of blows, harsh human cries, alarming splashes, whistles and rattles and all manner of pagan outburst. He seized his musket and scrambled up the steerage companionway. As he lifted the hatch, a brown hand smeared with red paint poked through the opening and grasped at his head. Jewitt's short hair saved his life; the ribbon slipped off; he fell backward, trying to ward off the axe blow that gashed his skull and sent him reeling into the hold as the hatch slammed shut. There he lay, stunned and senseless, for the next four hours, regaining consciousness occasionally, struggling to stand upright, toppling and fainting from loss of blood, while the war cries and triumphant songs of the Nootka echoed above and his shipmates died and were decapitated with their own knives.

The date was March 22, 1803. The place was Nootka Sound on the sodden western shore of Vancouver Island, as isolated from European civilization then as the coasts of Hokkaido or Togoland. Some three hundred miles to the north, Russian territory began; some six hundred miles to the south, the Spanish domain ended. The islands between, and the mainland drained by those two great rivers, the Fraser and the Columbia, yet unnamed, were the realm of the Indians. Only one white man, Alexander Mackenzie, had managed to force his way through the mountains from the interior plains to the Pacific Coast. The expeditions of Fraser, Thompson, and Lewis and Clark lay in the future. The wilderness stretched unbroken from the beaches of the Pacific to the shores of Lake Ontario.

And yet for a quarter of a century the white man's ships had been anchoring in Nootka Sound. At one time Spanish officers had feasted there from silver plates, proposed toasts from crystal goblets, and organized displays of fireworks. The natives were so friendly that James Cook named the little bay on whose shores their village stood, Friendly Cove. Now, deserted for a decade by the white man, it was friendly no longer.

In the dark of the hold, some time during that brutal March afternoon, John Jewitt regained his senses. He was a young man, barely twenty, with a long solemn face and full, sensitive lips. Above him he could hear the Indians yelling and chanting; were they saving him for torture? For a long time he remained in "this horrid state of suspense" until at last the hatch opened and a familiar face peered down – a noble face with an unmistakable Roman nose, smeared with black and red paint, belonging to a man Jewitt called king: Maquinna, the head chief of the village of Yuquot. At the Indian's bidding, Jewitt climbed to the deck and listened to his proposal.

"John – I speak," Maquinna said. "You no say no. You say no – daggers come!"

Jewitt did not say no. His life had been saved by the chief himself, who had ordered the hatch closed and had called off his assailants, not for reasons of compassion or prudence, but because he needed a man with a blacksmith's skills. His proposal was that Jewitt be his slave for life, work for him, repair his muskets and daggers, and fight for him in battles. Jewitt, drenched in his own blood, one eye swollen shut, surrounded by naked Indians clamouring for his death, their daggers raised to strike, had no choice. On Maquinna's order, he signalled his submission by kneeling before his captor and kissing his hands and feet.

In various corners of the globe at that time, white men were making slaves of aborigines. But here, against the dank backdrop of the rain forest, the position was reversed. For more than two years John Jewitt would be the personal property of Maquinna, accorded the status of a dog, a canoe, or a cedar-bark robe.

He was shivering uncontrollably from a combination of cold, weakness, and plain terror. Maquinna went to the captain's cabin and returned with a greatcoat, which he threw over the blacksmith's shoulders. He allowed his captive a swallow of rum, then led him by the hand to the quarter-deck, "where the most horrid sight presented itself that my eyes have ever witnessed." Arranged in a row were the decapitated heads of the crew, twenty-five in all. Maquinna ordered one of his people to bring a head to Jewitt to identify. It was the captain's. He was then forced to identify each head that was not too badly mangled to be unrecognizable. Jewitt now realized that every one of his shipmates had been massacred.

Maquinna continued his solicitude. He bound Jewitt's head wound with the blacksmith's silk kerchief and, at Jewitt's suggestion, dressed it with a tobacco leaf from the ship's stores. Then he ordered his new slave to set sail for Friendly Cove. Jewitt cut the cables and sent some natives aloft to loose the sails "which they did in a very bungling manner." Nonetheless, with a fair wind, he managed to get the ship to the cove where, on Maquinna's order, he beached her.

Here, at the village of Yuquot, the head chief was greeted with the hammering of sticks on the houses and blazing torches. Women and children ran out of the cedar lodges to hail him. Maquinna's own lodge was enormous – one hundred and fifty feet long and forty feet wide; it housed one hundred persons, half of them members of his extended family and half of them slaves. Five hundred warriors arrived to celebrate the capture of the *Boston*, but when it was suggested that Jewitt be put to death, the chief drove the visitors from his house.

Jewitt was young in the ways of the world, but he had a great deal of common sense. He understood (far better than most young men of that age) that it was foolhardy to battle overwhelming odds. He must make the best of things, and if that meant placating his captors, so be it. They had murdered his comrades, men who had slung their hammocks next to his on the long voyage round the Horn and up the coastline of the two Americas, but he put the memory out of his mind. He set out to ingratiate himself with his new master, charming Maquinna by taking his young son on his knee and stringing a necklace from the metal buttons on his coat as an impromptu gift.

But he could not sleep that night because of the pain of his wound and the anxiety he felt for his life. Maquinna had warned him that some of his people might try to stab him in the dark. He had never before felt so alone. Then, at midnight, an Indian rushed in to inform the chief that another survivor was on the beached ship – a white man who had knocked him down.

Lying in the dark, the captive allowed himself a glimmer of hope. A Christian companion! But who could it be? After some thought he concluded that the other survivor was John Thompson, a tough, surly sailmaker from Philadelphia who had been at work between decks before the massacre. There could be no doubt that the Indians intended to kill him. How might he be saved? Jewitt worked out a deception: Thompson was about forty and looked older; he would convince Maquinna that this man was his father and ask that his life be spared.

As dawn broke, he dozed off, only to be wakened by the chief who informed him that the man on the ship was to be killed. Jewitt followed the chief to the boat, taking Maquinna's young son by the hand. A palaver followed: did the men of the tribe wish to spare the life of the second survivor? With one voice they shouted for his blood.

Now Jewitt acted out his scheme. He pointed to Maquinna's son, still clutching his hand, and asked the chief if he loved him. Maquinna replied that he did. Jewitt asked the boy if he loved his father; the boy nodded. Whereupon the blacksmith cried, "And I also love mine!" With that he threw himself at his master's feet and, with tears in his eyes, begged him to spare his father's life. If his father died, Jewitt declared, then he too wished to be killed.

Maquinna was moved by this piece of theatre; moreover, as the blacksmith had shrewdly concluded, he was reluctant to lose his valuable new slave. The chief agreed that if the man on board should prove to be Jewitt's father, his life would be spared. He ordered Jewitt to find and bring the man to him. Jewitt climbed into the hold and was overjoyed to find that it was indeed Thompson, unharmed except for a slight wound on the nose. He outlined his charade to the older man explaining that his safety would depend on his playing the role of parent. Thompson's skill with a needle was also an asset. Maquinna realized that he would be useful making sails for the great forty-foot dugouts, which his people took to sea.

The following day, the Indians stripped the ship of everything movable – of arms, powder, sails, and masts. Jewitt managed to filch the captain's records and writing desk together with a Bible, a prayer book, and an account book in which he determined to keep a running chronicle of his captivity.

The Indians set up the ship's cannon on the beach, and when, three days later, two American vessels sailed into the sound, they were driven off, an incident that the impetuous Maquinna immediately regretted, knowing it would frighten other traders away. That was the last thing he wanted. His people were consummate traders, their shrewdness honed by twenty-five years of barter with English and Yankee seamen. The prize the visitors sought was the skin of the sea otter, a pelt that could fetch sums ranging from thirty to more than one hundred dollars. The day was long gone when a skin could be purchased for a dozen glass beads. Inflation had come to the Pacific Coast. The Indians wanted iron utensils, guns, metal jewellery, and, above all, the thick sheets of copper that were highly prized as gifts to be dispensed at the potlatch. Possessions in Nootka society signified status, and if Maquinna possessed more status than any other household chief at Friendly Cove, it was not only because of his inherited rank but also because of what he owned.

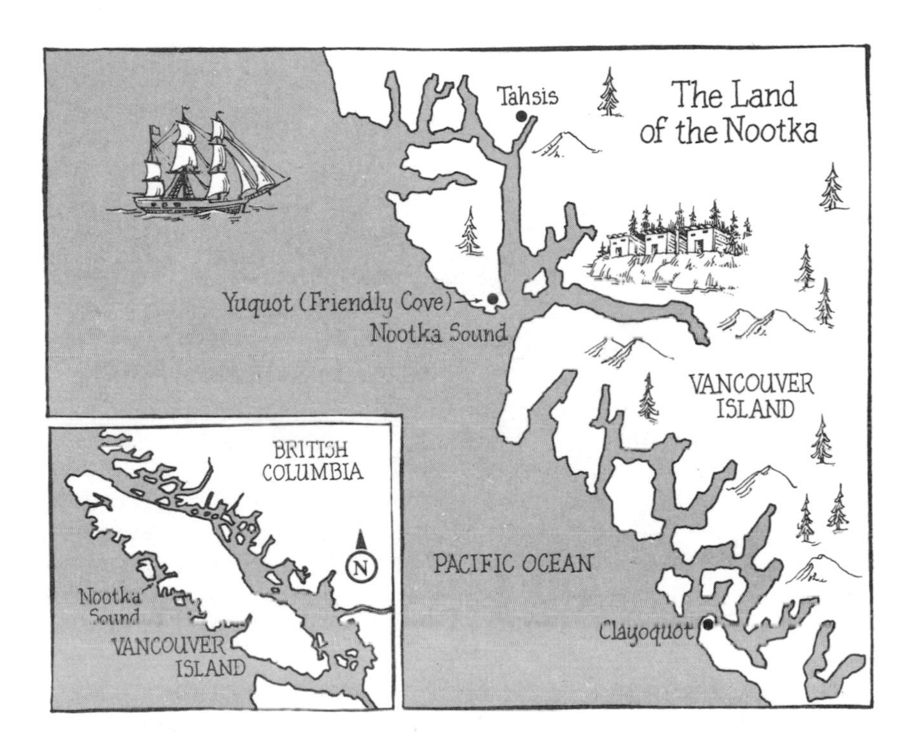

Now he was eager to show off his newest chattels to his peers. In the week that followed, people from twenty neighbouring bands poured into Yuquot to view the captives. Maquinna and Jewitt climbed to the roof of the lodge and drummed with sticks. Thompson was detailed to show off the plundered firearms. These the visitors examined with great curiosity, running up and down the beach, some carrying as many as eight muskets upside down. A feast of whale blubber and herring roe followed. Maquinna's son, wearing a wolf-mask, executed a spirited dance, followed by the chief himself in his sea otter robe, a whistle in his mouth, a rattle in his hand. For two hours Maquinna danced with enormous vigour, springing into the air from a squatting position and constantly turning on his heels as he landed to the insistent thrum of his fellow chiefs' drumming with sticks on hollow logs. There were presents for the visitors: one hundred muskets, one hundred looking glasses, twenty barrels of powder, for the giving of presents among the Nootka Indians, as among all the Pacific Coast tribes, was a means of achieving and maintaining status and the key event in the elaborate potlatch ceremonies, in which every tribe periodically indulged.

It might be said that this attitude toward conspicuous waste – the by-product of an affluent social system based on the largess of sea and forest – was not unlike that of the white civilizations of Europe, whose kings and lesser nobility were devoted to the profligate display of wealth. The parallel is superficial. For John Jewitt, late of Lincolnshire, the change in lifestyle must have been shattering, the culture shock numbing. Among the dripping cedars of Nootka Sound, there was little to remind him of the man he had been or the society in which he had been reared. The ethics, the customs, the human relationships were totally foreign.

Even the ship was gone, destroyed in a fire set accidentally by a pilfering native. Most of the cargo, and all of the provisions, were destroyed, a serious blow to the two slaves who had hoped to live on familiar fare and who would now be reduced to eating blubber, seal oil, and dogfish. All that Jewitt managed to save were his tools, a box of chocolate, and a case of port. The Indians preferred rum, some of which they salvaged. The resultant debauch was so rowdy that the two white men fled into the woods until midnight. When they returned, they found every man in Maquinna's lodge stretched on the floor, drunk. Jewitt thought immediately of escape – but to where? With no ships in the vicinity – and no white settlement of any kind – flight would amount to suicide. He was trapped. He thanked his Maker that the rest of the rum had been destroyed in the fire; otherwise, he knew, the Indians would surely have killed both slaves in the course of a drunken orgy. He found a cask of gin still whole, bored a hole in the side, and drained it on to the ground before the Indians were roused.

A less resourceful man, or a less adaptable one, could scarcely have endured the months that followed. But Jewitt belonged to that breed of men – they are to be found on every frontier – who are best described as "survivors." Thompson was not of this temperament. A rigid and stubborn seaman, consumed by hatred for the people who had massacred his comrades, he could not have lived a day without the steadying influence of his fellow captive. John Jewitt had yet to attain his majority, but it was he, not Thompson, who acted as a wise father toward a stubborn and quixotic child. Maquinna himself noticed it and was puzzled by it, remarking that Thompson had a disagreeable disposition compared to that of his "son"; the chief concluded that the good-tempered Jewitt must have had a very kind mother.

Jewitt's real father, also a blacksmith, had thought him intelligent enough to take him out of the local school in Lincolnshire in favour of an academy in a nearby town, hoping eventually to apprentice him to a surgeon. But young Jewitt preferred his father's trade and excelled at it. Later, when the family moved to the seaport of Hull, he began to yearn for adventure in lands beyond the ocean's rim, devouring books of travel, notably the *Voyages* of Captain James Cook, one of the best-sellers of the day. Cook and his crew were the first white men to enter Nootka Sound and the first to set foot on Vancouver Island. Reading the explorer's account of that incredible realm of gigantic trees, outlandish sea creatures, and bizarre ocean-going natives dressed in bark and skins, Jewitt was fired with a longing as old as time: to see a world that few other men had seen, to witness customs unknown and mysterious, and, of course, to profit from the experience. His chance came when Captain John Salter brought the *Boston* into Hull for repairs. Salter was headed for the northwest coast of North America and the sea otter trade. Jewitt jumped at the offer to sail with her as armourer. Away he went, mindful of his father's counsel to be "honest, industrious, frugal and temperate" and to "let the Bible be your guide" – advice that would serve him well in the travail that was to follow.

From the outset Thompson insisted that Jewitt keep a journal. He was himself illiterate but had been so long at sea that he considered a journal indispensable. He even offered to cut his finger to supply blood with which to write, but the resourceful blacksmith made his own ink by boiling blackberry juice with powdered charcoal. His inkwell was a clamshell; his pens were ravens' quills. The result was an invaluable anthropological document, a detailed account of the customs of a primitive people whose way of life had not changed greatly since the coming of the white man. Without it, our knowledge of early Nootka culture would be fragmentary.

Both men were the personal chattels of their master. This swiftly became obvious when Thompson, after being teased by Maquinna's young son, knocked him to the floor. The chief, entering at that moment, seized a musket. Thompson, who was strong, powerful, and an expert boxer, showed no fear but bared his chest and dared his master to fire. It was a brave but foolhardy gesture, and had Jewitt not entered at that moment, his comrade would have died. Maquinna made it clear that Thompson existed on sufferance; if anything should happen to Jewitt, the sailmaker would be killed at once. A council meeting followed at which Thompson's death was demanded to avenge the insult to the young prince. Again, Jewitt interceded for his "father" and again Maquinna spared the older man's life. Yet this narrow escape in no way curbed the sailmaker's temper. A few weeks later he struck the eldest son of another chief – an eighteen-year-old who had called him a white slave. For the third time, Maquinna saved him.

Jewitt saw no purpose in provoking their captors. He was later to write that he had determined from the first moment of capture to adopt a conciliatory attitude and to conform as far as possible to their customs and manner of thinking, "trusting that the same divine goodness that has rescued me from death would not always suffer me to languish in captivity among these heathen." He maintained a cheerful mien, joined in the sports and tricks of the Indians, made fishhooks and daggers for the men and ornaments for the wives and children. He also picked up some of the Nootka language to reinforce his knowledge of Chinook, the traders' jargon.

Thompson refused to learn a word, saying he hated the heathen and "their cursed lingo." He made no attempt to hide his bitterness, adding that he would destroy the entire race if he had the ships and guns to do so. He had spent almost his entire life at sea, running away from home in Philadelphia at the age of eight to ship across the Atlantic as a cabin boy. Pressed into service in England, he had served in the British Navy for twenty-seven years, being present at the great Channel battle of June 1, 1794, when Lord Howe defeated the French fleet. He was very much the arrogant sailor, taking bitter offence at the slightest insult, real or fancied, and continually bemoaning his lowered status. In this, oddly, he resembled his captors, who were equally obsessed by status and who took immediate and often violent umbrage at the most inconsequential slight. In Thompson's view, "to a brave sailor like him, who had fought the French and Spanish with glory, it was a punishment worse than death to be a slave to such a poor, ignorant, despicable set of beings." Jewitt's attitude was more elastic: life among the Nootka might be harsh, but it was better than the grave.

The people of Yuquot set their faces toward the sea. Behind the village – mysterious and gloomy – rose the green wall of the forest into whose dark recesses the Indians rarely ventured. Who knew what demons lurked among those creeping mosses, what spirits were concealed in that infinity of waist-high bracken? Above the tangle of salal and grape, above the webwork of rotting logs, above the grotesque shapes of plate-sized fungi rose the great trees – the monstrous cedars, the towering firs – blotting out the sun and cloaking the forest in perpetual twilight. The Indians preferred the wide beaches, the open ocean to this ghost world; what little contact they had with their cousins, the Kwakiutls, on the opposite side of the island, was generally made by sea.

The village was not large. It consisted of some twenty houses, most of them in a row, differing in size according to the importance of the chief of each family. The smallest house was forty feet in length; all were forty feet in width. The ridge poles were built of immense cedar logs – Maquinna's was eight feet in circumference. The roofs were lapped cedar shingles, covered by planks held down with heavy stones and extending out to shelter the lodge from the rain. The posts supporting the ridge poles were carved with human heads and painted.

The political structure was loose, its main unit being the extended family, whose members, presided over by a hereditary chief, lived under one roof. Maquinna, whom the white men called king, was in no sense an absolute ruler, being no more than the highest-ranking house chief in the loose confederacy that made up this one village. Twenty-five similar villages, containing perhaps ten thousand persons, were strewn along the western shores of Vancouver Island for two hundred miles.

As slaves, Jewitt and Thompson dined with members of their family, but not from the common tray. They sat on the ground, ate with their fingers, and scooped up soup and oil with clamshells. At feasts, where guests were carefully seated in order of rank, the slaves were allowed the leftovers. As Jewitt described it, this was "a most awkward thing for us, at first, to have to lug home with us, in our hands and arms, the blubber of fish . . . . But we soon became reconciled to it." Their feeding habits were erratic: porpoise meat one day, clams and fermented whale oil the next, boiled salmon the third, and often nothing but nettle stalks gathered in the fields. When there was nothing to eat in his master's house Jewitt would beg for food elsewhere; it was rarely refused.

The two men spent their Sundays in prayer and Bible reading; it helped alleviate their despair, for they felt that no ship would ever come to release them. They would walk to the banks of a freshwater pond about a mile from the village and here, after bathing and putting on clean clothes, Jewitt would read some chapters in the Bible and the prayer appointed for that day by the Church of England. The two men would end with a "fervent prayer to the Almighty that He would deign still to watch over and preserve our lives, rescue us from the hands of the savages and permit us once more to behold a Christian land."

Maquinna, who did not object to these ceremonies, reacted

strongly to Jewitt's keeping a journal. He was convinced that his slave was "writing bad about him." Jewitt made his entries secretly while his master was off fishing. That Maquinna was sensitive to what others thought or said of him is clear from the record. He was a man of mercurial temperament: as Jewitt learned, his touchiness had sparked the massacre aboard the *Boston*.

When the ship had anchored in Nootka Sound, about five miles above the village, on March 12, there had been no hint of hostility or discontent among the Indians. Maquinna came aboard the following day, wearing his knee-length mantle of black sea otter skin, accompanied by several villagers in long cloaks of woven cedar bark. The chief's appearance was extraordinary. His legs, face, and arms were covered with red paint; his eyebrows were painted black in two broad crescent-shaped stripes; his hair, shiny with oil, was fastened in a bun above his head and powdered with white eagle down. He had no difficulty in making himself understood in English.

Captain Salter gave him the obligatory presents of rum, molasses, and ship's biscuit and traded fishhooks and knives for fresh salmon. It was too early to buy otter skins; Salter had put in at Nootka for wood, water, and fresh fish because Maquinna was said to be friendlier than the Indian chiefs farther to the north. And so he appeared to be. He was invited to dine on March 15 and again on March 19, on which occasion the captain made him a gift of a double-barrelled shotgun; it pleased Maquinna greatly.

Two days later he returned with a present of nine pairs of ducks, complaining that the gun was no good. He had broken the lock. Salter was offended by the remark, which he perceived as a mark of contempt for the gift; touchiness, it would appear, was a common failing among whites and Indians alike. He called Maquinna a liar, seized the gun, and flung it into the cabin. He called out to his armourer, "This fellow has broken this beautiful fowling piece; see if you can fix it."

Maquinna understood exactly what Salter had said. To a man of his uncommon sensitivity, it was enraging; but he repressed his anger, repeatedly putting his hand to his throat and rubbing his chest, in order, as he later told Jewitt in a colourful and apt phrase, to keep down his heart, which was rising in his throat and threatening to choke him. In that instant, all the insults, all the demeaning incidents with the white traders over the past quarter of a century crowded in upon him.

Yet when he returned on March 22 to join a group of his fellow tribesmen on board the ship, he appeared good humoured. He was wearing a mask and carrying a whistle, which he blew as he and his men danced around on the deck. This feigned gaiety was a subterfuge; the chief's purpose was calculated and deadly.

As the ship was preparing to sail, Maquinna persuaded the captain to take on a load of fresh salmon. The first mate and nine men were accordingly sent ashore in a longboat on a fishing expedition. Thus was the crew's number depleted. It was at this point that Jewitt was in the steerage working at his bench and Thompson was between decks preparing sails. The steward also was on shore, washing clothes; Salter was on the quarter-deck; the second officer and the rest of the crew were hoisting the launch aboard, preparatory to leaving. Since there were not enough crew to complete this task, some of the Indians were pressed into service. None was armed, all having been carefully searched before boarding the ship. But they outnumbered the seamen four to one, and it was thus a simple matter, on Maquinna's signal, for each to reach into the pocket of the sailor beside him, pull out his knife, and dispatch him.

The signal was clear enough. Maquinna simply pushed Salter into the ocean, where a canoeload of Indian women beat him to death with paddles. With the decks running with blood, Maquinna sent a crew of Indians to kill the men on shore and cut off their heads. The corpses on the deck were also beheaded, the torsos thrown into the sea and the heads arranged in order of status on the foredeck, with the captain's at the top end and the cook's at the bottom. Status in death as in life was important to the Nootka, now capering about in a dance of victory.

How was it possible that a single remark could have had such bloody consequences? Though part of the answer lies in the character of Maquinna, the larger explanation has to do with the fierce competition for the sea otter trade in the sinuous fiords of the north Pacific Coast. It had begun in 1785, some years after Cook's men returned to England with a fortune from the sale of furs in China; it had reached its crest just after the turn of the century. At this time the trade was dominated by Americans, with Boston the leading home port for trading vessels, of which there might be as many as fifteen along the coast in a single season. The British, who had started the trade, melted away in the face of Yankee competition, which was fierce and sometimes bloody. With a single exception all Indian attacks on trading vessels were directed against American ships, whose crews used every artifice to obtain the increasingly scarcer pelts. In the words of the explorer Alexander Mackenzie, the coast trade had been "left to American adventurers, who without regularity or capital, or the desire of conciliating future confidence, look altogether to the interest of the moment

. . . . They, therefore, collect all the skins they can procure and in any manner that suits them." Some skippers thought nothing of kidnapping a chief and holding him hostage to obtain the coveted skins; others used threats, force, even theft. There was one instance of an entire village being destroyed because the natives were reluctant to trade. The British had always bartered at arm's length, avoiding the villages and insisting that the natives remain in their canoes at shipside. But as the competition grew fiercer, American captains began to allow them on to the deck so that the Indians considered it their right to be aboard. It was a classic case of familiarity breeding contempt.

Sporadic attacks on Yankee trading ships, tentative at first, had been occurring since the early 1790s. Revenge was a major motive. The Indians, holding to "a doctrine of vicarious responsibility," as F.W. Howay, the West Coast historian, has called it, made no distinction among sea captains. It was the class that was being attacked, not the individual. As Jewitt was to write, they would "wreak their vengeance upon the first vessel or boat crew that offers, making the innocent too frequently suffer for the wrongs of the guilty." And there was something else that perhaps did not occur to the traders: to the Indians, all white men looked much the same and thus were the same.

Maquinna confirmed much of this to Jewitt. As the chief came to know the armourer better, he regaled him with tales of white men who had shot Indians, specifically condemning Esteban José Martinez, the Spanish don who had established himself at Yuquot in 1789 and taken possession of the surrounding territory in the name of the King of Spain. Martinez was responsible for the murder of Maquinna's brother, Qualicum, and this indicated to Jewitt that a thirst for revenge as much as Salter's insult had driven him to kill the *Boston*'s crew. There was something else: the fierce desire, so deeply ingrained in all the West Coast tribes, to emulate and if possible outstrip their peers in such triumphs. The attack upon the *Boston* was the worst in a decade of sporadic incursions; it gave Maquinna enormous prestige.

The chief was determined not to lose his prize captives. He warned Jewitt that if he tried to escape, he would kill him. The same fate awaited him if he tried to defect to one of the other chiefs who coveted him. To emphasize his point Maquinna cited the case of seven deserters from another ship, the *Manchester* of Philadelphia, who had sought shelter with him and subsequently tried to defect to another chief, Wickinninish, his great rival, on Clayoquot Sound. Maquinna had had them all put to death.

His was no idle warning. The most valuable property among the

Nootka was a slave, and Jewitt was a pearl among slaves. Undercover attempts were made to lure both white men from Maquinna. Neighbouring chiefs secretly offered to help them escape, but Jewitt suspected, rightly, that this was only a ruse to steal them in much the same way that a society woman might steal her hostess's chef. A younger sister of Maquinna's chief wife purposely made Jewitt her favourite; because of a defective eye, injured in an accident, she could not marry. She tried to induce the blacksmith to return with her to the village of her father, the powerful Wickinninish. He refused.

In July a ship appeared on the horizon. It did not stop. "I shall not attempt," Jewitt wrote, "to describe our disappointment – my heart sank within me, and I felt as though it was my destiny never more to behold a Christian face."

Yuquot was the summer village of the Nootka. When September came, the whole tribe moved to winter quarters at Tahsis, about thirty miles up the sound, taking with them in their canoes all their belongings, including the cedar planks from the roofs. This meant there would be no further opportunity that season to spot a ship coming into the sound. At Tahsis, sheltered from the winter storms, the Nootka people could enjoy the harvest of the salmon run, catching as many as twenty-five hundred fish in a single day and feasting on roe, a great delicacy, which Jewitt found loathsome. "Scarcely anything," he wrote, "can be more repugnant to the European palate."

Thompson, who had annoyed many of the tribesmen by his habit of knocking at the stick ornaments projecting from their noses, now proceeded to gain favour by making Maquinna a sail for his canoe and clothes cut from European cloth, in particular a royal mantle of coloured patches sewn together, trimmed with the finest otter skin. On this Joseph's Coat were five or six rows of gilt buttons, closely set around the bottom above the fur. The chief wore it with enormous pride, strutting about as the buttons tinkled and exclaiming that no Nootka could have made such a garment. He was immensely vain and in the fashion of his people would sometimes spend a full hour painting his face, only to rub all the colour off and start afresh when the results failed to please him.

It is a sad commentary on Canadian history that only a handful of Indians stand out from the almost faceless mass of tribesmen as distinct individuals, subject to human strengths and weaknesses, vanities and whims, and all those diverse and contradictory qualities that differentiate real people from plaster saints or dark villains. Tecumseh and Joseph Brant in the East, Big Bear and Crowfoot on the Plains, Mackenzie's "English Chief" and Hearne's

Matonabbee in the North belong to this select few. But Maquinna, perhaps more than any other, comes through in the memoirs of a number of white seamen – the most detailed being Jewitt's – as a fully rounded character: volatile, vain, cowardly, bold, acquisitive, shrewd, passionate, sensitive, proud, vengeful, generous, selfish, sagacious, temperamental, and always fascinating. We may not understand him but, through Jewitt, we can feel we have met him.

The great mystery, which has never been entirely unravelled, is whether or not there were two Maquinnas. Was the Maquinna who, in 1778, spotted the tops of three sticks above the horizon and watched them grow bigger until they took the shape of a great canoe with white wings (it was, in fact, Cook's three-masted *Discovery*), the same Maquinna who, twenty-five years later, destroyed the *Boston*? We cannot be certain, for there is one piece of evidence suggesting that the original Maquinna may have died before Jewitt's day. In September, 1795, Captain Charles Bishop encountered him at Friendly Cove, extremely ill with ague. Some weeks later Maquinna's rival, Wickinninish, told Bishop that his fellow chieftain had died and that he had attended his funeral. In Nootka society a chief's name is not his property; it is passed on to others. (In the early twentieth century there was still a Maquinna living among the Nootka.) Thus it is possible, if Wickinninish spoke the truth (and that is open to question), that the man who enslaved Jewitt was not the one who greeted Cook and his successors.

Yet it is difficult to read Jewitt without coming to the conclusion that his master was the Maquinna of Cook's day. Jewitt does not himself question the assumption. He and the chief had long talks in which Maquinna went over the past and told of Qualicum's death at the hands of Martinez in 1789 and of the arrival of Captain James Hanna, who began the sea otter trade in 1785. Though descriptions of Maquinna differ, Jewitt's Maquinna, with his Roman nose (unique among his tribe) and his pencil moustache, bears an uncanny resemblance to an earlier sketch of Maquinna by a Spanish artist.

There is something more: Jewitt's Maquinna acts and sounds like the Maquinna of an earlier time. It is hard to believe there were two so similar. He came into the chieftainship in 1778, just before Cook's arrival, having avenged his father's death in a war with a neighbouring tribe. Maquinna led his men to the enemy villages, took them by surprise, and massacred the inhabitants. But if he was bold and precipitate he could also be prudent and vacillating. After his brother's death at the hands of Martinez, realizing that the Spaniards were too strong for him, he retired from Yuquot to Clayoquot, allowing the Spanish to occupy his village and make it their headquarters – an action he bitterly resented but was powerless to prevent. His failure to avenge his brother's murder, as he had his father's, rankled. It also lowered his prestige, because any Indian group (and Maquinna was the symbol of his group) that failed to act decisively in response to the injury of one of its members was considered impotent. An English captain, James Colnett, called him "a most miserable, cowardly wretch . . . [who] flies whenever he sees the Spaniards." But Colnett had also been bested by Martinez and driven half mad in the process. It would be just as fair to say that Maquinna preferred to live and fight again.

To be forced to skulk at Clayoquot under the protection of his rival, Wickinninish, was a humiliating experience. His fellow chieftain was as wealthy and as powerful as he – perhaps more powerful, for in the occasional battles between the two villages, the people of Yuquot always lost. When the time came, Maquinna would display his two white slaves before his rival with special glee; he did not like to be second to anyone.

He was touchy about his prerogatives. When the English adventurer John Meares left his village in 1788, the chief arranged a farewell ceremony but learned later that Meares judged this to mean that the Indian acknowledged the white man as his sovereign. The chief was enraged; *no* one was his superior. From that point on he referred to Meares as "Aita-aita Meares," meaning "Liar Meares." The Spanish captain, Pedro Alberni, who was stationed permanently at Friendly Cove, understood this quality in Maquinna. He took advantage of it to help break down Maquinna's suspicions by inducing his seamen to sing a song in Nootka, praising the chief. When Maquinna heard about it he asked that the song be sung to him repeatedly until he had memorized it. Two years later it could still be heard.

The following year, 1790, the Spanish navigator Alejandro Malaspina visited Maquinna at Tahsis, where the chief, "his face revealing both anger and fear," did his best to impress his visitors with his power, showing off his most valued possessions – a chest containing fifteen muskets, a set of elaborately carved boxes, and, of course, the sheets of beaten copper to be used as potlatch gifts. Of him, Malaspina wrote:

"Macuina's character these days is difficult to decipher, his temper seems simultaneously fierce, suspicious and intrepid. The natural course of his inclinations is probably stirred up, on the one hand by desire of the Europeans to capture his friendship, the treasures he has stored up in a few years, discords that have occurred among Europeans, and perhaps suggestion from one side or another to secure a monopoly of pelts; on the other hand consider the weakness of his forces, skirmishes suffered, profit from the traffic and excessive frequent presence of European vessels in these regions."

Because he held the key to the sea otter trade – a trade that was turning the young men from the traditional occupations of salmon fishing and whale hunting – Maquinna was able to pit the trading nations against each other. His one desire was to rid the coast of Europeans and return to his summer village with his personal prestige intact. But he did not reject those aspects of European culture or ingenuity that appealed to him or he found useful. The Nootka were ignorant of sails; Maquinna was quick to adopt them. And when that remarkably civilized Spaniard, Juan Francisco de la Bodega y Quadra, arrived at Friendly Cove in 1792 to negotiate a land settlement with George Vancouver (Spain and England having become allies after the French revolution), Maquinna joined him at his dinner table – a table that often sat more than fifty guests dining from 270 plates of sterling silver. Bodega wrote that "upon hearing the dinner bell, Maquinna comes daily, performs his courtesy with his hat and sits at the Commander's side. He asks for anything he pleases and uses spoon, fork and glass very well. He asks for wine and sherry, coffee upon finishing and if there is any chocolate in the morning . . . ." Though he was fond of wine, the chief was careful not to lose his dignity; he appointed a relative to watch that he did not grow intoxicated in front of the white men. Bodega gave him a steel helmet and a coat of mail and treated him and his followers to displays of fireworks. He was, the Spaniard noted, "endowed with a clear and sagacious talent and knew very well the rights of sovereignty. He complained a great deal about treatment from foreign vessels trafficking on the coast because of some of the outrages his people had received." The Spanish finally departed early in 1795, leaving Vancouver Island technically to the British, who did not occupy it, and the village site to Maquinna, who was given a Union Jack to hoist whenever a trading vessel appeared. All that remained was an excuse for revenge, and that came on the deck of the *Boston* in 1803.

His captives had given him enormous prestige; he delighted in displaying them. In January, when the salmon run ended, the tribe moved from Tahsis to Coptee, sixteen miles down the sound. Here they fished for herring and sprats. Maquinna could scarcely wait to take Jewitt in his canoe to show him off to Chief Upquesta of the Ai-tiz-arts. Few of these people had ever seen a white man; Maquinna's prize, still in European attire, was a fascinating novelty. They crowded about him, plucking at his clothes, peering at his face and hands, and looking into his mouth to see if he had a tongue, for his master had forbidden him to speak unless ordered to. At last he gave the signal: Jewitt might talk. They were astonished. Now, they told Maquinna, they understood that this strange creature was actually a man. But they thought his blue jacket and trousers were ugly and did their best to convince him to disrobe. Their best was not good enough; but they were mollified by Maquinna's spirited description of the massacre aboard the *Boston*.

From the north came a party of Indians to warn the chief that twenty-five ships were on their way to rescue the two slaves. This was probably a ruse to worry Maquinna, but it served only to anger him. If another ship arrived, he warned Jewitt, he would launch a second massacre. He guarded his captives as a miser guards his treasure. "Nothing could be more unpleasant than our present situation," Jewitt wrote. "Our lives were altogether dependant on the will of a savage, on whose caprices and suspicions no rational calculation could be made."

In February, the Indians returned to Yuquot, the summer village at the mouth of Nootka Sound. The following month a singular incident took place: Maquinna's brother-in-law went insane, something that no native had done in anyone's memory. He was a chief, Tootoosch, known as the greatest warrior of the tribe, a leading figure in the incident aboard the *Boston*. His madness was touched off by the death of his eleven-year-old son, a tragedy which he connected, somehow, with the massacre. He began to imagine that he could see the ghosts of two seamen, Hall and Wood, whom he had personally slain.

The tribe was shaken by this development. Maquinna took his two white slaves to see Tootoosch to ask if they had put a curse on him, but the deranged chief told Maquinna they were both good men. When Jewitt tried to persuade him that the ghosts were not there, Tootoosch replied, simply, "I know very well that you do not see them, but I do." Maquinna then asked Jewitt how his own people dealt with madness. The blacksmith replied that in his country lunatics were tied up and whipped. Maquinna tried this but found it too painful to watch and ordered it stopped, "saying that if there was no other way of curing him, he must remain mad."

This sensitivity to torment was curious in a man who had seen twenty-five seamen dispatched with knives, but it was genuine;

Bodega had reported a similar incident in 1792 when Maquinna had ordered the execution of one of his band for seducing a nine-year-old girl. Before the sentence was carried out, the chief arrived at the Spaniard's house "with an expression that betrayed his mental unrest" and told Bodega that "they are now inflicting the punishment, and I have come here in order not to suffer the pain of hearing his laments." As for the unhappy Tootoosch, the whipping drove him madder still, and he set about beating his wife who was forced to flee to Maquinna for protection.

In April, the whaling season began – a time of increasing tension, for the whale hunt was the supreme ritual of the Nootka people, giving enormous prestige to those who were successful and ignominy to those who failed. Only men of the highest rank were permitted to harpoon a whale. In the prow of each of the slim eight-man canoes stood two harpoonists – a head chief and his brother. Traditionally, the chief made the first cast; the final cut to the heart was his prerogative also. This undertaking was preceded by various ceremonies – a ritual cleansing with hemlock twigs, for example – for besides being a difficult and hazardous sport, the whale hunt was a symbolic act designed to ensure the prosperity of the tribe.

Maquinna's attitude at this time was, in Jewitt's words, "thoughtful and gloomy." He scarcely spoke and gave his captives very little to eat. The chief had good reason for this dark mood, for the whaling was not going well. He told Jewitt that if he did not kill a whale his people would kill him, and he ordered the blacksmith to guard him day and night with a brace of pistols and a cutlass.

Danger lurked at the forest's rim. Slave and master were united in a mutual fear of assassination. The Indians, apprehensive that a ship would appear, were determined to kill both white men the moment a sail appeared on the horizon; they wanted no witnesses to the horror of the previous summer. Two canoes arrived from Maquinna's old rival, Wickinninish – their occupants intent on dispatching both the chief and his slaves – but the cutlasses and pistols frightened them off. In his journal on May 16, Jewitt wrote: "We walked all last night before our huts to keep watch, and at twelve o'clock fired one of the great guns off for an alarm in order to terrify the natives who had left us the day before, and as a signal to them that we were on our guard."

Jewitt, meanwhile, had been working on a special harpoon with a steel shaft; perhaps with this his master might kill a whale and ease the tension. To the chief's delight and the blacksmith's relief, Maquinna was successful. He made his two captives a present of blubber, which they boiled in salt water with nettles and other greens – "tolerable food" in Jewitt's description.

May 21 was Jewitt's birthday; he could not foresee another. "I now begin to give up all hope of ever seeing a Christian country or a Christian face," he wrote, "for the season being so far advanced and not hearing of the arrival of any ship on the coast, we feel ourselves very unhappy . . . . We are much cast down at the thought of spending the remainder of our days among these savages."

Worse was to come. On June 5, the Indians took away their greatcoats and other clothing, which had also served as beds. The following week a native stole the canoe that Maquinna had given them to use for fishing. Maquinna retrieved it, confiscated the thief's catch, and gave it to his slave. But the situation was deteriorating. Both men were afraid they would soon be obliged to go naked, if, indeed, they survived at all. The chiefs of the various families continued to meet to decide whether they should both be killed if a ship appeared. Maquinna again held out for sparing their lives.

Their rations grew scarcer. On June 15, Jewitt recorded that they had eaten nothing for the past three days. He was forced to barter a handkerchief for a dried salmon and a little whale oil. On June 19, he wrote: "The natives take our canoe when they please. If we say anything to them they tell us we are slaves and ask us where our captain is, making signs that his head was cut off . . . ."

The Indians, too, were short of food. They blamed the deficiency on Maquinna, saying that the blood of the *Boston* crew had driven away the fish. At one point, Thompson and Jewitt, having managed to acquire some fresh salmon, reversed roles with their master and played hosts to him and his wife at dinner. A curious *rapprochement* was taking place between captor and captives, a kind of vague bond not unlike the so-called Stockholm syndrome of the 1970s, when hostages and terrorists in hijacking incidents found themselves drawn to each other. During the dinner, Jewitt complained that the common people abused and insulted him. Maquinna promised to put a stop to that. He went further, saying that anybody from another tribe who insulted the white men would be killed. And he warned them to go about armed.

A short time later, Thompson was washing his clothes, including a blanket owned by Maquinna. Several members of Wickinninish's tribe arrived to taunt him. One walked over the newly washed blanket. Thompson threatened to kill him. The Indian continued to trample the blanket, whereupon Thompson drew his cutlass and cut off the offender's head. He presented this grisly memento to his master, who professed delight. After this incident the two slaves were treated with some respect.

In July there came a new alarm – a threat of war. A canoe load of Indians arrived from the north telling of a battle in which a hundred men and women had died. The cause of this bloodshed was instructive. "We hear both from the north and south that the natives are massacring one another for want of cloth, muskets, etc.," Jewitt wrote in his journal. "Our chief expects to be obliged to make war with them as they have threatened him on account of destroying the ship, *Boston*, which they say has injured their trade very much, and that no ship will now come to their ports to trade with them."

Thus Maquinna's escapade was revealed as double-edged. It had helped to slake his people's thirst for revenge; it had given him enormous prestige through the possession of two white slaves and a vast quantity of goods and arms; but it was also seen as an impediment to further barter. Contrary to what has become popular cant, not all native peoples in North America lived an idyllic life in which the concept of private property was unknown. The Indians of the Pacific Coast were among the most acquisitive creatures in history. In 1778, Cook observed that he had never come across natives who had such a highly developed sense of proprietary right as these; not even the grasses on which they walked were public property, he reported ruefully. He had sent men ashore to cut forage for the ship's goats, never dreaming that the Indians would object. But object they did, insisting on an immediate and exorbitant payment.

"As soon as I heard of this," Cook wrote, "I went to the place and found about a dozen men who all laid claim to some part of the grass, which I purchased off [*sic*] them and, as I thought, liberty to cut as I pleased, but here again I was mistaken for the liberal manner I had paid the first pretended proprietors brought more upon me and there was not a blade of grass that had not a separate owner, so that I very soon emptied my pockets . . . ."

The beads-and-trinkets explanation of white duplicity among the native tribes tends to crumble a little in the case of the Pacific Coast; within a decade of Cook's arrival, the Indians had become the shrewdest of bargainers. John Meares reported in 1798 that "in all our commercial transaction with these people we were, more or less, the dupes of their cunning; and with such peculiar artifice did they sometimes conduct themselves, that all the precaution we could employ was not sufficient to prevent our being overreached by them. The women, in particular, would play us a thousand tricks, and treat the discovery of their finesses with an arch kind of pleasure that baffled reproach."

Now these people were being denied the pleasure of barter, the joy of possession – and the fault was Maquinna's. Hostilities were imminent. Maquinna would not wait for them to begin; he intended to fight a preventive war. To this end he ordered Jewitt to make daggers for his men and fashion a special weapon for himself – some kind of super-club designed to kill a man with a single blow, preferably when he was asleep. The resourceful blacksmith obliged with a truly fearsome device – a six-inch spike of sharpened steel set in a rough knob at right angles to a fifteen-inch handle of iron, crooked at the end to prevent it from being wrenched from the hand. The back of the knob was ornamented with a man's face, the mouth agape, the eyes of black beads fastened with red sealing wax. Maquinna, of course, was delighted.

The enemy were encamped fifty miles to the south. To prepare for battle, the warriors abstained from sex for several weeks and scrubbed themselves repeatedly with brier brushes. Maquinna urged his two captives to harden their skins in the same way; they refused. Finally, the war party embarked in forty canoes, each containing between ten and twenty men, armed with bows, arrows, and daggers. Jewitt and Thompson preferred cutlasses and pistols.

The battle was bloody and decisive. The attack came at dawn, many of the enemy dying as they slept. Thompson zestfully killed seven men, an act that considerably raised his status. Jewitt, who abhorred killing, took four prisoners. He was allowed to keep them to help him work and fish – slaves to a slave. Few of the enemy escaped; the old and the sick were dispatched on the spot. The slaughter over, the party returned to Yuquot for a victory feast.

Jewitt's value was increasing. Maquinna's old rival, Wickinninish, could hardly contain himself when he saw the club the blacksmith had made for his master. He *must* have him! To that end he made a formal offer to purchase; the price included four young male slaves, two highly ornamented canoes, a parcel of sea otter skins, and a variety of trade goods. It must have given Maquinna great satisfaction to refuse; his own prestige rose with his captive's price.

Another chief, Ulatilla, whom Jewitt considered the most civilized native he had encountered, also tried in vain to buy the blacksmith. Ulatilla, who spoke good English, was fascinated by European customs; when Jewitt satisfied his curiosity on this subject, the chief promised to try to get him aboard the first trading vessel that came to his country, if Maquinna would release him. Jewitt, who wrote sixteen letters begging to be rescued at different times and smuggled them out to various parts of the coast, sent one to Ulatilla, asking that he give it to any passing ship. That letter eventually led to his release.

But at the time there seemed no hope of rescue; Maquinna had no intention of losing his most valuable property. His intention was to turn the white man into an Indian, to marry him off to a local girl, and to convince him to settle down among the Nootka and conform to local customs. Jewitt had no choice; his master made it clear that he must marry or die. Since the blacksmith did not fancy any of the Nootka women, Maquinna agreed that he might marry outside the tribe. Accordingly, in September the chief took his slave and fifty men to Ai-tiz-art with a plenitude of gifts – cloth, muskets, sea otter skins – with which to purchase a bride. Jewitt, having to choose someone, chose the seventeen-year-old daughter of the chief, whereupon Maquinna, in a speech that rolled on for a full half-hour, extolled the blacksmith as a useful and well-tempered prospect. The girl's father replied with an even longer speech, praising his daughter and agreeing, at last, to part with her. Gifts were exchanged; feasting and dancing followed; joy was unconfined save in the heart of the bridegroom, whose diary entry for his wedding day is laconic: "This day our chief bought a wife for me . . . . It is very much against my inclinations to take one of these heathens for a partner, but it will be for my advantage while I am amongst them, for she has a father who always goes fishing, so that I shall live much better than I have at any time heretofore." Jewitt was nothing if not practical.

He now felt more hopelessly bound to the aboriginal life than ever, especially since Maquinna decreed that he must be considered a native and dress the part in a single mantle of red cedar bark. Again he had no choice: "He informed us that we must go naked like themselves, otherwise he should put us to death. As life is sweet, even to the captive . . . we thought it best to submit to their will without murmuring, even though it was a very grievous thing to us."

The two men were now accepted as Nootka and allowed to participate in the winter religious festival, a week-long ceremony from which they had been excluded the previous year. Jewitt scorned the ritual as a "farce"; it appeared to him to consist of continual feasting. "The natives," he wrote, "eat twenty times a day." At that moment, the Church of England, his strength and his comfort, seemed light-years away. It was as if he had been transported, through some warp in time, to an alien cosmos whose order and harmony bore no relation to any he had known. And so, in a sense, he had; adaptable he most certainly was, but after more than a year in captivity he was still not able to come to terms with an environment that was to him always unnatural and often grotesque. About this time he was called upon to perform a particularly distasteful task: Maquinna's older brother asked Jewitt to file his teeth, so that he might disfigure his wife by biting off her nose. She had refused his sexual advances and according to Nootka custom he was allowed to mutilate her so that no one else would wish to wed her.

The two slaves were eating better, thanks to Jewitt's father-in-law, the fisherman. Yet it seemed they had merely exchanged one hardship for another. On December 1, Jewitt wrote in his journal: "Frosty weather. Very hard times. All the European clothes being expended I am obliged to go almost naked like the Indians, with only a kind of garment a fathom long, made of the bark of trees to defend me from the inclemency of the weather. I have suffered more from the cold this winter than I can possibly express. I am afraid it will injure my constitution and make me very weak and feeble during the remainder of my life." Because neither man was allowed to wear shoes or stockings, their feet were cut badly and often frozen. Thompson suffered from rheumatism so severely that he was rarely able to leave the lodge.

In February, Jewitt had all but given up hope of rescue. In March, he was taken seriously ill "with a pain in my bowels, which I presume was occasioned by going naked in the cold." Too weak to stand, he could eat nothing. Soon, he expected, he would share the fate of another slave who had died and was "thrown out of the house as soon as the breath was out of his mouth" and pitched into the ocean.

Maquinna was convinced that the illness was caused by Jewitt's young wife. He offered to return her to her father – a flawed chattel, subject, apparently, to a money-back guarantee. To this Jewitt gratefully agreed. At last, however, the chief was made to realize that his slave's illness was actually caused by the climate, not sex, and he was allowed once more to wear clothes. One cannot read Jewitt's journal without concluding that Maquinna was genuinely fond of him, as a man is fond of a favourite horse or retriever, for he treated him with much greater affection than he did his other slaves.

As May ended Jewitt received news that rekindled an ember of hope: word came that Ulatilla had managed to pass his letter on to the captain of a trading ship, who was planning to come to the sound to rescue the white men.

When this news spread among the natives, it caused a buzz of consternation. What to do? Would the Yankees seek revenge? Would trade be resumed? What should be the Nootka response?

Jewitt and Thompson were the only witnesses to the butchery of 1803; if they were killed and their bodies hidden, who would be left alive to testify concerning that bloody spring afternoon? But perhaps the presence of two hostages might work to the Indians' benefit; perhaps *they* could be bartered, like sea otter skins, in return for a pardon. Some of the tribe began to treat the captives with greater kindness; others argued for their immediate death. The head chiefs of the lodges, in council, decided upon a conciliatory course: Thompson and Jewitt would be sent aboard the ship to mediate on their behalf and to re-establish regular trade.

Everybody waited; nothing happened. A month passed; no sail appeared on the dark ridge of the ocean. On July 2, Jewitt learned why: the ship had been involved in a skirmish with one of the northern tribes, losing ten men including the captain. He gave up hope of rescue. Of all the vessels trading on the Pacific Coast, the *Boston* had been the largest, strongest, and best equipped; hers had also been the most valuable cargo fitted out for the northwest trade. Clearly her destruction had filled all other captains in the area with a dread of Nootka Sound. He was doomed to spend the rest of his life as an Indian.

Deliverance came suddenly, without warning, on July 19, two years and four months after his capture. Jewitt was making chisels at his bench when one of the natives spotted the outline of a vessel on the horizon. Maquinna at once called him out to look. She was the brig *Lydia*, out of Boston. "My heart leapt for joy at the thought of getting my liberty," Jewitt wrote.

Maquinna dispatched a canoe at once with a letter from the blacksmith saying that there was no danger in entering Friendly Cove. The canoe returned with word from the captain, Samuel Hill, that he was coming in. The *Lydia* anchored off the cove about noon.

The Indians were in a quandary; if Maquinna went on board the ship, they reasoned, the captain would certainly put him in irons, at least until the two slaves were released. As one, they urged him not to go. Jewitt, meanwhile, had worked out a deception; he would hide his excitement and pretend that he was not anxious to go aboard. His plan was to have his master precede him and be held as a hostage for the two slaves.

The brig gave a salute of three guns. Jewitt replied, using the cannon from the *Boston*. Roles were now rapidly being reversed. Master turned to slave to ask what he should do. The slave urged his master to go on board the ship; the captain, he promised, "would use him well." But the chief was justifiably suspicious, whereupon his captive – scarcely a captive any more – offered to write a letter of recommendation to the captain, which, he said, would keep the chief from harm. Maquinna gazed at him quizzically, "eyeing me with a look that seemed to read my inmost thoughts."

"John, you no lie?" the chief asked.

Jewitt brazened it out. At Maquinna's request an odd little mime followed. The chief could not read, but he would run his finger across Jewitt's scribble, line by line, and have the blacksmith read out the words as his finger moved. Jewitt complied; the letter, he said, told the captain to treat the great chief kindly and to make him presents of molasses, biscuits, and rum. What it actually said was that Maquinna had been the leader of the attack on the *Boston* and that he should be confined "according to his merits" and not allowed to escape until the two white men were released.

At this moment, Jewitt reaped the harvest of his behaviour over the previous twenty-eight months. Maquinna had come to trust his slave. His wives and fellow chiefs crowded around him, pleading with him not to go to the ship, but Maquinna had decided upon his course. "John no lie," he said firmly. Would John go with him? he asked, tentatively. No, John would not. John made it clear that he had no desire to leave the Nootka.

Thus disarmed, Maquinna set off for the *Lydia* with Jewitt's letter and a present of four sea otter skins. The captain read what Jewitt had written, offered the chief a tot of rum, escorted him to his cabin, locked the windows, clapped Maquinna in irons, and placed him under an armed guard. The chief was surprised and terrified. He sent back a messenger who told the villagers that "John had spoke bad about him in the letter." An incredible scene followed: the villagers rushed up and down the beach, howling and wailing and tearing out their hair. The men ran for their weapons. The women threw themselves on their knees around Jewitt, begging him to save Maquinna's life. Some of the men circled him, brandishing their weapons, threatening torture. They would cut him into pieces no bigger than their thumbnails; they would burn him alive over a slow fire, suspended by his heels; they would – but it was all quite useless; their master was a captive and his captive had become their master.

"Kill me!" cried the blacksmith, dramatically, throwing open his bearskin robe. "Here is my breast . . . I can make no resistance but unless you wish to see your king hanging by his neck to that pole and the sailors firing at him with bullets, you will not do it." He knew they would not.

The chiefs were calmer than their followers. What should be

done? Jewitt assured them that Maquinna was safe and would be returned to Yuquot as soon as the two white men were released.

Thompson was allowed to go on board the ship at once. Jewitt then proposed that three natives should take him to within hailing distance of the brig to arrange an exchange. There was an affecting little scene as Jewitt was about to step into the canoe. Maquinna's young son, who had become very fond of the blacksmith and "could not bear to part," asked him if he would please not kill his father.

Jewitt's plan was to get on board the *Lydia* before Maquinna was released; in that way the chief could be held hostage for the return of the property from the *Boston*, notably the cannon. By threatening the native paddlers with his pistol, which he had been allowed to keep, he forced them to row directly to the ship. He climbed quickly aboard – a grotesque and astonishing figure, painted red and black from head to foot, dressed in a shaggy bearskin wrap-around, his long hair, which he had been forbidden to cut, fastened in a huge knot above his head and tied with a sprig of green spruce. The captain later told him that he had never seen anything in the form of a man, civilized or savage, who looked so wild.

Now the ex-slave faced his former master. Maquinna brightened. "*Wocash*, John!" he exclaimed, using the native word for "good." Captain Hill was intent on executing the chief at once, but Jewitt deterred him, explaining the circumstances of the massacre and all the events leading up to it. His life among the Nootka had made him the world's leading expert on the sociology of the West Coast Indians. He explained to Hill that if he had the chief executed, Maquinna's followers would be duty bound to exact revenge; the crew of the next ship to drop anchor in the sound would surely be massacred.

Maquinna constantly interrupted this discourse to plead with Jewitt to save him. He did not believe, however, that he would be spared, and when at last he learned that he was to be permitted to live, he was incredulous. His own notion of revenge would have called for death.

It was now past five in the afternoon. Jewitt told the Indians waiting in the canoe that their chief would be returned the following day in exchange for the remaining effects from the *Boston*.

He must have felt the strangeness of his new position. All through the night, the man who had been his undisputed master for more than two years, who had forced him into an unwelcome marriage, who had feasted or starved him at his own caprice, now kept him awake pleading for reassurance that his life was to be spared. Proud Maquinna had been reduced to a grovelling suppliant.

The following morning the Indians delivered the *Boston*'s cannon, anchor, sea chests and ship's papers, and – most important – Jewitt's personal journal to the *Lydia*. Maquinna sent for sixty otter skins, which he presented to Captain Hill. Now, he was told, he might return to his village. Ecstatic, he threw off his mantle and presented it to the captain, who, to his delight, gave him a hat and a greatcoat. Hill then asked Jewitt to tell the chief that he would be back in November to trade; Maquinna, in his turn, pledged that he would save for the *Lydia* all the sea otter skins his young men brought in.

There followed an affectionate and touching farewell between the two men whose lives had for twenty-eight months been bound together in such a curious fashion. Maquinna seized Jewitt's hand and told him he hoped he would return in a big ship loaded with blankets, biscuits, molasses, and rum; in return, he said, he would save all the furs he got for his friend. At the same time, he observed, with a shrewdness that was almost comic, that he would never again accept a letter of recommendation from *anyone*. He held no grudge against Jewitt for his deception; he simply said he would never trust himself on board a white man's vessel unless the blacksmith himself were present. Then he took both of Jewitt's hands in his "with much emotion while the tears trickled down his cheeks," and, releasing his grip, stepped into his canoe, waved a final farewell, and was paddled ashore. There is no record of John Thompson's role in the parting.

Jewitt, too, was moved: "I could not avoid experiencing a painful sensation on parting with the savage chief, who had preserved my life, and in general treated me with kindness and, considering their ideas and manners, much better than could have been expected."

He could not, of course, go directly home, for the *Lydia* had only commenced her voyage. She sailed north along the coast to trade with other tribes and then south again to the mouth of the Columbia, where, it was learned, Meriwether Lewis and William Clark had arrived just two weeks before to complete their famous land crossing of America. A good deal had been happening during John Jewitt's captivity; Napoleon had been crowned Emperor of France; the United States had purchased the Louisiana Territory; Beethoven had written the *Eroica* Symphony; Robert Fulton had propelled a boat by steam power.

The *Lydia* returned to Nootka Sound late that fall. The Indians were in winter quarters, but Jewitt, following Maquinna's earlier instructions – "when you come make 'pow' " – fired the brig's cannon, and a canoe shortly appeared with a message: Maquinna would come aboard only if his friend Jewitt would fetch him. Much to Hill's and Thompson's anxiety, the blacksmith agreed to return to the shores where he had been held captive. Maquinna welcomed him with joy and the two paddled to the ship with a small fortune in otter skins.

Maquinna had missed Jewitt; he urged him to return, promising, in the meantime, to look after the five-month-old baby son who had been born to Jewitt's Indian wife. But the armourer had no intention of coming back. The *Lydia* sailed once more up the coast and then, on August 11, 1806, more than a year after his release from captivity, set off for China. As Jewitt stared back at the green curtain of the cedar forest and watched it diminish until it was no more than a blurred line on the horizon, he resolved that "nothing should tempt me to return, and as the tops of the mountains sank in the blue waves of the ocean, I seemed to feel my heart lightened of an oppressive load." But he could not escape the frontier; it had affected him more than he then knew.

The *Lydia* left China in February, 1807, and arrived in Boston 114 days later. There Jewitt found a letter from his mother in England, expressing her joy at his safety.

He was no longer a captive of Chief Maquinna; but for the rest of his days he remained a captive of his experience. He could not put it out of his mind, nor, apparently, did he wish to. It dominated his remaining years, seduced him away from his trade, and turned him into a kind of wandering minstrel, repeating, over and over, the story of his trials on that far off coast.

He was determined to turn his experience to his advantage. The owners of the *Boston* gave him a small reward with which he financed the printing of his journal, of which only a handful of copies survive. Jewitt had intended to open a smithy in Boston but, instead, he spent most of his time moving about, peddling his little book.

He was married on Christmas Day, 1809, to an English immigrant girl from Bristol. They settled in Middletown, Connecticut, and raised a family of five children. But Jewitt remained obsessed by his captivity. After his marriage he encountered a flourishing merchant, Richard Alsop, who was a part-time satirist and poet. The two collaborated on a new version of the tale. Alsop interviewed Jewitt at great length and in 1815 produced *The Adventures and Sufferings of John R. Jewitt, Captive among the Nootka, 1803-1805.* It was an enormous success. For years it was carried in the sea chests of sailors all around the globe. It has since gone into more than twenty editions and several languages, has been bowdlerized in a children's version, and is still in print. But Alsop's nephew thought the book did Jewitt more harm than good, for he "became unsettled in his habits by his wandering life," peddling his books from handcart, wheelbarrow, or one-horse wagon all the way from Nantucket to Baltimore. In addition he hawked a broadsheet of a popular sea shanty, "The Poor Armourer Boy," which retold his saga in verse. In Philadelphia, he went so far as to play himself in a melodrama based on his experiences. Later on he joined a circus of sorts at the Vauxhall Garden, a summer amusement park near Philadelphia, where, dressed in Indian costume, he performed songs. He died in Hartford in 1821 at the age of thirty-eight, his life shortened, as he himself had predicted, by his ordeal in the harsh and distant land of the Nootka.

TWO

The adventures of Wilfred Grenfell

The Labrador Coast: 1896

" . . . Headland and shoreline were devoid of any colour – a drab monotone – no speck of green upon the dark ridges, no sliver of blue in the sullen skies, the grey cliffs sodden with spray, the grey rocks blurred by creeping fog, the grey beaches spattered by dirty foam, the stunted conifers rising darkly from a patchwork of soiled snow, the whole landscape like a faded photograph. And the people, too, were faded, old beyond their years . . . "

Wilfred Grenfell was the perfect schoolboy hero. "Perfect" is the proper adjective. For most people at the century's turn and in the three decades following, Grenfell – Sir Wilfred as he eventually became – *was* perfect: missionary to the dispossessed; surgeon to the abandoned; adventurer in a foreign clime; saint and healer, evangelist and teacher. The well-to-do of Boston, Philadelphia, Manchester, and Toronto, hypnotized by his every word, revelled in the certain knowledge that they were in the presence of a living legend. In an era when the word *charisma* was unknown, the Labrador Doctor glowed with a compelling aura. Seeing his restless, muscular figure pacing the stages of countless auditoriums and listening to his tales of hardship, despair, salvation, and adventure, thousands were moved to contribute small fortunes for the succour of Newfoundland fishermen and Labrador liveyeres, whose lives they could hardly comprehend and whose environment seemed as mysterious and as remote as that of Katmandu.

Grenfell knew everybody, and everybody knew that he knew everybody. He was equally comfortable in the presence of royal dukes, Eskimo hunters, and the swilers of St. Anthony. He hobnobbed with Mackenzie King, Winston Churchill, King George V, and Teddy Roosevelt. In the long list of young Ivy Leaguers who cheerfully paid for the privilege of serving under him (often performing the most menial chores) one finds such names as Nelson Rockefeller and Henry Cabot Lodge. To these the name Grenfell was magic: it bespoke Christian selflessness of the highest order, sacrifice rendered bearable – even glamorous – by the lure of high adventure beyond the rim of civilization.

To those who worshipped him – the newspaper readers who revelled in his Sunday supplement exploits, the doyens of society who gripped his hand at fêtes and levees, the thousands of members of the various Grenfell societies who gave him their unstinting support – the Labrador Doctor was a man who could do no wrong. He got results; he raised millions; he changed the lives of thousands of Newfoundlanders for the better. None could deny those accomplishments. Yet to those who knew him intimately, and who admired and even loved him, he was not entirely perfect; there were certain flaws of temperament and character that never crept into the public prints. He was not a good administrator, nor was he an especially good doctor; he was irritatingly casual about money; he could on occasion be perverse, bumbling, even juvenile; and he never seemed content to stay in one place for any length of time. There was a breathless schoolboy impetuosity about Grenfell that his colleagues found maddening yet at the same time attractive.

No incident illustrates this better than his miraculous brush with death on Easter Sunday, 1908. The Ice Pan Adventure, as it came to be called, cast Grenfell as larger than life. It was for the Labrador Doctor what Khartoum was for Kitchener, what the Livingstone encounter was for Stanley. But it was also a foolhardy and dangerous exploit that almost took the lives of several fishermen in addition to Grenfell's own.

He was forty-three, at the height of his abilities and approaching the peak of his celebrity. He was not handsome, but he was certainly attractive, with a pudgy, almost cherubic face that radiated geniality – a very English face with little crinkles around the eyes, a short, nondescript moustache (a little ragged, but not too bristly), and prominent teeth. His face was tanned, his muscles were taut, his body was elastic. He was, in his own phrase, "fit as a brickbat."

He had just returned from conducting Easter service in the little church at St. Anthony, a fishing village on the northeastern tip of Newfoundland, which he had made his headquarters. Two fishermen were waiting; they had come sixty miles from Brent Island to inform him that a boy on whom he had recently operated was critically ill with blood poisoning.

Grenfell dropped everything. Nothing would do but that he dash off, almost on the instant, without waiting for the two messengers who needed to rest their dogs before proceeding. There was no sense in it. Sooner or later he would have to wait for them to guide him to the island. But it was not in Grenfell's make-up to pause; movement for him was a tonic, idleness a soporific. Off he dashed in his *komatik*, his seven best dogs strung out in front of him, his little black spaniel, Jack, leading the way – off across the ice-covered boulders of the east coast and through the ragged forests. Grenfell to the rescue!

His dress was distinctly odd. Under his coat and overalls he was wearing, for reasons that have never been satisfactorily explained, a football uniform from his college days, which, after twenty years, he had unearthed from the mothballs in his trunk, consisting of Oxford University running shorts, red, yellow, and black Richmond football stockings, and a flannel shirt. This peculiar garb added a bizarre touch to the events that followed.

Brent Island lay on the far side of Hare Bay, sixty miles to the south. It was spring breakup – the most dangerous season for travel. It rained that night, and a bitter wind blew from the east, causing the ice to crack in the harbours. Grenfell's first stop was Lock's Cove, eighteen miles from St. Anthony on the north shore of Hare Bay. There he spent the night as the wind stiffened and veered to the west, as the temperature dropped and the snow hardened, as the ice in the bay broke into pans, growling and crashing eerily in the dark.

Grenfell was advised to wait until conditions became more settled; he refused. He was urged to follow the shoreline and not to venture on to the uncertain ice, and for a time he held to that plan. But he could not resist a short cut directly across the bay, and this nearly proved his undoing.

The wind dropped. Suddenly, the doctor became aware that the ice beneath him had turned to slush. So rapidly was it breaking up that there was no time to turn back. He tore off his outer clothes, flung himself on hands and knees in order to distribute his weight, and urged the dogs forward. The land lay a tantalizing quarter mile distant. But the harder the dogs pulled, the deeper the runners sank into the slob ice.

A long struggle followed in the slush-filled waters. Grenfell hacked the traces clear of the sinking sled and managed to get the dogs on to a tiny pan of ice. It was not large enough to hold them all. The doctor fashioned a rope from the traces, tied it to the lead dog, and tried to persuade the animal to swim to a larger pan, twenty yards away. The dog refused. Grenfell tossed a piece of ice to the other pan and commanded his spaniel, Jack, to fetch it. All seven huskies leaped into the water to follow, dragging Grenfell with them.

His situation was desperate. He had lost his cap, coat, gloves, overalls, thermos, matches, and fuel. Five miles to the north he could hear the immense pans grinding together and thundering against the cliffs. No vessel, he knew, could survive in that turmoil. And the wind was moving the ice out to the sea.

He was freezing to death, and he knew it. In one of his several accounts of the incident he tells how he considered stabbing himself to make a quick end of things. (It was clearly no more than a passing thought; it is impossible to imagine the Labrador Doctor attempting suicide.) Instead, he stabbed three of his dogs to death and was bitten in the process. He skinned them, wrapped the hides around his shoulders, and constructed a windbreak out of the carcasses. Behind this bloody bulwark he crouched, cuddling for warmth against his biggest dog, as the wind drove his precarious floating island out to sea. When the wind dropped he even managed to sleep until midnight. At dawn he rigged an extraordinary signal flag, using the frozen legs of the dead dogs as a staff and a shirt tied to it with bits of old harness rope as a pennant. By this time he was close to delirium.

He was saved by something very like a miracle. The only man on all that coast who owned a telescope happened to be standing late the previous afternoon on the south shore of Hare Bay. Into his field of vision, a tiny object moved: an ice pan "no bigger than a kitchen floor" on which were huddled a man and five dogs. He recognized Grenfell's wiry figure and set about organizing a search party. A boat had to be dug out of the packed snow and by the time that was done it was dark. There could be no attempt at rescue until morning, and by then the west wind would almost certainly have carried the marooned party far out to sea. Nonetheless the attempt had to be made: "Ef the doctor's gone, dat's the end o' the French shore and St. Anthony. 'Twill all go down . . . 'E's the one keeps us all going."

At dawn, the lookouts on the headland spotted the pan several miles to seaward but still within the bay. The intervening area was a chaos of broken, grinding ice. For no one but the doctor would five men have risked their lives in such seas, but "his life was worth many. We wouldn't let a man like that die without trying."

The sick boy's grandfather, George Reed, skippered the crew. He steered; the others rowed, often hauling the boat across ice pans or ploughing it through thick slush until they came within sight of their goal. Grenfell, when they reached him, looked years older, a scarecrow figure, bloody and ragged, his face grey and uncustomarily sober. They forced tea down his throat, but he could not speak. Later, on shore, he tried to argue that he be allowed to drive his dog team alone back to St. Anthony, but they would have none of that.

At the hospital he was given morphine to force him to sleep. Still suffering from exposure and shock, he insisted, when he woke, on dictating the story of his adventure to Jessie Luther, the occupational therapist at the hospital. That account, much embellished and often retold, became the basis for a best-selling book and numberless newspaper features and magazine articles. But was the trip really necessary? A day or so later, the boy whose life the doctor had set out to save was brought to the hospital by boat (the ice having temporarily cleared from the coast), where he quickly recovered.

There were some who would say that the whole adventure was a publicity stunt. It was scarcely that, though Grenfell was a master of publicity. It was simply the saga of a man who, having suffered a real peril through his own impatience, exploited it by his own zeal. There was nothing deliberate about Grenfell, nor was he troubled by self-doubt, second thoughts, or introspection. Like so many other nineteenth-century adventurers – Englishmen all – he was a man driven to risk with enough of a sense of drama to make capital from it. His was a special type of imperial derring-do – the same kind one finds in a Chinese Gordon. His was also, it goes without saying, a special kind of luck.

He was descended on his father's side from that Sir Richard Grenville of *Revenge* fame immortalized by Tennyson and Kingsley. His father, a classical scholar and sometime public-school headmaster, switched course in the midstream of life to become a slum chaplain in London. He suffered intermittently from mental illness and died in a nursing home in Wales when his son was twenty. There is some evidence that he committed suicide. However that may be, it was his mother who was the real influence on Wilfred Grenfell's life. She was always "Dear Old Mum" to him; he wrote to her regularly and at voluminous length until her death. When he was fifteen she had given him a book, *A Soul's Enquiries Answered*. He carried it with him all his life, scribbling homilies in it from time to time. In his fiftieth year he was still her little boy: there is a remarkable account by a Reverend Henry Gordon of Grenfell taking afternoon tea in her bedroom in 1914. "I can see him now," Gordon recalled, "stretched out on the hearth with his head in his mother's lap, and I have never doubted ever since that it was from her that he drew so much of his spiritual strength."

Yet one senses that his father's decline and death had its effect, for it was at that time that Wilfred Grenfell experienced an extraordinary religious conversion. He was studying medicine at the London Hospital Medical School, an indifferent scholar but an ardent athlete: swimmer, weight thrower, rower, and rugby player. Medicine became a passion only when he fell under the aura of Dr. Frederick Treves, a brilliant surgeon who would later be knighted for saving the life of Edward VII in one of history's earliest appendectomies. Treves, like Grenfell, was a man of action: swimmer, water-polo enthusiast, yachtsman and cyclist. Like Grenfell, he had a flair for the dramatic. The young student, hero-worshipping the older man, found his own natural propensity for self-dramatization heightened by the model of this second father.

Then, in 1883, Grenfell, nominally a low-church Anglican, wandered into the revival tent of Dwight L. Moody, the American evangelist, and was born again. For ten months, Moody and Ira Sankey, a gospel singer, had been offering Englishmen the theatre of tent evangelism. At first a thorn to the established church, they had at least received some measure of grudging acceptance. Grenfell arrived in the middle of a long prayer, found it boring and was about to leave when he heard Moody tell the congregation to sing a rousing song "while our brother finishes his prayer." Grenfell was inspired by the practicality of the act. He decided to give this down-to-earth form of Christianity his best try. He would attempt to "make religion a real effort as I thought Christ would do in my place as a doctor, or frankly abandon it."

Like many other young men of his class, he was yearning for a mission in life, and Moody's muscular Christianity offered it. It was, after all, the missionary age. A kind of lull had descended over the world; Britain had been the dominant nation for a century; the dark corners of the globe had been mapped and conquered; there was no war. Public-school boys, searching for an outlet for their energies, often found it in evangelism. Off they went to the jungles of Africa or the rice paddies of the Orient or the slums of Britain to save souls.

Grenfell did not immediately plunge into mission work. He had said that he would either take up religion or abandon it. His mother, in the end, convinced him to stay with it. In 1885 – the year of his father's death – his commitment was reinforced at another Moody meeting where the evangelist's showpieces were the famous "Cambridge seven," young men who were either crack athletes or army officers. To Grenfell, here was something worth paying attention to: these were not pious milksops, prattling endlessly about theology; these were *doers*, men of action. When the saved were summoned to their feet, Grenfell, not without a certain embarrassment, pulled himself up from his bench. He left the meeting feeling that he "had crossed the Rubicon, and must do something to prove it." He had scarcely been converted from a life of debauchery; in fact, he had nothing to give up. His interests in sport, religion, and medicine – none of them profound – had simply coalesced. The life that faced him could hardly be called a life of sacrifice because he so obviously loved every minute of it.

Dear Old Mum was consulted. She sent him to the local vicar, who put him in charge of a Sunday school class – dull stuff. Grenfell relieved the tedium by teaching his charges to box and was promptly dropped – violence was un-Christian, prizefighting was for the lower classes. Grenfell proceeded to doctor bodies in place of souls. He received his medical degree, though Dr. Treves in his reports marked him "very poor" and "indifferent." Yet the two became close friends. In 1888, Grenfell was appointed house surgeon under his mentor at the London Hospital and also helped out at Treves's boys' camp in Dorset. Eventually this led to an appointment to the National Mission to Deep Sea Fishermen, of whose medical section Treves was chairman. And that, in turn, led to Labrador.

Grenfell rose quickly from missionary doctor to superintendent, often maddening his superiors by refusing to follow the rules, taking matters into his own hands, vanishing occasionally on expeditions of his own, preaching, endlessly organizing everything from brass bands to sporting events, treating both fishermen and shore folk (thus annoying the local doctors), baffling everybody by swimming every morning in ice-cold water regardless of season, fighting the liquor sellers, and raising money by lecturing in drawing rooms – an attractive, vigorous young man in a romantic occupation who seemed to have boundless energy.

Three years after the young doctor descended on the mission, one of its council members, Francis Hopwood, returning scandalized from a week's visit to Newfoundland, wrote a scathing report on the conditions of the land-based fishermen – the five thousand permanent residents of coastal Labrador known as liveyeres and the thirty thousand "stationers" who worked from the stationary fleets off the northeast coast of the island. Hopwood roused all England with his descriptions of people living below subsistence level, in filthy conditions, on leaky vessels or in old sod huts, forever in debt to the merchants of St. John's, whose profit margin was often 200 per cent. On all that bleak coast, he reported, there was not one doctor. Once a year a government physician spent an hour or two among the people in the larger settlements when the mail steamer called; that was all.

The press response was instantaneous. Public opinion was further inflamed the following year when forty fishermen working out of Trinity Bay were lost in a blizzard. The mission determined to dispatch a hospital ship to investigate. Grenfell, of course, volunteered to sail with her.

She left Yarmouth in June, 1892, a 110-foot ketch called *Albert*. Grenfell was officially ship's surgeon but liked to call himself "master mariner," although his certificate qualified him only to command *Vagabond*, a small yawl he owned with Treves. He managed to irritate the *Albert*'s captain by practising navigation and comparing it with the experts' and by training his black retriever to fetch and carry on deck. But the crew liked him because he pitched in and helped with the painting and led them in rousing evangelical hymns.

St. John's was in ashes from its second disastrous fire when the *Albert* sailed into harbour. Even so the conditions of the eleven thousand homeless were not as bad as those of the people he was about to visit. A thousand schooners were sailing north to the fishing grounds. The *Albert* followed in their wake, along the bleak and mist-shrouded shores of northern Newfoundland and Labrador. Little had changed here since Cartier had damned it at first sight. Headland and shoreline were devoid of any colour – a drab monotone – no speck of green upon the dark ridges, no sliver of blue in the sullen skies, the grey cliffs sodden with spray, the grey rocks blurred by creeping fog, the grey beaches spattered by dirty foam, the stunted conifers rising darkly from a patchwork of soiled snow, the whole landscape like a faded photograph. And the people, too, were faded, old beyond their years, the children like aging dwarfs with peaked, grey faces, the women all bones and hide, the men, battered by the elements, shapeless in dun-coloured clothing. Yet all were marvellously hospitable and generous, for, having nothing, they gave everything.

Grenfell was horrified. He knew the slums of London, but here was poverty on a scale he had never known existed. It was not only the underdogs of society who were poor; *everyone* was poor. And half the population seemed to be sick. "The women seem to me all ill from one cause or another," he wrote to his mother in August. The concept of welfare aid for those unable or unwilling to work had no meaning in a society where men lived their lives in peril and exhaustion, hobbled by lifelong debt. Jolly sports, inspirational hymns, medical succour – none of these were enough. Life was unalleviated hell. Boats leaked, clothes were stitched together from flour sacks, huts were worse than hovels. The people suffered from rickets, tuberculosis, scurvy, infected amputations. Their remedies were lunatic: they tackled disease by swallowing lice or wearing charms of deer's teeth; they poulticed abscesses with a concoction of herbs mixed with paint; they warded off diphtheria with a cod's head tied around the neck. They resisted treatment because it meant time off from work, and those who did not work starved. To be sent to the nearest hospital (at St. John's) meant economic disaster. Some told Grenfell that the coast had no use for a doctor; only survival of the fittest made the economy possible. But Grenfell persisted: he recorded treatment that summer for nine hundred patients, many deformed, crippled, blinded, or incapacitated through continued neglect of such minor conditions as ingrowing toenails and tooth decay.

These people lived with death and with the harbingers of death: the fury of the intemperate seas; the grinding terror of the moving ice packs; the everlasting fog that shrouded the lurking rocks; the gales that tore houses and ships to pieces. In one storm in October 1867, forty vessels had been lost and forty fishermen had died while fifteen hundred people were driven, homeless, on to the shore. A North Labrador hurricane in October of 1885 had sent eighty vessels and seventy men to the bottom and flung two thousand men, women, and children on to that savage coast in a state of starvation. Grenfell became a walking repository of horror stories which he would use to advantage in his money-raising lectures in the years to come:

"One man nearly lost his life slipping under an [ice] pan. These pans rushed together with irresistible force. Another man told me that he had both his legs broken and eventually cut off by being nipped between two pieces in their sway."

"One man only was reported to me today as getting weak on the ice; that is, he gave in. When a man can go on no longer and resigns himself to sleep and ultimate death in the snow the saying is that he 'gets weak.'"

Under such conditions, Grenfell could not restrain himself. When the *Albert* returned to St. John's after its three-thousand-mile journey that summer, he went after the Newfoundland government. The government crumpled under his onslaught with surprising swiftness. It promised to build two hospitals on the northern coast. Grenfell organized a committee of merchants and politicians whose task was to get the mission in England to broaden its scope, which had hitherto been focused solely on the plight of North Sea fishermen, and to set up a permanent base in Newfoundland.

That done, he sailed for home in the *Albert*. There was only one extraordinary incident on the journey, but it was typical of Wilfred Grenfell. He had organized the crew into cricket teams. The ball went over the side. Without a moment's thought the doctor leaped overboard to retrieve it. The ship slowly tacked about. In its wake, Grenfell could be seen triumphantly holding his prize aloft. He was picked up, and the game continued. He was fond of games; life, after all, was a game – a contest with the self.

But the mission council in Britain was not happy with Wilfred Grenfell; nor would it ever be. It now had eleven ships under its wing, and Grenfell was supposed to be superintendent in charge, a middleman between the fleet and the London council; but the problem was that Grenfell would never remain in one place. The council moved him from his headquarters in Gorleston to London, where it was hoped he would stay put. He did not. He insisted on working throughout the winter aboard the North Sea ships. He went off on speaking tours to raise money for the new Labrador mission. He began to scrounge around for personnel. He spent so much time on Labrador business that there were no hours left for his official job. He wrote to the council explaining that he was too busy to be superintendent. The council, by now thoroughly concerned, forbade him to pledge mission money to Labrador without permission. That was as effective as asking a small boy to give up chewing gum for Lent. Grenfell, who had no money sense, ordered equipment on impulse and had the bills sent to the mission. For the mission council the doctor posed a constant dilemma: he was unavailable when wanted, sloppy, careless with funds, as perverse as a tabby cat, and not always responsible; but he *did* seem to have the knack of raising large sums, and he did have the public's ear. If only Wilfred Grenfell would conform! If only those marvellous talents could somehow be channelled as his superiors wanted them channelled! If only – but this was wishful thinking. The hierarchy threw up its collective hands and sent Dr. Grenfell back to Labrador in the summer of 1893.

Off he sailed in the *Albert*, taking two doctors and two nurses to staff the proposed hospitals at Battle Harbour and Indian Harbour. He had managed to scrape up funds enough to buy a forty-five-foot steam launch, which he christened *Princess May* after May of Teck, the future Queen Mary, and had talked the Allan Line into shipping the vessel to St. John's at a bargain rate. In this cockleshell he intended to steam up the Newfoundland and Labrador coasts, an undertaking that drew guffaws from seasoned seamen in St. John's.

Princess May had an eight-foot beam, and she rolled like an eel. Unlashed gear tumbled overboard every time she pitched, and she pitched constantly. The engine faltered; Grenfell had not bothered to check it over. The compass was two points out; he had not checked that, either. He was, at best, a Sunday sailor ignorant of the finer points of navigation. At the outset he almost ran into a cliff and was forced to hail a passing fishing boat to get his bearings. He had no charts worthy of the name, the only ones extant being those made by Captain James Cook in the previous century.

No matter: off he blundered through reefs and shoals, sheltering at night in coves thronged with the sick, pleading for treatment (for his arrival was always broadcast by some mysterious form of moccasin telegraph). Clearly he was having a wonderful time. He was also fostering a legend.

Late one evening he arrived at Battle Harbour, the site of one of the new hospitals. The *Albert* had preceded him. Grenfell dropped his medical staff but did not stay; he darted south again with only an engineer as crew, through the Strait of Belle Isle and along the southern coast of Labrador, picking up the occasional passenger, including a Roman Catholic bishop and a Methodist preacher whom he put to work as deckhands. Then north again, grounding in shallows and on rocks, struggling clear somehow, cruising deep into unknown inlets, shooting game birds, casting for salmon, sketching the foreshore, and rejoicing in the whole adventure. Up the Labrador coast he chugged to Indian Harbour, site of the second hospital, where he again encountered the *Albert*, and then on north to Hopedale, where he was firmly warned to go no farther. But, typically, he did go on for another 160 miles, watching for reefs from a ladder lashed to the mast, visiting with the people, preaching and doctoring and gathering material for a devastating report for the mission council. The living conditions of the liveyeres were almost unbelievable; the doctor discovered that a typical hut constructed of sod, mud, and old boards would house as many as fourteen persons and all their dogs. Equally infamous was the truck system, through which the merchants of St. John's kept the fishermen in thrall; their purchases always seemed to exceed the profit from their catch. In Grenfell's innovative mind, the idea of a system of co-operatives was beginning to take shape.

Back down the coast he went by fits and starts. The *Princess May* was the last boat to leave Labrador that winter. When she ran short of fuel, Grenfell tore the roof off the cabin and burned it. When he lost his compass overboard, he navigated by eye. When he reached Twillingate he learned that he had been given up for dead: a London newspaper had printed his obituary; only Dear Old Mum, with her abiding faith, refused to give up hope. When at last he reached St. John's he raced three steamers into the harbour, with one of his casual passengers – a Salvation Army captain this time – playing the violin on deck. His arrival was a small triumph. He had taken his improbable craft three thousand miles without lights or accurate charts. The *Albert*, on the other hand, had encountered a gale, run aground, and been hammered on the rocks. She was hauled off by a rescue boat and had lost her jib boom in Belle Isle strait. Her captain's comments, when the doc-

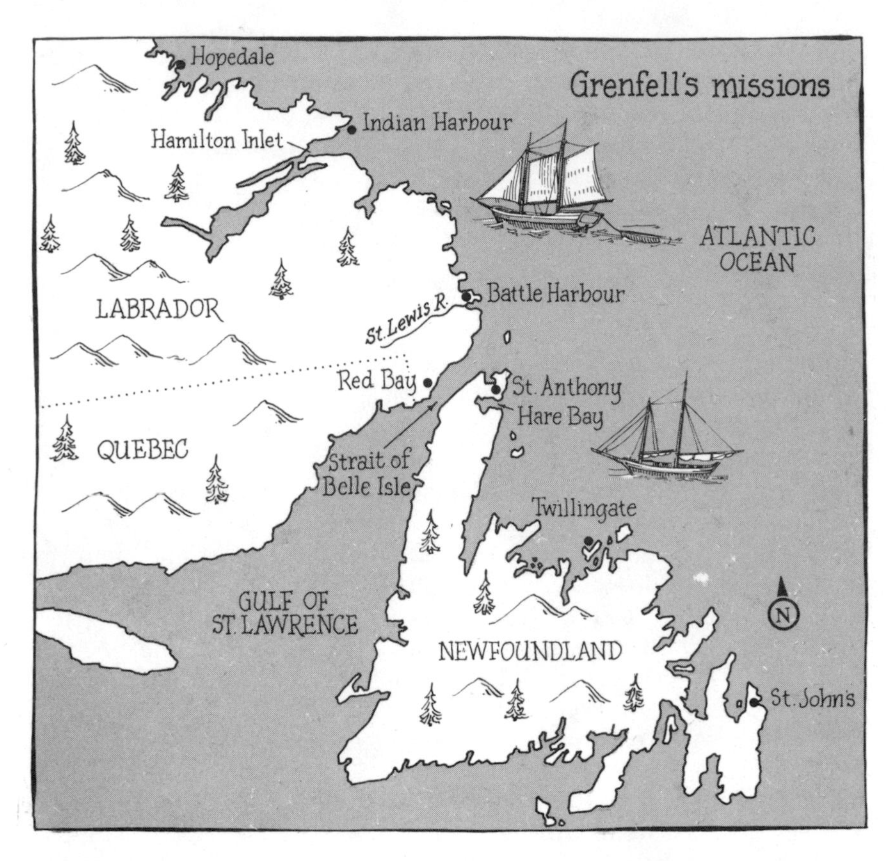

tor cheerfully moored the *Princess May* beside him, went unrecorded.

The *Albert* sailed back to England without Grenfell. He had decided to cross Canada at his own expense – and without permission – to raise money for a third Labrador hospital. When he returned to London the following February, the response from the mission council was decidedly chilly. The funds he had raised were not for the work of the mission as a whole but "for the work of Dr. Grenfell." The man seemed to be starting a fiefdom of his own!

Still . . . he *had* raised a great deal of money. He had crossed Canada on a CPR pass wangled from that old Labrador hand, Sir Donald Smith, the man who drove the railroad's final spike at Craigellachie. Now the mission learned that under Grenfell's gentle prodding, Smith had donated a steamer to the cause, to be named, of course, *Sir Donald*. It was valued at eighteen hundred dollars, a bit more than the fifteen hundred it had cost to repair the *Princess May* after Grenfell's summer journey. But the gift turned out to be a mixed blessing. It was a foregone conclusion that the doctor would captain the new vessel. Back to North America he went in late August of 1894, picked up the prize, and worked her through the Strait of Belle Isle. As he sailed her triumphantly into Battle Harbour, he struck a reef, damaging her so badly that she was out of commission for a year. With the *Princess May* also disabled and the *Albert* ordered back to England, he was forced to make do with a twenty-foot jollyboat. It served his purpose, which was to keep moving. "I never feel at ease," he wrote to a friend, "unless I am moving along day and night."

When he returned to England in December of 1894, the mission was forced to admit that he was an asset. He published his first book, *Vikings of Today*, and donated all the profits to the cause. He was now known as the Labrador Doctor and becoming a popular lecturer in spite of a nervous stammer and a rambling style. Subject matter triumphed over technique as the doctor spoke of a frontier few knew existed and a lifestyle that most could not imagine. The poverty and the isolation were beyond the ken of his listeners. It was hard to believe that St. Anthony, the major port of northern Newfoundland, with a bigger concentration of people than anywhere on the coast, had a permanent population of seventeen families. It was equally hard to believe that these cod fishermen and sealers were so badly off that their women often became reluctant prostitutes on schooners in exchange for food for their families. And was it really possible that white Christians with British ancestors treated rheumatism by wearing a haddock's finbone around the neck?

It was Grenfell's conviction that much of the poverty was the result of the system perpetuated by the Water Street merchants of St. John's, who paid the fishermen for their catch not in money but in sugar, vegetables, clothes, even liquor. So enslaved were the people that, in order to keep on the right side of the merchants, they preferred to maintain a slight debit balance. Grenfell's response was to launch a fishermen's co-operative at Red Bay, one of the poorest of the Newfoundland communities. He had scarcely accomplished this, in the summer of 1895, when the mission council pulled him back to England, apparently for good. Another doctor, Fred Willway, would take over the work in Labrador; Grenfell, whose profile was becoming alarmingly high, would go back to the North Sea trawlers.

The council thought it had divorced him from Labrador, but he was not easy to muzzle. Grenfell insisted on talking about it as if he were still involved. One of his most captivating stories concerned a crippled Eskimo boy named Pomuik, who had been on display at the Columbian Exposition in Chicago in 1893. Grenfell, with his flair for the dramatic, always referred to him as "Prince Pomuik" because he was the son of a minor chief. When the exposition ended, the boy was unceremoniously abandoned in Newfoundland and told to find his way home to Labrador. A Boston Congregationalist who had befriended the boy in Chicago called on Grenfell to help find him. Grenfell obliged. He traced Pomuik to the head of a Labrador fiord, near death, his crippled thigh badly infected. He sent him to hospital at Indian Harbour, where the leg was amputated. Pomuik died after Grenfell returned to England, and the Labrador Doctor wrung tears from his audiences as he recounted the story. The Boston link stood him in good stead, for it opened the door to connections with wealthy New Englanders.

The council was now determined to keep a tight lid on the irrepressible doctor. The very word "Labrador" was to be expunged from his vocabulary. At the General Meeting in 1898 he was specifically instructed not to mention it. But Grenfell would not be stifled. "I was told not to say a word about Labrador," he said as he began to speak, "but I am going to transgress . . . " and he was away in full spate. The following summer Dr. Willway asked to be relieved; Labrador was too much for his wife; the climate and the isolation had broken her health. The council was cornered; only one man could take Willway's place, and after an absence of almost three years that man returned to Battle Harbour, where crowds cheered, flags flew, and guns fired a salute. The legend was now secure.

The doctor's letters home to his mother – they are voluminous – are revealing. He delights in shocking her in the same way that he would deliberately shock an audience into a sense of guilt:

"Only two days ago I was in a starving man's hovel. I asked the mother, as usual, how many children? She replied: 'Only two now, the other two are better off.' Dead of chronic starvation."

Yet Grenfell's style is so brisk that the effect tends to be muted. His letters display a kind of bluff heartiness that plays down pain and despair:

"I was eight miles off visiting a poor fellow, out of whose leg I cut a large tumour . . . . The poor chap was half starved and fainted twice the first night when I began, so I had to give him food and begin in the morning again. I had only a local anaesthetic, cocaine, but it worked splendidly. I had to sew him up, six stitches with black thread from his wife's box as I had no sutures. These I sterilized and took them out last night. My driver and servant had to hold the man and get another man to hold the wound open. Luckily he did not faint, though, poor chap, the sweat ran off his brow like a sponge."

Grenfell was not an intensely sensitive man. Had he been, it is doubtful that he could have survived psychologically. His tales of hardship and heartache are rather like those of a college boy describing a game of rugger. In one letter home, written during his first trip to Labrador, he did strike a poignant note:

"One poor Eskimo called Jonas had both his hands shot off. I cut one arm at the elbow and would have taken off the other another day but mercifully he never recovered . . . . As I left the shore last night it was 10:30, dark and blowing. His poor wife heard my call for the *Albert*'s boat and came out to bid me good-by, she would not let go of my hand and I left her standing on the rocks after I had gone, crying as though she would break her heart. She could not speak English but just pointed up to signify that we should meet again in Heaven. It just made me cry outright."

This is a moving scene, but then Grenfell had to add: "Certainly these people are very affectionate and have the same feelings we have, though not, I believe, quite so acute." This is the gentleman missionary speaking, the country squire, the public-school boy, the Oxford blue. The lower classes, like domestic pets, must be looked after, but they cannot be expected to love or hate, to feel joy or sorrow to *quite* the same degree as their betters. "Missionary as I am," Grenfell had written to Dear Old Mum in 1896, "I fully believe in strict discipline as the best thing for the uneducated classes."

Yet it would be unfair to fault him for being what he was – the product of his time and of his background. His letters reveal him as the perennial schoolboy, rejoicing in the frontier life. He was at last able to spend a winter in St. Anthony and his gusto is infectious: "The first snow is on the deck – I'm just revelling in it," he wrote to his mother. As for the harsh Atlantic winters that drove so many fishermen to despair, it was "one long delight":

"My dog team is very smart. Red & blue tassels & every dog with a bell. My komatik with whale bone runners is a beauty. It is most exhilarating flying over mountain and valley, over sea flake behind the fast dog team."

Life was a lark to Grenfell and never more than when he was on the move: "It is a wonderful coast and I suppose I'm the only man on earth who can take a steamer down it at full speed."

Even his harshest descriptions of life in bad weather aboard his newest ship, the *Strathcona* (its donor now raised to the peerage) have a kind of *Boy's Own Paper* quality:

"Just fancy cleaning fish in the dark on deck in the blinding snow and rain of the past month with gales of wind blowing and constant waves coming over soaking all hands to the skin. The head piece that Granny made comes in after a night watch hanging with icicles and the men's beards and noses positively glisten with icicles. Just fancy, too, carrying water out of your stockings and putting them on again before going to bed and merely leaving your legs hanging out of your bunk to allow them to dry on . . . ."

At the end of his life, the doctor summed up his credo in a single sentence in a letter to a friend: "When two courses are open my plan in life has always been to take the most venturesome." To him life *was* a magnificent adventure. Did it ever cross that nimble but insouciant mind that the hardships of the Labrador and Newfoundland coasts, which he saw as a sporting challenge, were to the fishermen a source of unrelenting horror from which there was no escape? Only rarely in his letters home did Grenfell manage to capture the pathos of the situation. He was too busy flexing his muscles, dashing from one adventure to the next, pounding on the doors of the idle rich, to stop and reflect upon the reality around him. He was, after all, trained as an orthopaedic surgeon. All surgeons, one of his colleagues has said, are extroverts and orthopaedic surgeons more extroverted than most because theirs is a skill that deals entirely with bones and joints – solid things that either work or don't work; thus their occupation requires little self-examination.

Dr. Grenfell carried this lack of introspection into his evangelism. His faith was simple, all embracing, and untroubled by doubt; it never changed. He believed in deeds not words. His was a religion of action: "Christ's man should be a man first and foremost – a man among men." The muscular Christian saw faith as a contest, a wrestling match with the Devil. Early in his career, when suffering terribly from seasickness, he wrote his Dear Old Mum that "in Christ I can do all things and I just got up and had a run up and down. It's a nasty fight but can and must be won." He had little in common with the orthodox churches: "I've come to judge people's religion by their spirit and their works. Some of our honest talkers here are thieves and robbers in my estimation."

The worst thieves and robbers, in Grenfell's estimation, were the traders who exploited the peoples of the coast. He declared war upon them. As a justice of the peace, he prosecuted them for bootlegging. As an agent for Lloyds, he hit them for faking wrecks and scuppering old hulks for insurance money. His methods were unorthodox; he once threatened to take a man's wooden leg in lieu of a fine. He spread himself thin, yet he got results. By 1899, his first co-operative at Red Bay was able to declare a 10 per cent dividend. Within a few years, he had seven more in operation.

He saw the need to instil in the people a sense of community; without it the movement could not grow. And so that winter in St. Anthony he plunged into a flurry of activity: there were soccer games, shooting matches, duck hunts, obstacle races, concerts. St. Anthony was to be his headquarters, the hub of his empire; he would make it grow. Its people would build their own hospital; he led them into the forest to cut the lumber by hand. Other buildings would follow, and on each would be a Biblical quotation: "Whatsoever ye do, do it heartily for the Lord." That phrase, adorning the industrial workshop, summed up the Grenfellian credo.

In the summer he was off again up the coast. In London, the members of the mission council, who had deceived themselves into believing his sojourn was temporary, gave up their attempts to lure him home. The best they could hope for was to put a curb on his spending but this was more easily demanded than achieved. By 1900 his hospitals were treating four thousand patients a year, for everything from toothaches to brain tumours. Grenfell ignored all instructions to be frugal.

He plunged into new ventures. Apart from a little trapping, the people of the coast depended on two staple harvests – codfish and seals. The doctor set about to diversify their resources. He launched a co-operative lumber mill and an experimental farm. He founded an entire range of cottage industries, the manufacturing of hooked rugs, ivory and wood carvings, deerskin mitts and sealskin boots, the weaving of cloth and the preserving of foodstuff. He tried to get the coasts charted in order to bring in tourists, sent his own coastal sketches to the Royal Navy, urged the Canadian government to prospect for minerals. Some of the schemes worked, at least temporarily. Others aborted. At one point he ordered three hundred reindeer to be brought from Finland to launch a new industry; it was not a success.

He had, in the meantime, incurred the wrath of the traders along the coast and some of the merchants and ecclesiastics of St. John's. That opposition surfaced in 1905 with a vicious article in the St. John's *Trade Review*, which accused him of making a personal profit from his ventures. "We are not surprised," the *Review* declared, "to hear that he will soon retire from the Mission with what the sinful and the vulgar would call 'his whack of spondulicks.' " This opening shot touched off a volley of criticism led by the Roman Catholic archbishop, who had been irked by Grenfell's attacks on orthodox religion and his brand of evangelical Protestantism, not to mention his plans for non-denominational schools, which were opposed by Catholics and Anglicans alike. "Grenfell," the archbishop wrote, "is not needed on that shore and his work is not only useless but worse than useless. It is demoralizing, pauperizing, degrading."

The doctor fought back. He forced the *Trade Review* to apologize under the threat of a libel suit and, with the mission council publicly backing him, was able to prove false the archbishop's long list of charges against him. Meanwhile he had launched a new project, one of his most successful – an orphanage in St. Anthony for children found starving, deserted, naked, and homeless.

But the focus of his life was changing. He spent less time preaching and ministering to the sick and more time raising funds. He was an indifferent surgeon – some called him mediocre – who had succeeded largely through a remarkable bedside manner. A colleague, Dr. Theodore Badger, who worked with him on the *Strathcona*, has described Grenfell's medical approach as "almost like the laying on of hands. He didn't do much surgery. He had a few pills which he shook out of his pocket. But when you were talking to him it was as if nobody existed in the world but you." This personal magnetism made him uncommonly effective as a fund raiser. To Badger he was "one of the most unselfconscious men I have ever known. He would just walk onto the stage without a note in his hand and talk to the wealthy . . . tell them what he thought of them." The wealthy, in agonies of guilt, would dig into their pockets. In a single month in the United States, in 1906, Grenfell raised twenty thousand dollars for his work, an extraordinary feat when one realizes that this was an English doctor with an upper-class accent asking Americans to support welfare work in a British colony.

But, then, Grenfell broke all the rules of platform deportment. He was not a good speaker in the conventional sense. He rambled; he went beyond his time; he made appalling gaffes. He told one audience of Christian Scientists that they should have more sense than to spend millions on a monument to a "silly old woman" – the silly old woman being Mary Baker Eddy, the founder of the sect.

He was astonishingly blunt. "And what do you get out of all this work, Dr. Grenfell?" a plump businessman asked him. The doctor poked him in the paunch. "Not this, anyhow," he said.

He had no compunction in pointing to a string of pearls around a dowager's throat and exclaiming, "Those are worth twenty thousand dollars; that money would be better spent helping the people of Labrador."

He had a poor platform style, but he did have a sense of theatre. At a meeting in Boston, he introduced three orphans from Labrador, and on the impulse of the moment proceeded to auction them off to foster parents, taking the money for the mission. The children were, of course, returned to the orphanage at St. Anthony. Grenfell could size up an audience like a politician. His speeches, like his books, fitted the style of the period and his recital of life in Labrador never failed to grip his listeners.

He had a special appeal to Americans of the pre-war years. The British were already disturbed by intellectual doubts, but the Americans were still idealists, vastly impressed by the Labrador Doctor's image as a man of action, risk, and accomplishment and by his simple muscular Christianity. The sons of the well-to-do from Harvard and Yale flocked to Labrador each summer as WOPS – Workers Without Pay – to toil as stevedores, cooks, dish-washers, anaesthetists, and veterinarians and to follow their hero in a morning plunge from the cross-trees of the *Strathcona* into the freezing waters, followed by a ritual race to the closest ice pan.

By 1906, Grenfell was a world figure, awarded the CMG in the King's birthday list of that year and the hero of a variety of sentimental books and magazine articles. Edward VII had him to the palace; Andrew Carnegie made him a house guest and donated three thousand books to the mission; the Governor General of Canada put him up at Rideau Hall. Oxford bestowed upon him an honorary doctorate of medicine – the first it had ever given. In St. John's, the Bowrings were his hosts and companions. Did Grenfell, in the midst of dunning them for money, mention the unmentionable – the degrading conditions on the Bowring ships at the height of the seal hunt? We do not know.

He professed not to enjoy his honours. Fund raising, he insisted, was necessary but irksome; he hated asking for money. Possibly; but did he really hate the attention, the adulation, the recognition that he, Wilfred Grenfell, was receiving from heads of state? His very eccentricity was disarming. He would often turn up late on social occasions, improperly dressed. Was this entirely a pose? Probably not. He was in love with the sea and he enjoyed those exhilarating summers, testing himself against the rocky inlets of the Labrador coast. It was, after all, a continuation of his childhood, but with no parents in control. There was always something of the small boy in Wilfred Grenfell. "He did what he wanted to do and if somebody told him not to do something he would go ahead and do it anyway," Dr. Badger has recalled. He could be remarkably gentle; the word most often used to describe him is "lovable." But he could be ruthless when he did not get his own way; he could and did throw tantrums when others followed a course not his.

The Ice Pan Adventure of 1908, which increased his public stature, was typically Grenfellian. His impulsiveness, his incautiousness, his refusal to heed advice got him into trouble; his coolness and resourcefulness under pressure got him out. His sense of theatre and his courage turned the incident into an international act of heroism. The doctor had himself photographed in the costume he had worn that Easter Sunday – the Oxford shorts and the football stockings – waving aloft the shirt-flag on its staff of dog bones. The picture was taken in front of the hospital at St. Anthony, but the background was retouched to make it appear to have been made on the ice pan itself. Grenfell tended to play down the incident; he had the English flair for self-dramatization while appearing to deprecate his accomplishments. He knew the form – the form that makes a bloody siege "a bit of a rough go." The Ice Pan Adventure changed in the telling. When Grenfell rewrote it as a book for boys, he gave the impression that, immediately on being rescued, he had dashed back to St. Anthony behind a dog team. The truth was that he had been carried in, barely conscious.

By this date, the Mission to Deep Sea Fishermen wanted out. The doctor's disinclination to follow instructions, or even to report, was maddening. He was supposed to be a missionary, preaching the gospel; what was he doing organizing *handicrafts*? His charges were supposed to be deep sea fishermen; why was he working with shore folk, teaching them to weave and carve? And what on earth was happening to all the money – the money that was going into "special funds" (whatever *they* were!) that never reached England? Dr. Grenfell was ordering hospital extensions that nobody had authorized and ship repairs without a by-your-leave; he was inviting strange guests to the coast while forbidding others to come; he was behaving very like a dictator and – worst of all – he was changing the direction of the mission away from religion toward social reform. Too often his superiors read of his work in the newspapers before receiving his reports.

There were other changes. In 1907, he had helped set up a separate Grenfell Association of America in New York and another in New England. The mission council was upset at the use of the Grenfell name, but before it could move, the associations became legal entities. By 1908, the doctor was on bad terms with the council's agent in St. John's and a long, acrimonious, and complicated argument over funds erupted. No one questioned Grenfell's honesty, but his accounting methods were shockingly casual: checks were kited, funds were unaccounted for; records, when they existed at all, were incomplete. Grenfell belonged to that breed of enthusiasts – they have been called visionaries, and dreamers, and also bunglers and incompetents – whose ideas outrun their execution, who are impatient of detail, and who, in leaping from peak to peak, tend to strew behind them a litter of unfinished business and a perplexity of half-executed concepts, which lesser mortals must put in order.

The dispute over funds led to a not very satisfactory investigation, which, eventually brought about the formation in 1912 of the International Grenfell Association, almost entirely divorced from London, with Grenfell as Superintendent of Missions and a proper board of directors and a finance committee to look after the accounts.

Yet it must be emphasized that even those who were exasperated by the doctor's unorthodox approach found him an endearing man. His very offhandedness, his lack of pretension, his simple devotion to a cause that had seemed hopeless were attractive qualities. He had that rarest of abilities – it is found in certain politicians – of concentrating his full attention on whomever he encountered. The most casual stranger was made to feel important, convinced that Wilfred Grenfell was genuinely interested in him and in what he had to say.

In spite of his financial bumbling, none could deny that he got results. Without Grenfell there would have been no mission to Labrador. The secretary of the Mission to Deep Sea Fishermen who had originally been dispatched by London to investigate the financial tangle, had this advice for a later colleague:

"May I remind you and all associated with Dr. Grenfell that you have a man to deal with of peculiar temperament whose vices, paradox as it may seem, are his virtues. His extraordinary personality and his steam-power driving energy are his God-given virtues, which have led to his accomplishing an enormous amount of good . . . the gift of balance and judgment having been denied him, his strong personality and driving force result in his making errors and possessing methods and aims which an ordinary man would perceive and in littleness avoid. But whatever errors Dr. Grenfell makes and however wrong his methods may appear, judged by ordinary standards, you must never lose sight of the fact that his actions are prompted by the highest motives."

In the midst of this hullabaloo, Grenfell, at the age of forty-four, surprised everybody by taking a wife. He had seldom demonstrated any special interest in the opposite sex; his energies had been channelled in other directions. No doubt he found solace in the time-honoured and very Victorian therapy of the cold plunge, which, for him, was a ritual. He had said on one occasion in 1904 that he liked American girls – the Christian ones: they were so practical, so full of go and capacity. And it was to an American girl of impeccable social credentials that he became, at last, attracted.

She was Anne Elizabeth Caldwell MacClanahan, a twenty-three-year-old Chicago heiress and Bryn Mawr graduate, whose father, a successful lawyer, had been a Confederate officer in the Civil War and whose mother was the daughter of a Vermont judge. She had been "doing Europe" – the obligatory tour that was the birthright of every young American aristocrat (in Miss MacClanahan's case it was the last leg of a three-year trip around the world) – and was returning to America in May, 1909, when she encountered Grenfell on the deck of the *Mauretania*. More likely, he encountered her through her travelling companion, a prominent midwest banker and family friend named William R. Stirling. Grenfell was taking Dear Old Mum, then seventy-eight years old, on her first trip to the New World to see him receive an honorary degree at Harvard. It is likely that he saw in Stirling an important ally in his campaign for funds.

The doctor's own account of his first meeting with the autocratic and firm-minded Miss MacClanahan was highly romantic. He was, he said, attracted by her beauty and her background but proceeded to lecture her on the uselessness of her life as a social butterfly. "But you don't even know my name!" she retorted. To which he replied that he was interested only in her future name: Grenfell.

This charming anecdote seems a little pat. The future Lady Grenfell was no shrinking violet; the most cursory inspection of her character suggests that it was she and not the famous Labrador Doctor who was the dominant figure in a swift romance that led to a fashionable wedding in Grace Episcopal Church of Chicago in November of the same year.

Miss MacClanahan knew what she wanted. "All my life," she told a Chicago newspaper, "I have been interested in reading of those who have made sacrifices for the general welfare of mankind. I realized when I became a young woman that if ever my heart was won, the conqueror must be more than a mere figure in society or a successful business or professional man. The men I met – none of them – seemed to comply with my requirements. When I met Dr. Grenfell I realized at once that my ideal had been found." What Anne MacClanahan wanted, she generally managed to get.

The doctor brought his bride to St. Anthony by mail steamer in

January, 1910. It was not a propitious voyage for a honeymoon; the journey took nine days instead of the usual five because the ship encountered a blizzard and a gale, which drove the spray onto the vessel until it was "sugared like a vast Christmas cake." They arrived on a chilly night to a warm welcome. Skyrockets and flares lit up the sky; cannon and shotgun rent the air. A driver on a decorated *komatik* slid up to the dock, and the happy couple, perched upon the sled and followed by a long line of welcomers, were driven to the staff house where a bed-sheet banner flapped a "welcome to our noble doctor and his bonnie bride." The fisher families, silently lining the path, and the mission staff were treated to their first glimpse of the new chatelaine of St. Anthony: a tall, handsome, large-boned, and aristocratic girl, wearing a fashionable hat with a short veil on her piled-up hair. The American press had made much of her sacrifice in leaving high society for a life in the wilderness. One New York paper had gone so far as to depict her future home as a tiny log hovel. It was, in fact, to be a mansion, built on the hill above the mission – a two-storey edifice of local stone with a magnificent glassed-in verandah, central heating, and electricity, the grandest dwelling in the community. It was immediately dubbed "the Castle," a title that exists to this day.

Of this "Grenfellian mansion" (the doctor's own description) the new bride took imperious command. She had brought her own furniture from Chicago; the following morning she supervised its installation. She demanded a cook and got one. She ordered that a leaky roof be fixed; it was. Styles changed; informality vanished. People no longer dropped in, in the local fashion – not even Reuben Sims, Grenfell's guide, servant, and friend – they waited to be invited. Mrs. Grenfell was nothing if not regal. There was a quality about her that made the locals feel awkward. Clearly, she felt herself above them; and to this day in St. Anthony, stories are told to illustrate that point:

– About the time she held a dinner party and the cook, worried about the quantity of food, asked what would happen if anybody asked for second helpings. Replied Anne Grenfell, "They wouldn't *dare*!"

– About the workman who spent three days digging a trench for a drain and rang the Castle's bell, announcing that the job was done. Said Anne Grenfell, "Wait a minute, my good fellow," went back in the house, and returned with – an apple.

– About the woman who worked a sixteen-hour day in the summer preparing meals for the Workers Without Pay, a task so exhausting that she often slept in her clothes. When Anne Grenfell paid her for her week's work – a sum of a dollar and a half – she asked, "And what are you going to do with all that money now?"

In the first summer of their marriage, Grenfell took her with him on the *Strathcona* up the Labrador coast to show her the land he loved. He delighted in it all – in the people who brought him presents of rotting whale meat for his dogs; in the cool, northern nights when they bunked down amid piles of salt cod; in the smoky sod huts where they crouched down eating cod heads or "browse," which is soaked ship's biscuit mixed with cod and served with crisped pork fat. She loathed it – loathed every minute of it: the sea, the ship, St. Anthony; but, to her credit, she accepted it all without complaint, in her fashion.

She was a natural manager. She set out to organize her husband (a monumental task) and it is a tribute to her determination that she succeeded remarkably well. Without her, he would have been less effective. Dr. Badger remembers her, seated behind him on the stage at a fund-raising lecture, passing him a stream of little hand-written notes to overcome his notorious absent-mindedness: "Don't forget Mrs. Badger . . . Don't forget Dr. and Mrs. Little . . . etc., etc." She handled his mail and his appointments and took over from his brother, Algernon, the editing of his books and articles, some of which she virtually wrote herself. (Was that arch anecdote about the marriage proposal hers?) When Houghton, Mifflin, the publishers, congratulated the doctor on a story in the *Atlantic Monthly*, she replied: "I am much interested in it, as I did a great deal about it myself. I did all the polishing and worked for days over it." At St. Anthony she took over the marketing of goods produced by the cottage industries and raised a fund to send local children to schools in the United States and England. She also annoyed old friends by sending notes saying that her husband had no time for them. "She was boss; she ran him like a puppet," her son Wilfred, the eldest of the three children she bore the doctor, has said of her. He has also said that "she would have liked nothing better than to be the Duchess of St. Anthony" and that "she was one of those people who was never happy unless she was frantically engaged in activity for its own sake," a description which, he agrees, also applied to his father.

If these remarks sound less than filial, it is perhaps because the Grenfells were virtual strangers to their offspring. They wanted the best for them: a special cow to give them pure milk, a French governess – luxuries far beyond the reach of those who lived below and beyond the Castle – but they did not provide their children with the one gift that money cannot buy. Anne Grenfell rarely expressed motherly emotion. "The only time I ever remember her showing any sign of real love in the best sense of the word," Wilfred has said, "was when I was about four or five. As a sort of great privilege, handed down from above, I was brought to an upstairs room in the Castle and allowed to sleep in her room. I remember I regarded this as a sort of audience, as a tremendous privilege. It was manna from Heaven; but it's the only time I ever remember her showing anything. I don't remember her hugging or kissing me or any of us."

In later years the gap widened; Wilfred's memory is that he rarely saw his parents for more than two weeks out of a year. Anne Grenfell's time was reserved for her husband; *he* was her real child. She was determined that he would be even more famous than when she met him; to that end she would polish him as she polished his prose. She even managed to change the way he dressed; morning coats replaced the old tweed jackets; no longer did he wear mismatched socks and shoes. He had once been so indifferent to his appearance that he had been ticked off by court officials at the Palace and had appeared at Harvard wearing his Oxford gown over a yellow tweed suit and yellow shoes. There was something engaging about this; after all, it was part of the Grenfell legend. But he meekly accepted the change because "Anne told me I must dress properly because people expect it." The perverse boy, who in manhood had always had his own way, was once again under parental control.

She had decided from the outset that he would be most useful to the mission as a publicist and fund raiser. In this, no doubt, she was right; it also suited her own way of life, for she basked in the limelight. "Notables kept Wilfred talking for hours," she enthused in a letter to her mother when, in 1911, the pair crossed the Atlantic. "All London is crying out to meet us." Nellie Melba, the opera diva, occupied the adjacent deck chair on the *Mauretania*. King George sent for Grenfell and kept him talking for an hour about Labrador. Sir Ernest Shackleton, the Antarctic explorer, chaired a meeting at which Grenfell spoke. The Royal Geographical Society gave him a reception. Count Marconi offered to install wireless on the *Strathcona*. Dr. Treves, now knighted, invited the couple to stay at Windsor.

Anne Grenfell insisted that her husband leave the work on the coast to the team that he had trained, headed by Dr. John Little, a brilliant surgeon who had helped to eliminate beriberi in Labrador. By 1914 the little mission of the nineties had expanded into a vast and complicated organization: six permanent doctors and eighteen nurses, their ranks swollen each summer by fourteen additional doctors and one hundred and fifty WOP volunteers.

Four hospitals and six nursing stations treated more than six thousand patients every year. The annual budget, handled by a finance committee, had grown to sixty-six thousand dollars. All of this resulted from the inspiration of one man who had by now become a kind of walking flag for the enterprise that bore his name but who was spending less and less time on the coast. Instead, his wife commandeered the homes of the rich and powerful, where the couple stayed, accompanied by an increasing staff.

Grenfell was not immune from criticism. An entire generation of Labrador and Newfoundland traders had been forced out of business or compelled to cut prices because of the success of his co-operatives. In 1916, the merchants of St. John's petitioned the Newfoundland government to take away the mission's privileges because of bad publicity and unfair competition. Grenfell was presenting to the world a picture of a colony composed almost entirely of paupers; his institution was able to sell goods without paying duty or freight charges; the merchants wanted these perquisites curtailed or abolished. A commissioner was appointed to investigate the complaints. His report, laudatory of Grenfell and his mission, quenched the protests from Water Street, but there was little love lost between the doctor and the merchants of Newfoundland.

A few years before, when a customs officer had asked her if she had any spirits to declare, Anne Grenfell had let slip a revealing remark. "My husband," she said, "does not allow strong drink in the colonies." The Grenfell Mission was, in every sense, colonial. All of its doctors and nurses came from either the United States or England (except for one from Australia). Its young volunteer workers came from the good eastern universities. Most of its funds were raised outside of Newfoundland. No one in its hierarchy was a native Newfoundlander. And there were few if any Canadians among staff or volunteers. As one Torontonian remarked to Grenfell, the Canadians were quite used to ice and snow; to them there was nothing in the least exotic about the bald cliffs of Newfoundland or the bleak fiords of Labrador.

Grenfell's strength lay in his ability to romanticize one of the grimmest corners of the continent. But there was a potential weakness, too; the fact that the mission was an entirely foreign effort. One can understand, if not sympathize with, the feeling in St. John's that these were "outsiders" come to stir up the natives. There was something just a little patronizing about these strangers. The Prime Minister, Sir Richard Squires (to whom Grenfell privately referred, in a letter to a friend, as "a thief"), was infuriated by the doctor's impassioned descriptions of the sufferings of the liveyeres. Squires was trying to coax a good credit rating for the colony from the financial interests of New York and London, but everywhere he went he "came upon the bloody trail of a man named Grenfell." He openly accused the doctor of blackmailing the consciences of generous foreigners with lurid lies.

This view was not supported by the people of the coasts. At the height of one of the public attacks on Grenfell, one of them wrote to the St. John's *Evening Telegram*:

"He gets the salt brine in his eyes for he is out in all weathers .... Let those who speak ill of him follow after his heels .... Not only do the people of Labrador look for Grenfell, but forty thousand fishermen look for him sooner or later ... they know the magnificent work he has done .... There is not a fisherman I know or a fishing skipper that sails a vessel to Labrador has anything but good to say of Grenfell or his work, and it would be to our shame if one of us could not give Grenfell our everlasting gratitude."

Yet, as the years moved on, the doctor saw progressively less of the coast. He wintered for the last time in St. Anthony in 1918-19, the year of the great influenza epidemic, a tragedy that was to make the mission workers heroes in the world's eyes, for they struggled day and night against impossible odds. The statistics are shocking: in Okkak, a community of 270, every man died; only thirty-nine women and children survived. At Cartwright, forty children were orphaned. Dogs, neglected and starving, attacked the dying. Entire families succumbed, and their huts were burned over their corpses to kill infection. The plague put an additional strain on the mission. Grenfell, impulsively ordering more buildings, boats and repairs, sank it deeper into debt. But what if the doctor were himself to die? Face to face that winter with the uncertainty of life, the mission came to realize that the leader was not immortal. If he went, where would the funds come from? There was only one answer: Grenfell himself must raise an endowment fund of at least one and a half million dollars to perpetuate his work. Instead of cruising north that summer, he reluctantly agreed to return to the lecture platform.

To the great satisfaction of his wife, he moved his family to Boston and set off on a tour of the United States, Canada, and Great Britain. By crowding as many as three lectures into a day he was able, by the end of the first year, to raise more than half the required amount. He returned each summer to Labrador, but his visits grew shorter. His mother died in 1921. The following year the *Strathcona* was lost at sea. In 1924, nearly sixty, exhausted by fund raising, he was persuaded by the directors of the International Grenfell Association to embark on a nine-month cruise. It was designed to help him recuperate, but he could not relax; the lectures, the receptions, the appeals for funds, the constant correspondence with the mission all continued.

The following year he returned to London, formed the Grenfell Association of Great Britain, and cut himself off from the Mission to Deep Sea Fishermen, whose contributions to his Labrador work had for some time been minimal. Whipping about Britain in a second-hand car that frequently broke down, he was, as always, an enormous hit. He commanded overflow audiences; hotels refused to bill him; porters and waitresses handed back their tips as donations; typists worked for nothing; youngsters volunteered as WOPS. The lure of the Labrador wilderness – the lure of the unknown – tempted the imagination of young Englishmen as it had once seduced the doctor himself.

He had published thirty-five books and hundreds of articles, and his wife was busily revising and enlarging his biography. By 1926, both were in bad health. She had been treated for a tumour she must have suspected was malignant; he had suffered his first major heart attack. Yet in spite of this, and in spite of a worse heart attack three years later, he continued his fund-raising efforts.

He would have much preferred to cruise that dark and brine-encrusted coastline, diving into the freezing waters of a morning, prescribing for the fishermen, preaching to the liveyeres, and living a carefree adventurous life; but this was not to be. One February he found himself at his "lowest ebb" in a hotel room in Birmingham, Alabama, and sat down to pour out his thoughts in a letter to his friend George Warburton, the General Secretary of the YMCA for North America:

"Talking for money – talking – talking – talking – sometimes to individuals, sometimes to crowds. But talking. I wasn't bred that way and I look forward to the day of my deliverance. Do you love the open and the silence of the woods and the next-to-nature life, and the challenge of the wild? Here I hear of it in Labrador. I see it and pass by – never still, always urged on and on, as if I must fall off the edge some day . . . ."

He was laden with honours: Lord Rector of St. Andrew's, a Livingstone Gold Medal, a Fellowship in the Royal Geographical Society, and a knighthood. He was now Sir Wilfred Grenfell. The title was shared, with considerable pride and not a little hauteur, by his wife. In St. Anthony a local acquaintance committed the unpardonable error of addressing her as "Mrs. Grenfell." "*Lady* Grenfell to you!" came the frosty reply.

He had reached the pinnacle but had passed his prime. He was like a sports hero who has lost his crown but refuses to admit defeat – a boxer vainly attempting one more comeback. At the hospital in St. Anthony he was tolerated and sometimes indulged; but he was not always welcomed, for he could be a disturbing and irritating influence. Dr. Charles Curtis, in charge of the hospital, lacked Grenfell's brilliance and bedside manner, but he was a better organizer and a better surgeon. For some years he had been the real head of the mission, and it irked him when his mentor would suddenly turn up, come roaring into the hospital, seize a white coat, and go into the wards or the operating room to tackle cases of which he knew very little. There is one tale in which Curtis, having prepared a patient for operation, arrived to discover Grenfell kneeling at the bedside in prayer. "I would prefer you to leave off praying," Curtis said acidly. "My patients are not dead yet."

Grenfell had always been a creature of impulse. Now the trait became more erratic. He would drop groups of children into the already crowded orphanage without knowing their names and forgetting where he had found them. He would walk into one of the co-operatives, pick up armfuls of clothing, and order the clerk fired when she told him he could not take the items without their being listed on a receipt. The WOPS continued to be his sole responsibility; sometimes they turned out to be drug addicts or alcoholics, shipped off by their parents for a cure and useless when they arrived. He invited important guests to visit St. Anthony and then went off cruising, leaving them to be entertained by others. He took on patients and left their after-care to the staff. He once brought in a dying man who had no identification and whose body had to be disinterred from the Protestant graveyard when his worried wife, a Roman Catholic, wrote to inquire about his whereabouts.

Nelson and Laurance Rockefeller, whose father was a financial supporter of the mission, were WOPS in Labrador in 1929; they found the experience a little disillusioning. When Laurance was stricken with appendicitis and brought into the hospital at St. Anthony after a difficult trip down the coast, Grenfell offered to perform the operation himself. In the words of a Rockefeller aide, the offer was "politely declined – the young Rockefellers were having their doubts about putting Laurance in the hands of an ailing man functioning under rather primitive conditions as to antisepsis."

Yet in spite of it all, he retained his ability to mesmerize. Curtis encountered it one day, after a shipload of tourists arrived at St. Anthony. "I'm going down to have a talk with them," Grenfell remarked. Curtis urged him not to; he was not invited – it would be an intrusion. "I don't care whether I'm invited or not," Sir Wilfred retorted. "I'm going." He approached one of the ship's officers and identified himself. He was told that the passengers were at lunch and would not want to be disturbed. "Well," said Sir Wilfred, "I'll just talk to them anyway for a couple of minutes." He walked into the dining saloon and began to talk as his listeners nibbled. He talked for five minutes; the nibbling ceased. People began to ask questions; Grenfell replied. The five minutes stretched to forty-five. At last Grenfell was finished. "Thank you very much for letting me talk to you," he said. "I would like to be able to go back to the hospital with three thousand dollars in my pocket." He got it.

He made one last voyage to Labrador in 1932. As always there were photographers and cameramen present as the sixty-eight-year-old doctor was shown gliding across the sea, propelling a kayak. But he suffered a stroke that year, and the directors suggested he resign as superintendent. Lady Grenfell was having none of that; but he did agree to give up his sole right to choose and send volunteers.

The couple retired to a handsome white-painted house in Vermont where he continued to write long, rambling articles and letters until his doctor forbade the activity. Anne Grenfell was in great pain from cancer and the resultant X-ray treatments, but she continued her work, raising funds herself, sorting out her husband's mail, protecting him from irritating letters and calls, and polishing up the best of his earlier writing for a new book to be entitled *A Labrador Logbook*.

By 1938 both were invalids. Grenfell's high blood pressure made him increasingly irrational and intolerant. Sometimes, it appeared, he was not quite sane. He had been forced to resign as superintendent of the mission in 1937, henceforth to be known as Founder. It irked him. In a letter to Harvey Cushing the following year he quoted Huxley: "The idea that one is becoming useless is the greatest shock a real human organism can experience."

Anne Grenfell was sent to Boston in October of 1938 for what was to be the last in a series of operations. She had been in great pain for years and had born it stoically; no whisper of discomfort, no murmur of complaint ever passed her lips. She worked until the end, as she had for almost all of her adult life, in the interests of her husband. When he checked into a small hotel near the hospital with his male nurse-cum-secretary, she made sure that he was not told she was dying. All of her considerable ambition had been channelled in one direction. In those final days, when she knew her disease was terminal, did she come to regret the narrowness of that devotion? There is evidence that she did. "For God's sake," she told a friend at one point – and she was in tears – "keep your children with you always. Don't farm them out." When she died, hers were not at her bedside; nor did they attend her funeral.

Her husband, with his abiding faith in the afterlife, accepted her death. She had left him a touching note, which she had managed to scrawl just before the end: "I'm going to leave today, I think – but I shall never be far away." Only after she was gone did he discover that she had squirreled away all his records, papers, drawings, and photographs for posterity.

Clearly he missed her, and yet there is more than a suspicion that he felt the kind of release a schoolboy does when the term is over. After the funeral, he came back to the home of his friend Dr. Badger, who was suffering from pneumonia and had been unable to attend the last rites. Grenfell went to his friend's bedside, then crossed to the window and, staring out, remarked, "You know, Ted, for the first time I can lead my own life." It is possible to believe that, at that moment, he was staring not at the Boston skyline but at those far shores where the cry of the gulls is lost in the clamour of the storm.

It was characteristic of Anne Grenfell that to please her husband she had asked that her ashes be scattered either at sea or at St. Anthony – the two places she most heartily detested. And so, in the summer of 1939, Sir Wilfred Grenfell set out on a final visit to his headquarters on the northeastern tip of Newfoundland. It was a far different community from the frontier settlement he had first seen almost half a century before. The hospital was thriving. The fishermen were raising crops and cattle. Old men were at work carving; the women were sewing clothes from deerskin and from the tightly woven cloth that Grenfell had suggested and that still bears his name. He cruised north on the mail steamer to welcoming crowds and then, on his return, was given the mission tender to skipper across the Strait of Belle Isle. When he left in August, the years seemed to have fallen away; his health, both physical and mental, had improved to an astonishing degree.

His recovery was close to miraculous. At one point he had been so totally disoriented that he had forgotten where Labrador was and could not recognize even such old friends as Ted Badger. Now he was alive once more. He returned to the lecture platform, and only those who had heard him in his prime knew that he was less than what he had been.

Death held no terrors for him. He had been living with death since his first heart attack, had brushed against it long before that among the ice floes of Hare Bay. He had always seen it, as he saw all of life, as a great adventure. "When I actually was looking at death, sitting on that ice pan with no material hope whatever of ever seeing land again," he wrote to his friend Warburton, "I was just as keen about what I was going to see on the other side of the horizon as I was to get back and see what I thought I had left forever behind me."

And did not death also bring freedom? For all his life, the schoolboy in him had chafed at restriction, rebelled against the constraints of convention, financial responsibility, executive red tape; his happiest moments had been spent on the frontier of the Labrador coast, alone in the wilderness of the ocean, captain and crew of his own craft, free to voyage wherever whim took him, father to his flock, protector of his people, master of his own fate and that of others.

Freedom. It is a word that crops up in his correspondence over the years. In one of the last letters he wrote (to a woman friend), on September 5, 1940, he mentioned it again:

"I'm supposed to be under sentence of death from heart trouble. You know how I look on death – as the greatest advance in life . . . soon we shall ourselves get free of this human temporary habitation and know what real freedom is . . . ."

The following month – the date was October 9 – at the age of seventy-five, he played a rousing game of croquet with his secretary and a visiting professor. He went upstairs for a rest before dinner and there, in his sleep, the Labrador Doctor embarked upon his last great adventure.

THREE

The saga of Sam Steele

The North West: 1874

" . . . Between Fort Garry and Fort Edmonton there were only two buildings occupied by white men: the log forts, Carlton and Ellice. Nothing else. Nothing but grass, poplar copses, and wolf willow; nothing but rolling hills, blue lakes, coulées, and vast river valleys; nothing but marshes, buffalo wallows, and more grass – no bridges, few trails, no supplies of any kind. The young men in their pillbox hats would have to be farmers as well as police or they would die of starvation . . . "

Steele . . . Sam Steele . . . Steele of the Mounted . . . Steele's Scouts

The alliteration echoes with the sibilance of a great whisper down the canyon of history. Some men are fortunate in the accident of their names, but few more fortunate than Samuel Benfield Steele of Simcoe County, Canada West. They fitted him as neatly as his puttees: the given one, rendered both blunt and familiar through abbreviation, and that marvellous surname – suggestive of both flexibility and toughness – utterly appropriate to the man who bore it. In tandem, the two names sing like a well-tempered sword whirling in battle, and the sound they make is the sound of command. It is hard to imagine a bank inspector calling himself Sam Steele – he would, no doubt, sign himself "S. Benfield Steele" – but in Steele's case the name *was* the man – a born leader: resolute, barrel-chested, keen-eyed (all the clichés apply), "erect as a pine tree and limber as a cat," to quote the best-known description. When James Oliver Curwood, the frontier novelist, first came across the name, he stole it. *Steele of the Royal Mounted*, the title of one of his most familiar novels, became a phrase in the language.

When Steele died in 1919 – an orphan boy who had risen from private soldier to major-general – he had seen more of Canada and more of Canadian history than any man or woman of his time, and not as a mere observer but as a participant and usually as one of the central figures. "I have," he wrote in a private letter to the NWMP comptroller in 1902, "taken part in almost everything of importance in the history and development of the country west of Lake Superior from the time Canada took over Manitoba and the West." Steele was in the thick of all the major adventures whose dates subsequent generations of school children have had to memorize and whose climactic moments have provided the raw material from which films, novels, plays, and stories of high romance have been fashioned: the Fenian raids, the two Riel rebellions, the long march of the Mounted Police, the arrival and departure of Sitting Bull, the Indian treaties, the building of the Canadian Pacific, the Klondike stampede. Steele was involved in all these landmark adventures before he reached the age of fifty. Another two decades of service were left to him – as Boer War commander, South Africa policeman, and Great War general. Through it all, his reputation remained impeccable. It was said of him in 1907, by the Manitoba *Free Press*, that "though there are few living men who have met more men in conflict than Colonel Steele has met in his forty years of soldiering, yet there is none who has fewer enemies."

If there is a flaw in Steele's epic it is the very lack of flaws. His massive figure strides though a dozen memoirs, but nobody who encountered him has had an unkind word to say about him. Descriptions of Steele are invariably couched in superlatives: he is "the greatest roughrider of them all," "the most spectacular roughrider in the world," "the quintessential Mounted Policeman," "the world's greatest scout," and "the Lion of the Yukon." Steele himself was so modest that his autobiography suffers from self-effacement. He cannot bear to tell us of his promotions, and he makes his many triumphs – his pursuit of Big Bear, for example, during the Saskatchewan rebellion and his superb handling of the Klondike stampede – sound almost routine. It comes as a relief to the researcher, burrowing through a mass of archival documents, to discover that Steele did exhibit certain human frailties: that he hungered for the top post in the Mounted Police, for instance, and was bitter because he was passed over; that there was little love lost between him and his superior, the flinty-eyed commissioner, Lawrence Herchmer; that he was prepared on occasion (as almost everybody was in those times) to use his political connections in his search for advancement; and that he was not in the least shy when it came to pressing for what he considered his rightful due in the matter of pensions, pay, and military decorations.

His saga begins in 1866, the year in which the Fenian Brotherhood of New York mounted a series of raids into the Canadas as part of its attempt to support the Irish revolutionary movement in its struggle with Britain. When the United Canadas called for ten thousand volunteers for defence against the Fenians, fourteen thousand responded: Sam Steele, aged sixteen and newly orphaned (his mother had died when he was eleven, his father the previous year), was one. It would have been remarkable had he done otherwise, for he came from a family steeped in military tradition. One forbear had been with Wolfe at Quebec, another with Nelson at Trafalgar, a third had died of wounds after Waterloo. His father had been the midshipman who, from the decks of the British ship *Leopard*, fired the broadside that touched off the *Chesapeake* affair of 1807, one of several naval encounters that helped bring America into the War of 1812 against Britain. All five of Steele's uncles had died in the service of their country.

When Steele joined the militia, the Fathers of Confederation had only recently concluded their first meeting at Charlottetown. Canada was not yet a united country. The North West was a no-man's land, ruled by the Hudson's Bay Company. The frontier began at Orillia on Lake Simcoe where Sam Steele, the oldest of six children, was raised. More than half a century later, he would recall that period:

"In those days every man and boy, and many girls and women, could shoot, swim and find their way through the forests, which were then a trackless wilderness, and all men and boys could ride well. I had the benefit of all this, and in winter could skate, play any game, wrestle and box; our bouts at school were without gloves, as all boys could not afford to purchase any, and we had to do without . . . . With my cousin . . . I roamed the woods during the holidays, built boats and rafts, assisted Hugh [another cousin] to make gunpowder and ball, using the heavy rifle or fowling pieces as soon as we could carry them. There was nothing in the life of a backwoods pioneer that we did not know and desire to learn."

The desire never left him. When he qualified for an infantry commission, he took the best certificate going, receiving 100 per cent in drills and discipline. Shortly afterward he qualified for artillery and cavalry as well. When the Fenian scare ended, he returned to civilian life as a clerk. It is difficult to imagine a man of Steele's temperament in such a post; his main interest was the militia. He raised a company in his spare time but refused to take the command offered him on the ground that he was too young. When in 1870 the chance came to serve in the expedition to the Red River under Colonel Garnet Wolseley, he seized it. He might have gone as an officer but made up his mind to serve as a private. He wanted to experience military life at the grass roots and "to appreciate the trials of other men to the extent that I should never have been able to do had I been promoted."

Every young man in the new Canada, it seemed, wanted to

march off to the Red River, that distant, almost mythical land of the Métis, beyond the Precambrian barrier of the Canadian Shield. There, under the leadership of Louis Riel – whom all of Ontario saw as the Devil incarnate – a half-breed nation had come briefly into existence, an Orangeman named Thomas Scott had been summarily shot, and loyal Canadians were being held hostage. Orange Ontario was in an uproar. Twelve hundred soldiers would be needed to restore order. Who would not be one of them? Adventure beckoned in a land that few had seen but all had extolled; now it could be experienced under the guise of patriotism. Life in settled Canada was unutterably dull; more than one farmer's son had exchanged the ruts and furrows of the back country for the glamour of the American frontier. Now the way was open to the Canadian North West, an empty domain newly relinquished by the Hudson's Bay Company, an ocean of grass, so it was reported – like no other realm in all the world. There was only one problem: it was damnably difficult to get there. But Colonel Wolseley would take care of that.

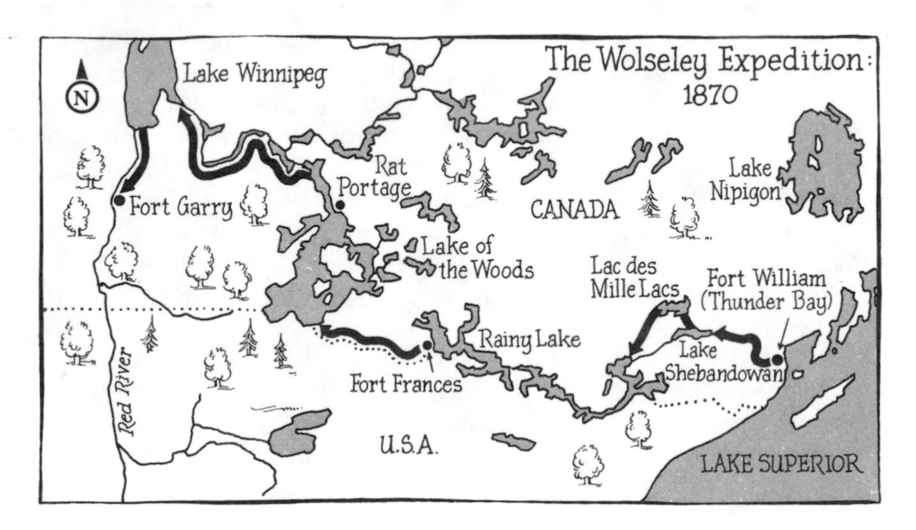

So began the expedition that has been called "one of the most gruelling military movements in history" – an exhausting, ninety-four-day trek across a six-hundred-mile wilderness of naked rock, stunted forest, wild water, and muskeg. Of the twelve hundred men, four hundred were British regulars who knew little of wilderness travel and eight hundred were Canadian militiamen who knew little of soldiering. Steele was an exception; he was one of the few who had experience with both.

The journey began when the troops disembarked from the lake steamers at Thunder Bay. It was a backbreaking nightmare. The fur traders who had been among the few white men to roam the unmapped country between the lakehead and the Red River, believed that nothing heavier than a birchbark canoe could navigate the serpentine rivers and slippery portages that made up the "Dawson Route" to the North West. But Wolseley had determined to use large bateaux, and these flat-bottomed barges had to be hauled or pushed on rollers cut from poplar logs over steep inclines, often at angles of forty-five degrees. The farm boys from the East were faced with forty-seven such portages, many of them several miles in length. Everything – cannon balls, sails, oars, rifles, artillery pieces, ammunition, blankets, clothing, and food – had to be manhandled around the interminable rapids that foamed over the broken face of the Shield. Up these armoured inclines and through uneven trails hacked from the forest Steele and his comrades clawed their way bent double under barrels of pork or cumbersome ammunition boxes, each weighing two hundred pounds, and often sinking to their knees in mud. Prodigious feats were noted on that trail. Steele, who was with the 1st Ontario Rifles, thought nothing of shouldering a two-hundred-pound barrel in addition to his personal kit. Redvers Buller, a British regular later to become famous as a Boer War general, was known to carry three hundred pounds. Ensign de Maur of the 60th – the future Duke of Somerset – went him one better by carrying two barrels of pork, a total of four hundred pounds. One of Steele's voyageur guides carried two barrels of pork and a thousand rounds of ammunition, a record 529 pounds.

To add to the misery, it rained for forty-five of the ninety-four days; yet the troops, soaked to the skin often for days at a time, maddened by blackflies and mosquitoes, bathed in mud and staggering under their burdens, rarely complained. For young Sam Steele, barely twenty-one and about to be promoted to corporal, it was a time of testing. A contemporary photograph shows him as a clear-eyed youth, but there is a leanness to the face, a firmness to the jaw line that suggests an inner resolution, a toughness of character.

At Fort Garry and at the neighbouring hamlet of Winnipeg Steele had his first view of the legendary North West. In his own lifetime he would see it totally transformed. The sea of buffalo grass, which stretched unbroken past the farthest horizon, the dark herds of buffalo themselves, the squealing Red River carts, the Métis in their toques and sashes, the flocks of passenger pigeons that darkened the sky – all these would pass. Winnipeg would be transformed from a cluster of hovels into Canada's third-largest city. But Steele remembered it when the only street was a sea of black mud in which "voyageurs, whites, half-breeds and Indians fought, wallowed and slept in all stages of drunkenness, induced by the poison dispensed over the bars of the vile saloons of the place. They made the night and day hideous with their yells, shrieks and curses . . . "

As a corporal, Steele had to deal with a ruffian element in his company, several of whom "were as bad as I ever met." When two got into a fight, knives were produced and a near riot ensued. Steele faced the mob with a clubbed rifle, his favourite weapon on such occasions, and drove them out of the barrack room. Shortly afterward, during an election riot – and few elections took place without a riot – he again used the weapon to ward off three "hostiles" who attacked him.

The soldiers who had marched across the Shield with Wolseley and who had found little to do at Fort Garry (since Riel had decamped and fled to the United States) were given three choices. They could remain at the garrison for another year; they could return to civilian life and stay in the North West with a land grant of 160 acres; or they could go home. Steele chose to return to Ontario, where he enlisted as a permanent force soldier in the newly formed Royal Canadian Artillery. In little more than a year he was an instructor at Kingston. But then, in August of 1873, he learned that a new force of mounted men was being raised for police duty in the Far West. William Francis Butler, Wolseley's emissary to Riel, had already captivated the nation with his descriptions of what he called the Great Lone Land, which lay between the Red River and the Rockies. As Steele put it: "I had the Great Lone Land before me, where it is a man's own fault if he fails while he has his health and strength." He was one of the first to join the new force – a source of considerable pride to him in later years – and set off on his second great adventure.

He was enrolled as a sergeant-major in the North West Mounted Police and stationed for the winter at Fort Garry to instruct recruits, many of them young upper-class Englishmen drawn to Canada by a thirst for adventure. They called him Simcoe Sam, but never to his face. They trained out of doors in subzero weather from six in the morning until darkness fell, learning to ride broncos that flung them off repeatedly on to the frozen turf. In June, 1874, these hardened constables, joined by recruits from Toronto, set off on a thousand-mile march across the plains to the foothills of the Rockies.

Again Steele was helping to make history. The western trek of

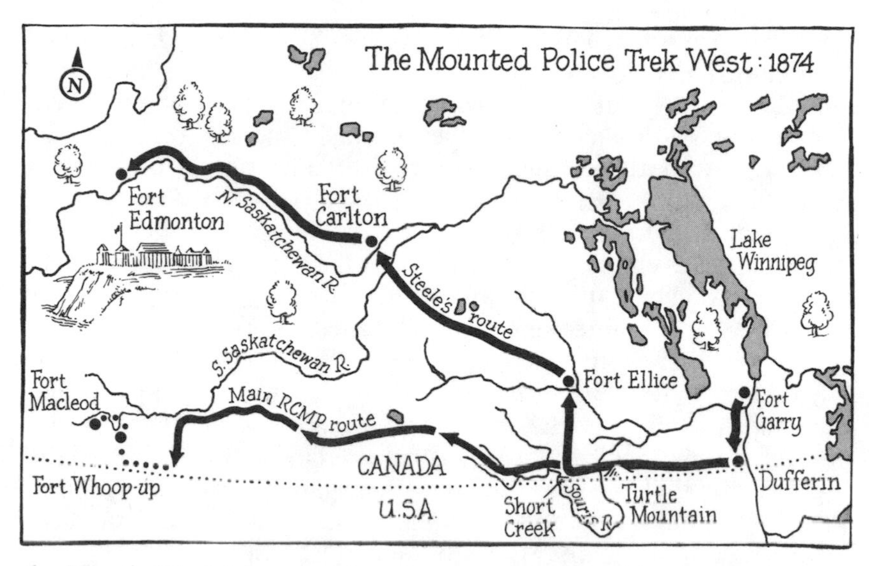

the North West Mounted has become enshrined in the mythology of the Force, and with good reason. Between Fort Garry and Fort Edmonton there were only two buildings occupied by white men: the log forts, Carlton and Ellice. Nothing else. Nothing but grass, poplar copses, and wolf willow; nothing but rolling hills, blue lakes, coulées, and vast river valleys; nothing but marshes, buffalo wallows, and more grass – no bridges, few trails, no supplies of any kind. The young men in their pillbox hats would have to be farmers as well as police or they would die of starvation. The column that wound its way west (it was later split into three) was almost three miles long, for it contained everything the police would need to stay alive: not just guns, ammunition, clothing and barrack-room paraphernalia but also ox carts and wagons, cattle for slaughter and milking, mowing machines, ploughs and harrows, and, of course, seed.

The men, toughened by the winter's training, withstood the journey better than the animals. Almost at the outset the horses were driven berserk by a freakish thunderstorm that sent a bolt of lightning directly among them. The terrified beasts broke their fastenings, trampled six men who tried to stop them, smashed their way through the tents, and stampeded for almost fifty miles into Dakota. Days were wasted rounding them up; all that year the slightest unexpected sound caused them to rear or shy.

At Turtle Mountain, the police were engulfed by a swarm of grasshoppers that blotted out the sky and smothered the trees, grass, and carts in a blanket so thick that nothing showed but the glitter of a million beating wings. The locusts attacked everything, even devouring the paint on the wagons. Steele and his men had to work furiously to save the tents.

At Short Creek on the Souris, one division under Inspector William Jarvis, with Steele as sergeant-major, peeled off from the main train to push northwest toward Fort Edmonton, taking with it fifty-five sick horses together with oxen, cows, calves, wagons, and ox carts. The horses were so weak they had to be changed twice daily; even then they could manage no more than eight miles a day. The cattle, exhausted and footsore, slumped to the ground every few miles; men were detailed to prod them forward. Out of Fort Carlton, when the weather grew cold and wet, the horses were so stiff they could not rise in the morning without help. Steele called his men from their sleep during the night to lift up each animal and rub its legs to restore circulation. So often did this happen that the men themselves began to flag from fatigue. Finally, the horses became too weak to carry riders and the men were forced to walk the rest of the way to Edmonton.

The last few miles were for Steele the hardest he had undertaken. It was late December. The trail was a mired horror. Floundering knee-deep in black mud, the men faced a labyrinth of sloughs. Every few hundred yards they were forced to unload their wagons and drag them through by hand. The horses, thirsty and feverish, rushed to the ice-covered ponds to drink, fell in, and had to be dragged out by ropes. Jarvis had moved on ahead to Fort Edmonton and Steele had been attempting to follow orders to reach that goal in one final day-long spurt. At five in the morning, he admitted defeat. The men and animals had been on the move for twenty-one hours without a break and, in Steele's words "appeared to have reached the limit of their endurance." But there was no rest yet for the sergeant-major. A horse had fallen half-way through the ice of a waterhole. Just as Steele hung a lariat around his neck the ice gave way; Steele and his men found themselves struggling in ten feet of icy water, wrestling with a kicking animal. Somehow they managed to pull free.

It was now past 6:00 a.m., but Steele, who had been awake and working for more than twenty-four hours, could not rest. He changed his clothes and set about cutting poles to make a bridge across the last creek. When, later that day, he and his men arrived at the fort, Jarvis was able to write in his report that besides "being untiring in his efforts to assist me . . . he [Steele] has performed the manual labour of at least two men." The division had been on the trail for more than six months and in that time had travelled 1,225 miles. Its work had only begun.

Over the next decade, as Steele rose from sergeant-major to

inspector to superintendent, he occupied a ringside seat at the drama of the emerging North West. He was present when the three great treaties were signed with the Plains Indians at Fort Pitt, Fort Carlton, and Fort Macleod. He was one of the few white men privileged to witness the so-called Sun Dance (more properly the Thirst Dance) of the Blackfoot in the Cypress Hills, a heart-stopping ordeal in which young braves were required to prance and leap around a central pole until thongs from it attached to skewers in their chest muscles were pulled free. He met Sitting Bull, newly arrived in Canada after the Custer massacre, was present during the Sioux's historic and abortive parley with General Terry of the U.S. Cavalry; and, some years later, saw the famous medicine man and his followers move reluctantly back across the border. He watched while the last of the great buffalo herds vanished forever. He fought typho-malarial fever, which came close to killing him, and snow blindness, that most painful of all afflictions, which all but put him out of action. When the Marquis of Lorne became the first governor general to visit the prairies, Steele was on hand to welcome him.

Steele, in his laconic way, tells a story that conveys something of the hazards faced by a Mounted Police patrol during the prairie winters of the 1870s. He had left Fort Walsh, in the southern foothills, with two constables, Mills and Holtorf, and a half-breed interpreter, Foley, to undertake a census of mixed bloods in the region between Fort Macleod and Calgary. The weather, bitterly cold, grew worse. Rations and forage gave out. For four days the men and their horses were without food. And then, just seventeen miles from Fort Macleod and safety, a blizzard sprang up, so fierce that the whirling snow blotted out the trail. Steele, whose sense of direction was well developed, was in the lead when he heard Foley cry out: "The man behind you is freezing to death!" It was Holtorf. Steele reined his horse, dismounted, and pounded, shook, and slapped the freezing man out of his death sleep. The four riders then continued through the blizzard at a slow walk. Suddenly Steele, looking about, shouted to Foley that the man behind *him* was freezing to death. Mills was dragged from his horse, shaken, cuffed, and shouted at until he revived. The party blundered on, with Steele alternately slapping and reviving both constables and despairing of their lives, until they stumbled upon the sod hut of a pioneer and were saved.

In that period, Steele was about as far from Canadian civilization as it was possible to be. The closest settlement was Fort Benton, across the border in Montana. Mail to Toronto posted at Fort Calgary carried U.S. stamps and was carried south across the border by bull teams. But when in February of 1882, Steele took his first leave and was given permission to travel East on private business, he encountered at Brandon a spectacle that would change the face of the prairie. In the burgeoning railway yards piled high with steel rails and ties and crawling with men, was the first locomotive he had seen in nine years. The Canadian Pacific was on its way, and Steele would be given the task of policing its construction.

He was to be magistrate as well as policeman, dispensing justice most often from beneath a marquee, which also served as mess room and sleeping quarters, but sometimes from a Red River cart, open to the sky, with a plank stretched across it for a bench and the flap of his dispatch bag as a desk. In the winter of 1883 – the great prairie construction year – Steele's quarters in the new territorial capital of Regina were so primitive that the bath water froze and his clerks were forced to thaw out their ink before they could record evidence. Steele himself worked all hours – far into the night – as he would for most of his life on the frontier.

His style contrasted sharply with that of lawmen on the other side of the border. Unlike the county sheriffs and town marshals who were creating their own legends in the cattle towns and mining camps of the western United States, Steele represented more than the immediate community he served. He wore the Queen's uniform; behind him stood all the resources of the Empire. He had been appointed by the Crown to bring order to the North West, and any who opposed him recognized that fact. The Mounted Police were inviolable; it was useless to come up against them in the kind of *mano a mano* gunfight cherished by aficionados of the American West. For if one were shot, another would immediately take his place and, if necessary, another and another until, in the finality, the long arm of justice, reaching all the way from Westminster, would pluck the culprit from the wilderness and bring him to book.

That explains why Steele, with only two constables and a half-breed interpreter, was able to walk into a hostile Blackfoot camp and arrest a wanted man without a hand being raised against him. The incident took place in 1884 near Calgary, and is one of several that helped create the enduring legend of Mounted Police invincibility. Steele's quarry was a half-breed who had escaped custody and was hiding in the lodge of Crowfoot, the greatest and wisest of the Blackfoot chieftains. Leaving his men outside, Steele strode into the lodge accompanied only by the Indian agency interpreter, John L'Hereux.

Inside the great teepee, the leading men of the tribe had formed a half-circle about their chief. Crowfoot sat at the rear, facing the door. The wanted man occupied the place of honour to his right. The atmosphere was so antagonistic, the chief's gaze so fierce, that L'Hereux turned pale and his knees actually knocked together from fright. Steele, without raising his voice, told Crowfoot that he must take the wanted man back to Calgary. The chief's reply was so defiant that Steele realized that his interpreter had not the courage to convey his demands in strong enough terms. He told L'Hereux that he would permit no temporizing, and the reluctant interpreter at last relayed the policeman's demands exactly as given.

At this Crowfoot sprang to his feet and seemed about to attack Steele. Steele waved him back, warning that at the slightest move made against himself, Crowfoot would be the first to suffer. He spoke quietly but firmly looking into Crowfoot's eyes and moving slowly toward him. Crowfoot backed away. Steele then ordered the flap over the entrance to the lodge to be lifted. Placing his right hand on his rifle butt, then, with his left he seized the wanted man by the back of the shirt collar, whirled him about, and dragged him head foremost through the opening and outside before he had time to resist.

Crowfoot's lodge was surrounded by hundreds of infuriated Indians. Steele's two constables hoisted their prisoner onto their buckboard and fastened him to the seat. Then Steele, through his interpreter, spoke to the Indians, telling them that when the Mounted Police came for any man, Indian or white, that person had to come, and that anyone who interfered would be punished for it. Steele then called out for the chief, who emerged from his teepee to receive a tongue-lashing for failing to co-operate. Having humbled Crowfoot before his followers, Steele arranged for him to be given a CPR return ticket to come to Calgary, witness the trial, and see the Queen's justice done. The chief did just that. It is undoubtedly ironic and possibly significant that the prisoner was acquitted.

Steele's strength, and that of his fellow policemen, was that he did not have to respond to an electorate as American lawmen did. On the American frontier there was not the same clear line of demarcation between citizen and policemen. The town marshal held his job on the sufferance of the voters. One day he might be a gambler, living on the edge of the law, as was Wyatt Earp; the next he could be wearing a star. A citizen could find himself briefly transformed into a policeman, deputized as part of a posse. Sometimes as a member of a vigilante group or a lynching party he took the law into his own hands.

The Canadian style – actually the British colonial style – was markedly different. After all, one of the most influential groups in the country was made up of those loyalists (and their descendants) who had refused to take the law into their own hands at the time of the Boston Tea Party. Steele made the point when he quieted a potential lynch mob in Calgary, following the murder of a young storekeeper by a Negro:

"You lads are all tenderfeet and have visions before you of taking part in a Neck-tie Social. There never has been a lynching in Canada, nor will there be as long as our Force has the police duties to perform, so go away like sensible men and remember that any attempt at lynching will be bad for those who try it."

The mob dispersed.

Steele was, at this point, temporarily in charge at Calgary, which he had seen change overnight from a timbered fort to a booming railway town. He was shortly afterwards given a more important post, the charge of all Mounted Police along the line of the CPR's construction in British Columbia. The job gave him a double responsibility: he would be a commissioner of the peace as well as a police inspector. It would not be easy, for "large numbers of gamblers, whiskey men, in fact every description of criminal . . . were . . . establishing their dens on every little creek along the line." Many were Americans, used to the undisciplined life of the American frontier. Saloons, dance halls, and bawdy houses crept along the line as it inched upwards through the mountains. James Ross, the CPR's construction boss, was later to declare that he did not believe that "on any other portion of the Pacific construction or any Trans-continental line, had they ever such a tough lot." Ross described the Americans as "refugees from justice from the United States, murderers, gamblers, etc." But Steele was equal to the occasion. He wrote: "The fun began at dances to which the navvies and toughs went, but as half the police were on patrol the greatest order possible with such a class of men prevailed."

"Order" is a word that turns up time and again in Steele's memoirs. It is, after all, a policeman's word. The Americans wanted freedom before order – the history of their own frontier demonstrates that: freedom to choose their lawmen, freedom to drink openly in saloons, freedom to carry a gun, string up an outlaw, gamble with their savings. On the American frontier, freedom often led to anarchy; north of the border, order often meant dictatorship, albeit paternalistic. Steele effectively closed the saloons along the CPR's right of way by insisting on a "dry" zone for twenty miles on both sides of the line. After ten hours of tamping ties, few navvies were prepared to walk twenty miles and back for a drink. Bootleggers, of course, were not unknown, but Steele was hard on bootleggers; he made a jail term mandatory on a second offence. "We had right on our side . . . " he wrote years later, with a policeman's conviction. "The building of the great work must not be retarded."

To maintain order and further the great work, Steele and his handful of Calgary volunteers were forced to work harder than the navvies. Since their days were spent dealing with prisoners and since the towns along the line were awake for most of the night, they were seldom in bed before two or three in the morning and up again at seven.

Steele's most dramatic moment came in March, 1885 at Beavermouth, his new headquarters at the foot of the Selkirk mountains, a mile from the end of the track. The incident, which has since become imperishable legend, needs no embroidery. In the century that followed, Hollywood would make scores of motion pictures extolling the exploits of the Mounted Police, but no producer has filmed the tale of the Beavermouth riot, possibly because the sequence of events was too improbable for even the most credulous audience to swallow.

The railway had run out of funds. The greatest construction project on the continent was about to go under. The navvies were desperate to send home their pay to their families in Manitoba, Minnesota, and Dakota. But the promised pay car did not arrive. The mood along the line grew surly, the embers of discontent fanned by large numbers of "ruffians, gamblers and murderers from the Northern Pacific," to quote Steele.

He saw trouble coming and warned the contractors; they refused to take him seriously. He wired the prime minister, who did not reply. He could feel the tension growing, but now two events occurred that left him virtually helpless.

First, word came of an imminent rebellion by the Métis and Indians at the forks of the Saskatchewan under the leadership of Louis Riel. Steele realized at once that he could expect no reinforcements.

Second, he was himself felled by an attack of Rocky Mountain spotted fever, one of the most dangerous and mysterious diseases of its time. He was so ill that he could not raise his head from his pillow.

As Steele lay prostrate, a sequence of events exploded. On March 26, at Duck Lake, the first shots in the Saskatchewan rebellion were fired; a dozen Mounted Policemen and volunteers lay dead or dying on the snows. A few days later the Crees under Poundmaker and Big Bear joined the Métis uprising. On April 1, the navvies in the Selkirks struck the CPR over lack of pay. On April 2, at Frog Lake, nine whites were massacred by Big Bear's young men.

The prairies were close to panic. A telegram from the mayor of Calgary pleaded with Steele for help: "For God's sake come: there is danger of an attack by the Blackfeet." But Steele could not go because at that moment the strike west of Beavermouth was developing into a riot. Work on the vast Mountain Creek trestle, one of the biggest on the continent, had slowed to a halt. Mobs of armed men were marching down the right of way, heading for Beavermouth.

At the end of track – chaos. James Ross, the construction chief, had personally driven a trainload of strikebreakers through the mob, oblivious of a fusillade of shots. Steele's second-in-command, a sergeant with the appropriate name of Fury, fended off the strikers with a loaded rifle. Then occurred an incident that brought matters to a head. One of Steele's constables, Kerr, had gone up the line to find some medicine for his stricken superior. En route he encountered "a well known desperado," one Behan, inciting the mob to riot. Kerr attempted to arrest him on a charge of drunkenness but was prevented by the mob, which forced him to release the prisoner and retreat. That was too much. No Mounted Policeman could be allowed to fail in his duty. Steele, rising shakily from his bed, ordered Sergeant Fury to take as many men as were needed and arrest Behan.

Fury and two constables waded into a mob of two hundred armed men but were again overpowered, their uniforms ripped and their quarry still at large. This Steele could not countenance. The police had tried to do their duty according to the manual without bloodshed or gunplay; the time for that was past. "Take your revolvers," Steele ordered Fury, "and shoot anyone who interferes with the arrest."

An incredible scene followed. Steele, hearing gunfire, was unable to resist crawling to the window, just in time to see two of his men dragging their prisoner across the Beaver Creek bridge, followed by a crowd of seven hundred infuriated strikers and a woman in a red dress, screaming imprecations. Sick or not, Steele knew he must act. He called on George Hope Johnston, the stipendiary magistrate, who had been in the sick room, to run to the orderly room to get the Riot Act. Then, seizing a Winchester rifle from the constable on guard at the jail, he ran to the bridge and faced the mob.

"Look at the sonofabitch," somebody cried (or perhaps he shouted "bastard" – the various Victorian accounts discreetly leave the epithet blank). "His own death bed makes no difference to him!" But the crowd came to a halt.

One of Steele's men clubbed the prisoner insensible and pulled him across the bridge like a rag doll.

"You red-coated bastard!" screamed the woman.

"Take her in, too," ordered Steele, still advancing on the crowd, his Winchester levelled.

At this climactic moment there came an interval of high theatre. Steele, holding off the crowd, was desperately awaiting the arrival of Johnston with the Riot Act. But Johnston could not get the act from the orderly room because the O.R. was locked and the constable who had the key was helping to hold back the crowd. Johnston lunged, kicked, lunged and kicked again, knocked the door off its hinges, seized the book, and dashed to Steele's side.

"Listen to this," shouted Steele, "and keep your hands off your guns, or I will shoot the first man of you who makes a hostile movement." The crowd fell silent. It was and is a tradition with the Force that a Mounted Policeman never draws his gun unless he intends to use it. Fury had already shot one of their number through the shoulder. There was no doubt in any man's mind that Steele would kill the first man who made a move for his weapon.

Steele read the act, his full force of eight policemen standing behind him in line, rifles cocked.

Said Steele: "I warn you that if I find more than twelve of you standing together or any large crowd assembled, I will open fire upon you and mow you down! Now disperse at once and behave yourselves!"

The crowd broke up, and the next day Steele was able to report that the line was as quiet as "a country village on a Sunday." Order had been restored; the great work could continue; eventually the men were paid.

A remarkable coda to the incident was Steele's own recovery from fever. He never returned to his sick bed. In the days that followed, he presided over the cases of the rioters he had arrested (each was fined one hundred dollars or six months in jail), and then left for Calgary to organize a cavalry battalion to pursue Big Bear, the rebel Cree chief. The battalion was named, appropriately, Steele's Scouts. Two weeks of training were followed by two months of skirmishing, culminating in the battle of Loon Lake, where Steele's small force attacked and scattered five times as many Cree and Salteaux in "a trackless and unknown wilderness on ground of their own choosing."

By the time Big Bear walked into Fort Carlton with his eight-year-old son and surrendered – the date was July 2, 1886 – the railway was solvent. It had been the means of speeding troops to quell Riel, and the government could hardly ignore its request for a further loan. Back in British Columbia, Steele watched the rails pierce the wall of the Selkirks and snake their way across the Columbia Valley towards that bleak corner of Eagle Pass where the line from the Pacific had come to a halt.

Once again Sam Steele was to occupy a reserved seat at the stage of history. On November 6, a train from eastern Canada picked him up at Revelstoke. In its private cars, *Matapedia* and *Saskatchewan*, were several of the great figures in the drama of Canadian railway construction – massive, bearded men in dark, formal wool – W.C. Van Horne, Sandford Fleming, Donald Smith. Next morning, standing in the shroud of the mountain mists, with fresh snow dripping from the firs, Steele watched while Smith hammered in the last spike and Van Horne made his famous speech about the work being done well. It was typical of Steele that of all the members of that company – navvies, surveyors, track bosses, and executives – the policeman chose to remain faceless. When the camera clicked he stood aside; he is not to be seen in that famous photograph.

But he was aboard the train on its historic passage to tidewater, and he wrote that "the recollection of that journey to the coast on the first train through is far sweeter to me than any trips taken since. It was an exultant moment of pioneer work, and we were all pioneers on that excursion." It was, by all accounts, a terrifying ordeal. The train roared in and out of the tunnels and whistled around the narrow curves of the Fraser canyon, two hundred feet above the boiling waters, at a speed of fifty-seven mph. Steele was one of only two men on the trip who did not succumb to motion sickness.

His iron constitution was legendary. The young man who had carried two hundred pounds of pork on his shoulders on those long portages across the Shield was now thirty-six, straight backed, deep chested, stern faced, clear eyed. Old-timers in their memoirs always remarked on his carriage. John Locke Jamieson, who was a constable under Steele, remembered him "walking 60 paces to the minute from his home to the office in a tremendous Chinook wind, almost being blown off the sidewalk." Col. G.C. Porter recalled him "on his 1,500 pound dark bay stallion, with his Stetson flopping and his 240 pounds of bone and sinew swinging in the saddle ... a compelling figure of romance and competence." Steele's features were as impassive as a brick wall, as taut as army canvas. His photographs resemble a sculpture. His moustache, waxed at the points, gave him a fiercely military look that belied an intrinsic amiability. Steele was no martinet; he understood that rules were made to be bent; as a magistrate he had developed a broad streak of compassion. He was never vindictive; the sentences meted out to the riot leaders at Beavermouth were light by the standards of the day, just enough, in Steele's words, to deter further trouble without causing undue bitterness.

It is easy to admire Steele; but the admiration is for the exterior. It is not easy to get inside him, for he was not one to reveal his inner feelings. Did he ever suffer from self-doubts, from fear or loneliness? Did he feel despair or defeat or disillusionment? There is some evidence that he did; but when he did he kept it deeply buried. It is doubtful whether he was often, if ever, racked by personal uncertainties. He was not the kind of man who is given to self-analysis. Had he been, he would have been less effective as a policeman. He emerges from the pages of history as a man meeting each situation, attacking each problem as it comes along, accepting the established order of things, which rarely conflicts with the dictates of his conscience.

There is little poetry in Steele's account of his days on the frontier – none of the eloquence, say, of William Francis Butler, his military contemporary. Steele had a policeman's eye for detail: he gives us a good picture of social life in Fort Macleod during the 1890s, for instance – the summer quadrilles, the tennis parties, the race meetings, bronco ridings and ropings, the annual winter ball, and the festivities at Christmas. Reading his memoirs, one gets a sense of raw prairie communities developing and changing with the coming of the railway, but neither his recollections nor those of his contemporaries tell much of the man himself. Emotion is sublimated to impersonal description. He writes that he went east in 1890 to be married to Marie, the eldest daughter of Robert Harwood, MP, at Vaudreuil, Quebec; we are left in the dark, however, as to the circumstances of the courtship and engagement. But perhaps a policeman cannot afford to be emotional any more than can a doctor, nor can he express opinions. If Steele had views on the rights and wrongs of the strike at Beavermouth he kept them to himself. His job was to keep order, not to indulge in politics. He was the same in his relationships with the native peoples. In 1887 he was sent to Wild Horse Creek in the Kootenay mountains of British Columbia (it is now known as Fort Steele) to maintain peace among the Indians who, rebelling at a reservation system that exchanged their traditional lands for new ones, were refusing to vacate property on which they had lived for years. Steele dealt with the chief, Isadore, whom he came to admire:

"I told him . . . that we were in the district to maintain the laws of the Great Mother and that both whites and Indians would receive just treatment and would be equally severely punished if they deserved it. The effect of this interview was a marked improvement in the demeanour of the Indians."

But what was meant by "just treatment"? Steele worked out a compromise with the Indians. But, reading between the lines of his account, one cannot escape the conclusion that it was the white landowner who got the better of the deal.

He could not, of course, ignore the politics of the day; no one paid with public funds could hope to. The road to advancement lay in party patronage. Yet advancement came with disappointing slowness for Steele, and politics was undoubtedly at the root of that disappointment – the politics of the nation and the politics of the police. In 1882, when Steele was an inspector, a friend of Sir John A. Macdonald's wrote to the prime minister on the policeman's behalf, urging that he be promoted to superintendent: "I have been requested to write to you by some friends of ours in reference to the position of Inspector S.B. Steele of the Mounted Police, who is a staunch conservative and bėing so his services were of course overlooked by the Mackenzie government . . . . He has frequently been passed over and now the wrong can be redressed by appointing him to the vacant superintendentship in the Force. He is well connected and all his friends and associates are conservatives . . . ." But it was not until Big Bear's surrender, three years later, that Steele got his promotion, for services rendered during the rebellion.

Steele's eyes were fixed on the top post. He wanted very badly to be Commissioner of the North West Mounted. But the position eluded him. Some of the most powerful men in Canada, including D'Alton McCarthy, a leading Conservative, James Ross, the millionaire contractor, W.C. Van Horne, president of the Canadian Pacific, and Father Albert Lacombe, the voyageur priest, supported Steele's cause but without effect. As early as 1886, McCarthy urged the prime minister to appoint Steele to the vacant office of assistant commissioner, pointing out that Steele's half brother, John, had contested the local riding "in our interest and his promotion would be well received by the public and I believe also by the force." But Steele was passed over. Why? On the record he was eminently qualified – by seniority, by experience, by temperament. He had, however, incurred the displeasure of the newly appointed commissioner, L.W. Herchmer, a martinet who considered the slightest complaint against his orders an act of insubordination. In 1886 – just before McCarthy wrote to the prime minister – Steele rebelled at a series of complaints that Herchmer had made regarding his handling of the Battleford post. When Herchmer threatened to remove him from the post for misconduct, Steele demanded a hearing and investigation under the Police Act. The contretemps never was resolved, but the correspondence between the two sizzles with animosity. Herchmer charged Steele with "gross negligence," with condoning malingering among his men, with keeping liquor in the dispensary, with paying too much for potatoes – accusations which seem remarkably picayune and, when applied to a man of Steele's calibre, scarcely credible.

Steele took none of this lying down. His reply bristles with umbrage: "I have been accused by you of extravagance. I most distinctly deny it. I found this post a nest of corruption and the men in a mutinous state. It is no longer so, part of the credit must belong to me. I have, as all know, changed the feeling of the people here from terror of the police (mingled with contempt) to respect and friendship . . . your language has continued to be such as neither I nor any other officer in the Force has been in the habit of receiving from anyone . . . . 'Gross negligence' is a favourite term for the faults of *others*, but is used towards *me*. If any officer not recently appointed had treated me as you are doing, I would have complained or remonstrated at once. Being no change in your treatment, I must demand my rights . . . ." This only served to enrage the new commissioner, who used the word "insubordination" in describing it to the Mounted Police comptroller in Ottawa. Steele was transferred to Lethbridge, his chances of advancement badly damaged. The post of assistant commissioner went to Herchmer's brother, William, better known as "Colonel Bill."

Steele was not a political animal, and when he tried to be, he was uncharacteristically clumsy. In 1891, hearing that there was a vacancy at the rank of assistant commissioner, he wrote to the minister of customs, Mackenzie Bowell, asking him to "use your powerful influence on my behalf" and explaining that "my friends and relatives have always been supportive of the Conservative party." Later, during his Yukon duty, when the Liberals were in power and he thought he was about to be made subordinate to a regular army officer, he wrote to Clifford Sifton, the minister of the interior, urging that he be retained in command and declaring that he had "hundreds of relatives and connections who support the government, one in the cabinet and one a member . . . ."

In that instance, Sifton supported him, but no one – not the Liberals, not the Conservatives, and not his own superior officers, most of whom were his juniors in service – seemed ready to advance him beyond his rank of superintendent. He took no part in the politics of the NWMP; as he put it in a letter to Herchmer, "I am not a toady." One gets the impression that he was considered a little too regular, a little too straight – "square" might be the modern word – to hold a position that required a certain political suppleness, an ability to bend with the political winds for the sake of the Force. There was the instance of the potatoes at Battleford. Herchmer was outraged at Steele's apparent extravagance: "What authority had you for buying so many potatoes in May?"

Steele was equally outraged in his reply. These were potatoes "to which the men *are entitled by law*" (Steele underlined the words) "and without which their health is apt to suffer seriously . . . ." The reply was not politic, but human well-being was a serious matter to Steele. In October, 1895, following a fire in a school on the Blood Indian reserve, Steele discovered to his horror that the children were locked in the building at night. He took it upon himself to change the system and to warn the principal that if a second fire occurred and there was loss of life, he would be tried for manslaughter and other persons connected with the mission would be charged as accessories. The commissioner was irritated; Steele was rocking the boat. The school was the responsibility of the Indian department and "it is little matters of this kind . . . having the appearance of interference with another department, which give the Indian Department ground for insinuating that the Police encroach within their jurisdiction."

Steele never betrayed in public his bitterness over what he felt, with considerable justification, was a deliberate attempt to bypass him for promotion. In 1892, he gave vent to his feelings in a confidential letter to his father-in-law, Robert Harwood, a prominent Conservative, who was working on his behalf:

"I am informed that an effort will be made to put us off by saying that I am not the senior officer of the Superintendents, and therefore not entitled to the next step, and as I am also informed that you purpose going up to Ottawa . . . I beg to draw your attention to the *solid fact* that I was *at one time* senior to *everyone of those who have the luck* to be above me . . . . I was the second N.C. officer in the Force at the formation . . . neither Cotton nor Gagnon were then in the corps. McIllree was a Sergt. under me . . . . He was promoted over my head shortly after the downfall of Sir John Macdonald's Govt. on the 'Pacific Scandal.' Cotton joined in '79 and through currying favor with Colonel Irvine our Commissioner at that time and others, was promoted over the heads of the whole of the Inspectors, myself included in '82 . . . . Supt. Gagnon joined in '74 as an Inspector, coming in over the heads of a number of Non Com officers who could justly consider that having assisted materially to organize the Force they were entitled to what promotion was going. Supt. Gagnon had never been in a mounted corps in his life nor do I believe that he *had ever mounted a horse.*

"None of the gentlemen I have mentioned *have served under fire* . . . ."

That he was qualified for higher office was made abundantly clear during the Klondike stampede of 1897-98. There Steele showed, conclusively, that he was capable of commanding something far more complex and undisciplined than a quasi-military force of a few hundred trained men. He ran the gold rush like an army manoeuvre; hundreds owed their lives to his prescience and common sense. Yet, ironically, the Klondike was the instrument of his final disillusionment and his exit from the institution he loved.

When the gold rush began in the late summer of 1897, Steele, in charge of the Fort Macleod district, had no idea he would become a part of it. But the following February, when tens of thousands of men were toiling over the passes and thousands more were frozen in along the headwaters of the Yukon, he found himself heading north, with orders to take charge of the police detachments at the summits of the Chilkoot and White passes and along the shores of the headwater lakes, Lindeman and Bennett.

Steele was one of two hundred men crammed aboard the tiny sealer *Thistle*, which pitched so badly in the heavy seas that he had difficulty staying in his bunk. The tables were crowded from morning until night with six sittings at every meal. Storms and hurricanes raged without cease. When the ship reached Skagway, the temperature had dropped to thirty below, Fahrenheit, the chill factor forced to an unbearable low by a paralyzing wind blasting down from the mountains. Yet these conditions were mild compared with what Steele encountered on the trail and at the summits of the two passes.

At the time, there was no agreement on the exact location of the border between Canada and Alaska. The Americans insisted that, under the terms of the 1867 purchase from Russia, Alaskan territory extended inland to Lake Bennett and even beyond. The Canadians, needing a bargaining point, claimed that British territory extended to tidewater. The Mounted Police, regardless, were instructed to seize and hold the mountain summits and to collect customs duties from every American crossing through. Possession is nine points of the law; the compromise was tacitly accepted; the border today runs exactly where Steele and his men set up their

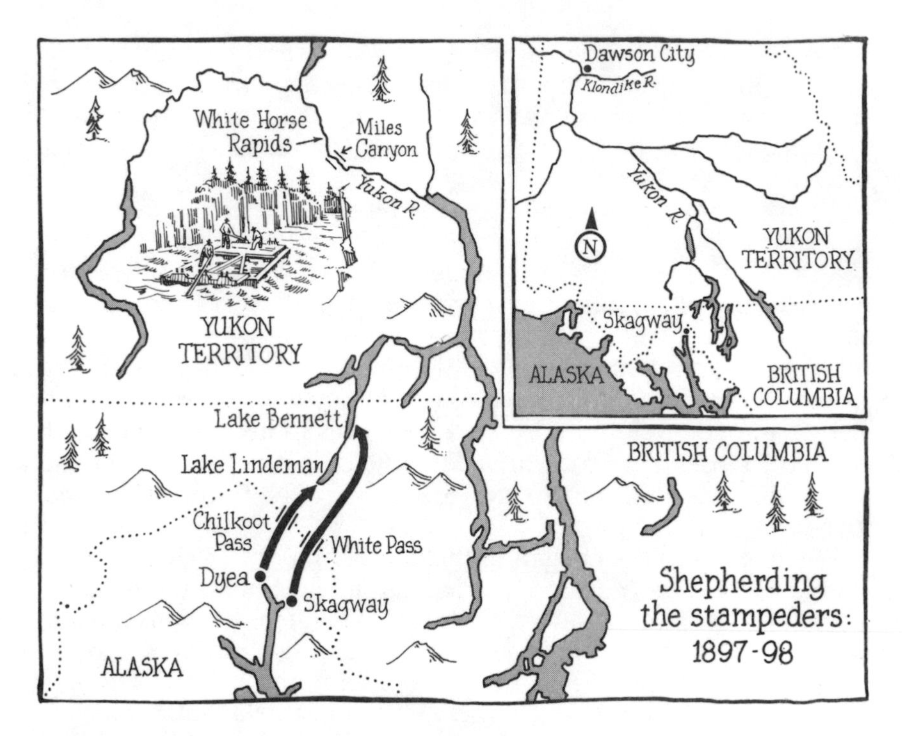

Maxim guns.

On both sides of the border, turmoil reigned. The twin Alaskan ports of Skagway and Dyea were a chaos of men, dogs, and pack animals, a wilderness of mire and slush. The trails that led to the passes were a disarray of abandoned supplies, broken sleds, tattered tents, and rotting horseflesh. High above this human slough, storms of unbelievable fury raged, one upon the other, with only brief periods of respite. When Steele headed for the Chilkoot a violent blizzard had halted all movement. But the policemen kept on:

"As we proceeded up the pass we faced a wind so cutting that we often had to make a rush for the shelter of a tree, or walk in a crouching position behind the tailboard of the sleighs for a moment's respite. We saw no people moving on the trail, they were afraid to venture out in the storm, in fact it was useless to do so, for no one could work in such a wind; even the horse had the greatest difficulty making headway against it."

At noon, Steele and his companion were forced to halt at a huddle of stables. The next morning, with the storm still at its height, they set off again. Steele overtook many men staggering blindly up the steep incline, bent double under ungainly burdens. Some had lost the trail and were searching blindly for it with their feet;

Steele helped them. Finally he reached the Scales, a cleft in the mountain where professional packers weighed the goods to be taken on their backs to the summit. Here the incline was more than thirty-five degrees. Above, lost in the swirling snow, was the notch in the mountain wall that marked the Chilkoot Pass.

Steps had been cut in the ice of the slope. Steele groped for the lifeline that helped guide climbers upward; he could not locate it. The two policemen sought shelter in a camp of engineers constructing an aerial tramway to the top, but, it too proved impossible to locate. Then, Skirving, the constable with Steele, happened upon a tunnel in the snow leading through an immense snowdrift which covered two large tents. Two men were toiling in the tunnel, shovelling out snow to keep the occupants from suffocating. Within a few weeks both would be dead, smothered with more than sixty others in the great snowslide of April 3. The following morning, a constable made his way down from the Chilkoot summit, located Steele, and reported that a customs post had been established. Steele sent him back with orders to commence immediately collecting duty on all goods brought across the hastily established border. Then he headed back to the coast.

At Dyea he boarded a small boat to take him across the bay to Skagway. They arrived when the tide was out and Steele had to wade the half-mile to shore in the freezing shallows. He was soaked to the thighs, his clothes frozen solid, but had no time to change, for it was essential that he get his report to Vancouver by the first available boat; Canadian sovereignty was involved. Even Steele's iron constitution could not stand that punishment; he came down with a severe attack of bronchitis, which lasted several weeks.

Most of the Mounted Police were suffering similar attacks. On the Chilkoot summit, where seventy feet of snow fell that winter, Inspector Bobby Belcher, who had been Steele's sergeant at Fort Garry in 1873, was snowbound in a shack that resembled a shower bath. The nearest firewood was seven miles distant. Snow fell so constantly that every stitch of clothing was permanently damp, every official paper greasy with mildew. In one twenty-four-hour period, six feet of snow fell, burying the post. Conditions were no better on the White Pass summit, where the police tents were pitched on solid ice. Here, with the nearest firewood twelve miles away, a blizzard could howl without let-up for as long as ten days. When Steele arrived, he ordered the ailing inspector in charge, D'Arcy Strickland, to go down to Tagish Post on the Canadian side to recuperate. The superintendent, though suffering just as badly, stayed on in his place.

On his side of the border, Steele maintained his reputation for keeping order. The Alaskan side was as night to the Canadian day. Skagway was a camp of vultures, "about the roughest place in the world . . . little better than a hell on earth," to use Steele's own description. "Robbery and murder were daily occurrences . . . . Shots were exchanged on the street in broad daylight." One morning, Steele and another policeman were awakened from their sleep on a cabin floor "by the cries, curses and shouts of a gang having a pistol fight around us. Bullets came through the thin boards, but the circumstance was such a common event that we did not even rise from our beds."

Skagway was in bondage to a local dictator, Jefferson Randolph "Soapy" Smith, a suave, spade-bearded confidence man out of Creede and Denver, who had come north with the intention of taking over the port. His sovereignty extended to the border but not one inch further. "There was no danger of Soapy Smith and his gang," wrote Steele. "They dare not show their faces in the Yukon. The 'gun,' the slang term for a pistol or revolver of any description, was put in the sack or valise, and everyone went about his business with as strong a sense of security as if he were in the most law-abiding part of Canada."

Steele astonished one banker who was en route to the goldfields and concerned about the safety of the paper money in his care. The policeman took the bundle – a small fortune – and tossed it under his bunk where, he assured the banker, it would be quite safe.

Gunfire was almost never heard in Steele's command. One evening in May, while at his headquarters cabin on Lake Bennett, he heard two shots. Incredible! A sergeant was dispatched at once to discover the cause. He reported that an American had accidentally fired his gun while cleaning it but added that the man looked like a member of the Soapy Smith gang.

"Arrest him, lock him up and go through his things," Steele ordered. The search revealed a complete shell game outfit and a marked three-card monte deck. Protesting that he was an American citizen, the culprit threatened to take his case to the secretary of state. Steele's reply was terse: "Seeing you're an American citizen, I'll be very lenient. I'll confiscate everything you have and give you half an hour to leave town." Before the con man could utter a word, he was marched out of the cabin at rifle point and hurried up the trail for twenty-two miles to the border with an armed policeman at his heels.

At Lake Bennett Steele's day was once again eighteen hours long. The tents of some twenty thousand gold-seekers whitened the rocky shores of the lake and its smaller neighbour, Lindeman. Each was trying to construct some sort of craft with which to navigate the Yukon river system when the ice finally broke. Steele's morning began at four. By ten, his routine work completed, he started seeing stampeders "who came all day and far into the night, asking advice and assistance with every imaginable phase of their lives." Numb with cold and exhausted to breaking point by unending toil in the sawpits, partners were quarrelling, dividing up their outfits, even to the point of sawing sleds and boats in half; all requiring of Superintendent Steele the judgment of a Solomon.

By late May, a hedgerow of seven thousand homemade craft lined the shores of the two lakes. Steele – determined that all should be conveyed safely down the more than five hundred miles of water to the Klondike – ordered that every boat, scow, canoe, catamaran, raft, barge, kayak, bateau, and dugout be given a number, and that the names and addresses of each passenger be recorded. In this way he and his men could keep track of the entire flotilla, for each boat would be required to check in at various police posts along the way. If a boat failed to arrive in a reasonable time, the police went searching for it. As a result, of all the thousands who floated down the river in the summer of 1898, only twenty-three were lost.

Seven of them drowned in the first days of the armada in Miles Canyon and in the White Horse Rapids, before Steele and his men could reach them. One hundred and fifty boats had been wrecked in the white water by the time the superintendent arrived. At the head of the canyon, a bottleneck of several thousand boats had formed. Some men were afraid of going through, others were trying vainly to push past; thousands stood on the banks wondering whether to chance the fury of the current or manhandle their goods around those gloomy walls of conglomerate rock. Below the canyon and beyond the rapids were hundreds more – a demoralized mass of shipwrecked souls who had lost all their possessions in the raging waters.

The scene that followed has been described many times. Canadian frontier authority was never more paternal than on this occasion when Sam Steele, a strangely comforting father figure, gathered his flock around him and spoke to them sternly. It should be remembered that most of those who listened so meekly were Americans, many of whom had resented the authoritarianism of the Canadian constabulary. Steele was aware of this and made the most of it: "There are many of your countrymen" he began, "who have said that the Mounted Police make the law as they go along and I am going to do so now for your own good, therefore the directions I give shall be carried out strictly . . . "

His instructions were explicit. No women and children would be allowed to shoot the rapids. Every boat would be examined before entering the canyon to make sure it had sufficient freeboard to ride the waves. Only competent men would be allowed to take a boat through. One of his corporals, an experienced boatman, would be in full control of all passages. There would be a fee of five dollars for every boat taken through and a fine of one hundred dollars for anyone who broke the rules. No one did, and there were no more drownings.

A month later, Steele was given command of all Mounted Police in British Columbia and the Yukon. In September, he arrived in Dawson to establish his headquarters. He was now in effective control of the largest and gaudiest city west of Winnipeg. Prices were prohibitively high. The commissioner's funds for administering the government, which were supposed to last for a year, ran out in a few weeks. The town's administration, such as it was, was bankrupt. The hospitals, crowded with typhoid and scurvy victims, were also out of money. Steele, who was neither mayor nor territorial commissioner, solved the town's financial problems in a few months by levying fines on what he called "loose characters" (the proceeds going to the hospitals) and by licensing every saloon, gaming house, dancehall, and wayside inn that sold liquor. Before the snows had melted he had collected ninety thousand dollars in licence fees to be used for administration.

His day had now stretched past nineteen hours. He rose at six; dropping into bed at two the following morning, but never neglected his five-mile walk each day along the frozen Klondike. He organized a mail service to the outside world for some thirty thousand people in the town and along the creeks, arranged to collect gold royalties, appointed a sanitary inspector, made himself chairman of a board of health as well as of the licence board and, when necessary, actually did make up the law as he went along. "We were not," he wrote, "tied down by foolish precedent."

Under Sam Steele, the Yukon was close to being a police state; no other frontier in the world was so tightly controlled and organized as this. As Steele put it, in his blunt fashion, "The situation was before us and had to be faced. Nothing was omitted that was for the good of the community." For those who complained there was the object lesson of Skagway's anarchy. Dawson's crime statistics for 1898 – the stampede year – are so remarkable that many a novelist and screenwriter has found them impossible to believe. More than forty thousand souls poured through the town that summer – gamblers, confidence men, fugitives, prostitutes, ex-convicts, petty thieves, saloonkeepers, cutthroats, American gun-fighters, and prospectors hungry for gold and women, thirsty for hooch, and, in Service's phrase, "loaded for bear." Yet in those twelve months there was not a single murder or a major theft.

"We have some of the greatest criminals on the continent here," Steele wrote to his father-in-law in February 1899, "and yet the vigilance exercised has made the place as orderly as Montreal, in fact, as far as public resorts go, the city is much rougher than this town . . . . The change that has come on this place since September is marvellous. Crimes are all brought to justice promptly. The town is so orderly that any lady can walk with more safety from insult (in the middle of the night) than in any place I know of . . . ."

If Steele's law was arbitrary, it was also sensible and flexible. He did not ban prostitution; he knew that that would not be possible. He simply confined the whores to a single area and barred them from walking the streets before four in the afternoon. Nor did he ban gambling. "There were worse men in the world than the gamblers of the Klondyke," he was to write. But he controlled gambling and maintained the Lord's Day, closing every game at one minute before midnight on Saturday and keeping them shut until the following Monday at 2:00 a.m. No man could run a crooked wheel or a three-card monte game in Steele's jurisdiction. He had ensured that the CPR right of way was free of liquor, but he had no such scruples about drinking in a mining camp. The saloons ran all night (though never on Sunday), but no minor could enter for work or for play. Steele's idea of "the good of the community" extended to theatrical performances. He had no compunction about censoring remarks that he considered disloyal to Queen, country, or Empire or dances that he considered lewd or obscene. He allowed no one to work on Sunday; one man was fined for chopping his own wood on the Lord's Day. The policeman, not the clergyman, was the arbiter of Dawson's morals.

He allowed his men considerable latitude in their off hours. Anyone who has examined the default sheets of Mounted Policemen from the past century will be struck by the insistence on adherence to the letter of the regulations. A button unbuttoned, a stable badly cleaned, a minute's tardiness on parade, a salute sloppily given – any such misdemeanour could bring a reprimand, a fine, or a confinement, but when one night the sergeant-major reported to Steele that some of the young constables were not at their beds at roll call, the superintendent dismissed the breach.

"They're young," he said, "and they'll never see a mining camp like this again. So long as they do their duty it won't hurt them to go a bit large."

No policeman in Canada has ever had the power that Steele wielded during his days in the Klondike. He needed only to raise his finger to have a man deported, and since almost everybody in town had risked his neck and fortune in the struggle to reach the goldfields, this "blue ticket to the Outside," as it was called, was the worst of punishments. It was admirable, but it was scarcely democracy; and it is more than possible that Steele's behaviour was the precedent for a continued and extralegal interference by later generations of Mounted Policemen with the rights of dissenters for what the police have considered to be "the good of the community." Steele was absolutely certain that he knew best what the good of the community was. In his memoirs he tells of the time an American performer made some anti-monarchical statements from the stage of a Dawson theatre. Steele, the imperialist, was having none of that: the performer was told to cut it out or face banishment. "This," Steele wrote, "had the desired effect."

Unorthodox situations often demand unorthodox methods. Without Steele and his police, it is possible that the Canadian Yukon might have become part of Alaska. In Steele's view, more than half of the Americans constituting 90 per cent of Dawson's population were "of a shady character." The biggest patriotic celebration of the year was not Dominion Day but Independence Day. The most popular newspaper, the *Klondike Nugget*, fanatically anti-government, was American-owned. There was talk of rebellion and, perhaps, some plotting. Shortly after the gold rush a quaint novel was published, apparently founded on facts, that described an organized attempt at a Yukon takeover known as the Conspiracy of the Midnight Sun; it had as its central figure and hero the man who put down the fictional revolt: Samuel Benfield Steele. No conspiracy could possibly have been successful during Steele's reign.

His real problem was the rapacity, incompetence, and often the crookedness of appointed government officials. His *bête noire* was the political spoils system. This he could curb but not control. Steele was appalled at what he saw going on around him and poured out his dismay in a long letter to Harwood: prominent civil servants, sent by Ottawa, having milked the public of large sums, were entertaining each other lavishly on champagne at forty dollars a quart and keeping expensive mistresses. The Crown timber agent was taking money for handing out concessions to insiders. The Crown prosecutor and most of the local lawyers were so "mixed up with mining interests that one cannot tell who one hits." The new government legal adviser was stealing clients from rivals by claiming political pull. It was ironic: Steele had cleaned up the town, had halted every form of plunder except the political variety. "I do not think," he wrote, "that so much rascality has been done since the country commenced to open up the West. And to make matters worse, there are others who have been sent up lately."

The "others" included J.D. McGregor, a close friend of Clifford Sifton's, who had been handed the plum of liquor licence commissioner for the territory, an appointment which, in that graft-ridden community, was an invitation to illicit wealth. Steele was having none of that. As chairman of the licensing board, he had seen to it that all applicants were treated equally and that all money went into the public coffers. As a member of the Territorial Council, he now used his influence to block McGregor's appointment.

It was to be his downfall. McGregor, a strong Liberal, who was also mine inspector (and would later become lieutenant-governor of Manitoba), dispatched a hand-written and confidential letter to the minister telling him the worst: the police were "practically running the country." They were even out on the creeks collecting millions from the miners in government royalties – a job McGregor felt should be left to civilian appointees (meaning political favour-seekers). It was "a dangerous thing," McGregor wrote, that "there is not a politician on the council." That body was "the weakest thing you can imagine and the sooner you can get a couple of good strong men on it the better." It was implicit that the good strong men be Liberals. "The Torys," McGregor disclosed to Sifton, "are on top in this country." The Liquor Licence Board and the Board of Health were both run by three members of the hated opposition party. Steele was on both; Steele was a Tory; Steele was out to get McGregor. And then Steele compounded his sins by refusing to let a meat contract to another friend of Clifford Sifton's.

He had looked forward to a long stay in the Yukon – had asked permission to bring his wife and young son north – but his days there were numbered. On September 8, 1899, a brutally concise telegram arrived for Steele, advising him that his duties in the Yukon were ended and ordering him to report immediately at Regina without waiting for the arrival of a successor. It was signed by Sifton.

An unholy uproar followed. All three Dawson newspapers – bitter journalistic rivals, that seldom agreed on anything – closed ranks to support Steele. "WRONG IS TRIUMPHANT," cried the anti-government *Nugget*, not unpredictably, in its main headline. What followed is a remarkable example of the trenchant frontier journalism that the Klondike enjoyed:

"The nefarious schemes of the Sifton gang of political pirates could not suffer the continuance of even one honest and competent member of the outlying government . . . a government constructed solely to acquiesce in the blackguardedly spoilation of a defenseless territory . . . . Without one word of warning which might have led to a national protest Colonel Steele is relegated to obscurity, that not even one pair of keen, cold, honest eyes should witness the villainous prostitution of the governmental prerogative in turning over to private bodies of henchmen the public property of this great and growing Artic [*sic*] commonwealth . . . . The confiscation plans and concession programs of the gang temporarily in control of Canadian affairs caused them to look askance at the growing reputation of a man who was becoming famous for virtue, not for duplicity; for honesty and not for avariciousness; for temperance and not for debauchery; for merit and not for usefulness to his masters; for truthfulness and not for equivocation; for efficiency and not for political brilliance; for good faith and not for treachery; for sterling qualities of manhood and not for pliability to the base uses which Siftonism imposes upon its office-holders . . . " and so on and on, for four columns, the words fairly spitting from the newsprint.

The editorial comment of the rival newspapers was only slightly less strident. The *Dawson Daily News* deplored Steele's recall by the government as "an act of unwisdom." The paper felt sure "that it voices the sentiments of every resident of the territory when it says that the loss to the country is almost irreparable." As for the Liberal *Yukon Sun*, its editor, Henry Woodside, shot off an urgent telegram to Sir Wilfrid Laurier, the prime minister: "For the good of Government beseech you to suspend order removing Colonel Steele from command here will be terrible blunder will create intense indignation."

The intense indignation was whipped to fever pitch at a mass meeting on September 16 at the Criterion Theatre. Although it was a Saturday night, merchants left their stores in charge of clerks to turn out; miners poured in from the outlying gold creeks; and "most anyone of any local prominence was there." Joseph Whiteside Boyle, soon to be famous as the dredging king, presided; Woodside was elected secretary; both were prominent Liberals. Speaker after speaker, representing both political parties, rose to eulogize the absent superintendent. A memorial was drafted to be sent to Ottawa (a petition from prominent citizens had already been dispatched); it was passed unanimously. A copy was struck to be circulated among the miners working on the creeks; Joe Boyle, who would one day run the nation of Rumania with the same efficiency with which Steele had run the Yukon, offered to circulate it personally; thousands signed it. Andrew Hunker, the discoverer of one of the Klondike's richest tributaries, Frank Swanson, one of the Eldorado "kings," and C.W.C. Tabor, a prominent lawyer shortly to become more prominent by virtue of his marriage to the notorious Diamond Tooth Gertie, offered to underwrite the cost of sending all the signatures by telegraph to Ottawa. It was all in vain. On September 26, Sam Steele, who had not since his removal spoken one word publicly or written one privately left the Yukon for good.

He wanted to go quietly, without fuss, but that was not possible. He was, in the *Nugget*'s words, "by all odds the most highly respected man in the Yukon today." To his astonishment thousands blackened the river bank to see him off – not just the townspeople but multitudes also from the outlying creeks. As a special concession the steamboat on which he was to leave came upriver from the dock to the Mounted Police barracks to take him on board, but not before Big Alex McDonald, the "King of the Klondike," had presented him with a poke of gold as a going-away present. For days McDonald, a taciturn bull moose of a Nova Scotian – the richest man in that rich community – had been coached in his farewell speech, but when the time came all he could do was to thrust the poke into Steele's hands and mumble: "Here y'are; poke for you, Sam! G'bye." For Steele, who hated such ceremonies, it was undoubtedly a relief. Minutes later, when the boat threw off her lines and puffed out into the grey river, every whistle in town blew a salute, and the crowd on the bank cheered and waved until the scarlet paddlewheel vanished round the bend and only the white plume of smoke could be seen above the yellowing aspens.

What now for Steele? Fred White, the NWMP comptroller in Ottawa, perhaps to soften the blow, offered him a variety of posts that might once have been considered plums. Steele agreed to meet him in the capital en route to Montreal, but due to a delay in communications they missed each other. It did not really matter; he was lost to the police – and, for much of the rest of his career, to Canada. He saw no chance for advancement, and when that fall the opportunity arose to take command of an unorthodox regiment of mounted riflemen to fight the Boers in South Africa, he seized it. As colonel of Lord Strathcona's Horse he distinguished himself. A British royal commission appointed to look into the conduct of the war gave him the supreme accolade: "There was no better commander than the rough riding colonel from Canada." His heart was still with the North West Mounted, but when the war ended he chose a foreign frontier at the request of General Sir Robert Baden-Powell who, in addition to founding the Boy Scouts, was planning a South African constabulary on the model of the NWMP. In his heart, Steele must have known that he could not go back, and yet he could not bear to cut the umbilical cord. He wrote a wistful letter to Laurier asking for leave of absence without pay so that he could serve with the South African force. "Having no prospects with police this will give me the means of saving a little, which I cannot at present and I may stand a chance for the better times allowed later on in the police."

The better times never came. In 1907, he returned to Canada as a soldier, not a policeman. With war impending, he was given the task of building up the country's military forces. When hostilities broke out he was sent to England to take charge of all Canadian and Imperial troops in the Shorncliffe Command, and there he reorganized the Canadian Expeditionary Force. But he was too old for active service. Honours were heaped upon him. On New Year's Day, 1918, he was knighted. He was now Major-General Sir Samuel Benfield Steele, C.B., M.V.O., K.C.M.G., in a cocked hat with a plume. Everything, it seemed, had come to him, everything but the one thing he really wanted – the supreme command of that Force which had been a father to a fatherless boy, which had nurtured him, tested him, honoured him, and, in the end, rejected him. In July, 1918, after fifty years of service, he retired. But retirement was not for Sam Steele. Six months later he was dead.

FOUR

The martyrdom of Isaac Jogues

Huronia: 1636

" . . . Like everybody else who visited the Georgian Bay country in that century, Jogues could not help but be struck by the contrast between the funereal Precambrian land through which he had just passed – a wilderness of sombre conifers and rubbled gneiss – and the luxuriant domain that now greeted him. Verdant with stands of oak and pine, the land rolled gently toward the water, rendered pastoral by small plots of cultivated maize, the Indian corn that was basic to the Huron culture. The forests were alive with deer, beaver, and bear; the surfaces of the lakes dark with wildfowl; the waters beneath teeming with trout, pike, and sturgeon. Unlike the nomadic Algonkins, the Hurons had no need to roam the Shield. Provender lay at their doorsteps . . . "

It is not easy for the twentieth-century mind to come to terms with Isaac Jogues's zeal for martyrdom. To others of his faith, death by torture in the name of their God was certainly an occupational hazard, but to Jogues it was much more: it was a dream to be cherished, a goal to be fulfilled, a sublime climax to a life of sacrifice. The evidence suggests that Jogues longed to be a martyr and that he sought out that fate as fervently as medieval knights pursued the Grail. He revelled in discomfort, welcomed pain, endured the most dreadful torments, and went off to what he knew was certain death on a forbidding frontier with an enthusiasm that today would be equated with lunacy.

But Jogues was no madman, nor was he a witch, as the Indians with whom he lived tended to suppose. He was a seventeenth-century Jesuit priest who believed with absolute conviction in a literal Heaven and an actual Hell – a Hell in which every unbaptized adult, be he Frenchman, Iroquois, or Hottentot, was doomed to suffer eternally the torments of the damned.

To Jogues, one of the greatest services he could render God and man was the hasty and often secret baptism of a dying Huron baby – wiping its brow with a handkerchief dipped in water hurriedly made sacred while feeding it raisins and pretending to take its pulse. Without that act of absolution Jogues was convinced (as were his fellow priests) that the infant would be confined to limbo, denied forever the presence of God. That was a circumstance almost as horrifying as the one which awaited those adult Indians who refused the sacrament and who were thus condemned to be roasted forever over a slow fire or parboiled through all eternity in a lake of molten brimstone. Jogues was better able than most to understand the horror of that fate, for he had himself seen humans roasted alive; indeed, he half hoped that his own life would end in the same fashion. He did not fear the flames, for he knew they would not be eternal; his earthly life was brief and transitory, the pain of his passing momentary. What did a few years of hardship matter when at the end lay the delights of Holy Paradise?

Such convictions are as foreign to us today as were those of the Hurons whom Jogues was trying, without much success, to convert to his way of thinking. Indeed, it has been said that in terms of their beliefs in supernatural forces, the Jesuit and the Huron had more in common than either does with modern man. But that does not mean they were on the same wavelength. The Indians were mystified by Jogues and his black-robed colleagues: what on earth were these bizarre celibates doing among them? They did not even want to trade! And they seemed obsessed by the idea of death. The priests, for their part, were confused by the Huron lifestyle, which they never did understand. The sexual licence common among the unmarried natives appalled them; they were themselves so modest that they shrank from undressing in front of one another. But another aspect of the Huron behaviour shocked them even more – the refusal of the Indians to use physical punishment to discipline their children. These mutual gaps in understanding were exacerbated by the conviction on each side of its own social, spiritual, and intellectual superiority.

Jogues was born in Orléans, France, the middle child of nine in a prosperous merchant family. At the age of ten he was accepted for instruction by the Jesuit order. He was a willing pupil. He seems, in fact, to have been almost *too* devout, for by the time he was a novice at seventeen, he had to be restrained from over-meticulous observation of the most trivial rules. He was a small, agile youth, not strong but wiry, a good swimmer and runner, an excellent scholar and an adequate poet. The contemporary portraits, which are, of course, idealized (for Jogues eventually became a saint), show him in later life as a slight figure, thin-faced and hollow-cheeked, with downcast eyes and a somewhat ragged beard. His ambition was to be a missionary in one of the far corners of the earth – he had thought of Constantinople, but his superior made a more accurate prediction. "Father Jogues," he told him, "you will not die anywhere but in Canada."

His choice of a patron provides a clue to his ambitions. He selected Father Charles Spinola, martyred in Japan in 1622; he carried a picture of that unfortunate priest being burned at the stake. He prayed to him, we are told, "and envisioned a similarly glorious ending for his own life."

He was ordained at the age of twenty-nine and ordered at once to Canada. The year was 1636; Louis XIII was on the throne of France; Richelieu, his first minister, had just four years before given the Society of Jesus exclusive missionary rights in the New World. The Thirty Years War had been raging for a generation; the citadel of Québec, a pawn in the struggle, had changed hands twice – from France to England and back to France again. In Europe, the Renaissance had reached the period of high baroque; Rembrandt in Holland, Velázquez in Spain, Rubens in the Low Countries, were at the peak of their talents. Paris, applauding the work of its rising new playwright, Pierre Corneille (himself a product of Jesuit education), thought itself exquisitely civilized.

On the far side of the ocean barrier – eight weeks' sail for the handful who attempted the journey – lay New France, a vast, virgin wilderness, stretching west from the Atlantic to the unknown shores of Lake Superior and south from Hudson Bay to Lake Erie, a domain far larger than the parent land and scarcely explored. Only one white man, Jean Nicollet, had actually seen Superior and then only its eastern tip near the present site of Sault Ste. Marie. Two pinpoints of civilization, Trois-Rivières and Québec, existed on the St. Lawrence. The rest belonged to the Indians – to the nomadic Algonkins and their relatives, the Montagnais, who roamed the Precambrian forests between the St. Lawrence and James Bay, and to the sedentary Hurons, who occupied the agricultural lands in the neighbourhood of what is now Lake Simcoe. To the south of the Great Lakes lay Dutch territory and the five nations of the Iroquois League, whose language and culture were similar to those of their enemies, the Hurons.

To many on arrival from Paris or Rouen, the culture shock of this wilderness world must have been numbing; to Jogues it acted as a tonic. From Québec he wrote to his mother: "I do not know what it is to enter paradise, but this I know, that it would be difficult to experience in this world a joy more excessive and more overflowing than what I felt when I first set foot in New France and celebrated my first mass here . . . I felt as if it were a Christmas day for me, and that I was to be born again to a new life, and a life in God."

This super-enthusiasm would never be quenched in spite of the dreadful ordeals that lay ahead. One hardly knows whether to pity Jogues, even in his moments of greatest anguish, for he continually gives the impression that he is in a state of ecstasy.

He did not want to stay in Québec; he hungered to be sent to the farthest reaches of New France, to the pagan realm of the Hurons. Since a Huron trading party was due at Trois-Rivières, his superiors dispatched him to meet it. And there the little priest encountered his first example of the Indian lifestyle: he witnessed the torture and death of an Iroquois brave at the hands of a group of Algonkin women and children. This grisly spectacle would have deterred most newcomers, but it merely strengthened Jogues's resolve to "soften their hearts and tame their wild savagery."

A second shock lay in store. Accompanying the Huron trading party was an old acquaintance, Father Antoine Daniel, a skeletal figure, barely recognizable, body wasted, skin leathered and wrinkled, eyes sunk deep in their sockets, cheeks hollowed, beard and hair ragged and matted, cassock in shreds. To Jogues, the other priest was a saint and a hero; he begged to be allowed to return with the Hurons in Daniel's place and, after some palaver, the Indians agreed.

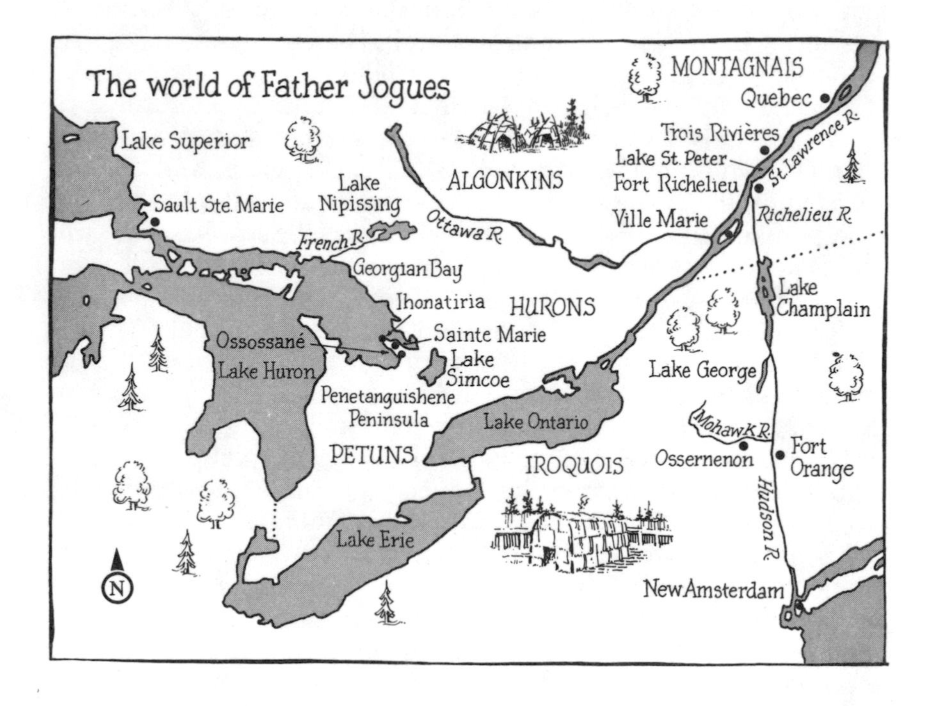

The land of the Hurons lay some eight hundred miles to the west; that meant at least a month of hard travel by canoe and portage, a gruelling experience for a young missionary fresh from France. Jogues was forced to sit motionless in the canoe, his knees drawn up to his chin, afraid to move lest he disturb the balance. His food consisted of a little corn, pounded between two stones and boiled in water without seasoning. At night he slept on the hard ground "or the frightful rocks lining the great river," suffering the torment of mosquitoes and black flies. On the portages – there were more than forty – he scrambled over huge boulders and crawled along slippery ledges, burdened for much of the journey with an eleven-year-old boy who was too exhausted to struggle on his own. Yet, for Isaac Jogues, all this was bliss because "the love of God, who calls us to these missions, and our desire of contributing something to the conversion of these poor savages, renders this so sweet, that we would not exchange these pains for all the joys on earth."

The route led up the St. Lawrence to the Ottawa River, through Lake Nipissing, and along the French River until Georgian Bay was reached and finally the Huron village of Ihonatiria on the Penetanguishene peninsula. Like everybody else who visited the Georgian Bay country in that century, Jogues could not help but be struck by the contrast between the funereal Precambrian land through which he had just passed – a wilderness of sombre conifers and rubbled gneiss – and the luxuriant domain that now greeted him. Verdant with stands of oak and pine, the land rolled gently toward the water, rendered pastoral by small plots of cultivated maize, the Indian corn that was basic to the Huron culture. The forests were alive with deer, beaver, and bear; the surfaces of the lakes dark with wildfowl; the waters beneath teeming with trout, pike, and sturgeon. Unlike the nomadic Algonkins, the Hurons had no need to roam the Shield. Provender lay at their doorsteps. They occupied two dozen semi-permanent villages, located near streams and fertile soil and connected by some two hundred miles of narrow trails. Upwards of eighteen thousand persons lived and lived well in the seven-hundred-square-mile strip between Lake Simcoe and Georgian Bay. It was the most populous wedge of land in eastern North America.

For the missionary, however, life was not easy. Father Jean de Brébeuf, who had been the superior since 1634, warned Jogues that first evening what to expect: six months of continual discomfort and cold during the winter, confined to a draughty cabin constantly crowded with Indians, with whom they must share their food. The hovel in which the six priests and their five helpers would live was, in fact, a smaller version of the traditional Huron longhouse. This windowless structure ("no Louvre, no palace" as Brébeuf warned) was fifty feet long and eighteen feet wide. The smoke from the open cooking fires that ran down the centre of the building was so thick that it was impossible to read. It would be hard, Brébeuf told Jogues, to find in France a hut so wretched.

Worse, he explained, they would live under the shadow of death: "A malcontent may burn you down or cleave your head open in some lonely spot. Then, too, we are responsible for the sterility or fecundity of the earth, under the penalty of our lives. We are the cause of droughts; if we cannot make rain they speak of nothing less than murdering us." There was, of course, from the Jesuit viewpoint, a positive side: the hardships and enforced poverty provided a glorious opportunity to deepen their devotion to God.

Jogues arrived at the Huron village brimming with enthusiasm but broken physically by the hardships of the trail. He was shortly felled by a serious attack of influenza, one of a series of epidemics which, between the years 1634 and 1640, reduced the Indian population by half and turned them against the white men, whom they believed, not without cause, to have spread the sickness among them. Most of the French were stricken by the disease from which they recovered only with difficulty, partly because they could get no peace from the Indians who crowded around their sickbeds from sunrise to dusk. They had never seen white men sick before and could not understand why they lay prostrate rather than sitting, Indian style, with knees drawn up to chin. The priests did their best to keep the cabins quiet, but the Hurons thought it preferable to chant, dance, and feast about the sick in order to drive off evil demons. The cabins were jammed with men, women, and dogs, in a continual uproar.

The French recovered. The priests saw this as a sign of the power of prayer, but the reason was more likely their acquired resistance to a disease unknown to the natives. While the epidemic spread across the whole northern section of the peninsula, each side remained arrogant in the assumption that its remedies – and its alone – were the cure for the affliction. The Hurons turned to their medicine men, one of whom offered to cure the Blackrobes with roots, herbs, and potions, all for the price of ten glass beads; Brébeuf dismissed him as a charlatan. The priests preferred to bleed their patients, a treatment equally superstitious.

Jogues, the first to recover, helped minister to the sick. He was more concerned, however, with their spiritual welfare. Regardless, they stubbornly resisted his attempts to baptize them. It was most puzzling, not to say annoying. These primitive creatures did not seem to comprehend the delights of Heaven or the agonies of Hell. "I have no desire to go to Heaven," one man said, "for I have no acquaintances there, and the French would give me nothing to eat." Another said he would not go to Heaven because his relatives would not be there. Another refused because he understood there were no fields, no corn, no trading, fishing, hunting, or marriages in Heaven.

These responses, which ought to have given the Fathers an insight into Huron values, were lost on them. The Hurons rejected conversion because it would cut them off from their culture and their friends, and, to a Huron, everyone was either friend or enemy. The basic unit of friendship and co-operation was the extended family. Friends shared everything; from an enemy one could expect only hostility, injury, or death. Death was something the Hurons did not care to contemplate, yet it seemed that these peculiar white men in their outlandish dress were obsessed by it. They did not appear to care much about life; they seemed to talk of nothing but the hereafter. Nor were the Hurons immune to the flawed logic of cause and effect. They noticed – how could they not? – that when a priest sprinkled water on somebody, that somebody almost invariably died. From the priests' point of view, it was better for the Indians if they died as soon after baptism as possible, for death prevented them from sliding back into heresy.

The Jesuits had taken pains to learn the native tongue. Brébeuf spoke it fluently and so, eventually, did Jogues and the others. They could speak, but they could not communicate, nor could the Indians with them. Yet both were united in a common belief in the supernatural – in demons who could control human lives. Brébeuf was convinced that the Indians were guided by Satan and his attendant devils whose presence was as real as the maple trees. (Some priests actually "saw" these evil spirits and banished them by making the sign of the cross.) The Hurons were divided about the Blackrobes: one faction believed them to be witches, responsible for the influenza epidemic; another held that they were powerful shamans who could drive off the demons of illness.

Witches, in Huron society, were considered the most dangerous of enemies. Anyone could slay a proven witch with impunity, for his relatives were not permitted the usual practice of seeking compensation or blood revenge. And how was a witch to be identified? By a process not unlike the one then being practised in civilized Europe and white America: any deviation from the accepted social norms was sufficient to arouse the suspicion, especially in times of crisis. A failure to be polite, a tendency to speak harshly, a refusal to be generous with presents or feasts, an unusual desire for privacy – these were seen as un-Huron activities. This was exactly the way the Jesuits behaved, albeit unwittingly, among a people they thought stubborn and ungrateful. Little wonder then that, during the six years he lived and travelled among the Hurons, Jogues and his fellow priests laboured under the menace of execution and torture.

In spite of threats and plots to massacre them, the Blackrobes travelled from village to village, often in waist-deep snow, seeking to baptize the Indians. Jogues had never felt such fulfilment. In June, 1637, with his usual enthusiasm, he wrote to his mother that he and his fellows had managed to baptize two hundred and forty Hurons: "The life of a man, could it be better employed than in this noble work?" he asked. "All the labours of a million persons, would they not be well compensated for the conversion of one single soul, gained for Jesus Christ?" It did not in the least concern him that all but one of these two hundred and forty had been baptized on their deathbeds, often not comprehending the rite. To Jogues, this was irrelevant; he had snatched them from the pit – literally at the eleventh hour. Of all that number, only one healthy adult had voluntarily accepted the Christian faith.

The Hurons believed that the Jesuits were trying to destroy their society and their culture. This was not the intention of the priests, who had specifically learned the language and gone out to the villages to preserve the Indian culture, or so they thought. It did not occur to them that in accepting Christianity, an Indian was rejecting his own lifestyle. For among the Hurons, religion and culture were indivisible; they could not comprehend the European attitude in which the two were conceived of as separate. The blindness on both sides can be seen in the impressive ceremony and feast that marked the baptism of the one healthy Indian. The priests, with a singular myopia, thought it salutary to exhibit a large and grisly painting of the Last Judgment, depicting serpents and dragons tearing out the entrails of the damned. The Hurons completely missed the point. They were convinced that the victims were Indians like themselves whom the Blackrobes had caused to die the previous winter.

By the end of October, 1637, the sporadic voices demanding the execution of the priests had developed into a unanimous chorus. The Huron council, convening after dark on the twenty-eighth, blamed the pestilence on the Blackrobes. No one defended them. So convinced were the Fathers that they were going to die that they adopted the Huron custom of holding a ritual farewell feast in which friends and enemies alike were invited to their cabin and offered prodigious supplies of fish and corn. Yet they were not killed, in spite of continued threats, largely because of the Hurons' greed for European trade goods. They feared, with good reason, that any harm done the Jesuits would result in a break with New France.

Each side continued to misunderstand the other's motives, beliefs, and customs. The priests thought the Indians fickle and inconstant because those who accepted Christianity continued to practise the old rites. The Jesuits could not understand the Indians' ability to borrow from various religions. As far as the Hurons were concerned, Christianity was another healing society; it did not occur to them that membership in one group precluded membership in another. Moreover, the priests failed to realize that politeness was part of the Huron code of behaviour; in dealing with others, a Huron was expected to be gentle and considerate and to repress feelings of frustration or hostility, which were reserved for the common enemy. These are also Christian virtues, but the Christian priests were confused by the Indians' apparent friendliness, by their readiness to accept and to listen, which went hand in hand with an inability to assimilate the truths of Christian teachings. The Hurons, on the other hand, were greatly offended when the priests censured or ridiculed their own explanations of their customs and culture. More than once they gently reminded the strangers that each side had different customs and should respect the other's beliefs. But the Jesuits could not bend.

In the summer of 1638, the Hurons were plunged into a savage war with the Iroquois who, short of European goods, were bent on plundering trading parties in New France. Captured Iroquois were burned, mutilated, scalped, and sometimes eaten by their captors, who, in spite of their paganism, engaging in double-think, became enraged when the captives were baptized by the Jesuits before their ordeal. The Hurons did not think it proper that their enemies should be granted the happiness of paradise – in the event that paradise actually existed. They tossed the bones of their victims into the Blackrobes' cabins. The priests responded with a Christian burial.

The ritualized torture of prisoners of war by all the Iroquoian peoples, which reached its apogee in 1649 with the death of Brébeuf and others, has fostered an image of these Indians as unspeakable savages given to orgiastic excesses. Yet to what degree did their customs differ from similar practices in Renaissance Europe? Pain is pain; horror is horror. Was the mutilation and burning of Spanish heretics, the roasting alive of witches (common to most European nations) and the public disembowelling of living traitors in England less reprehensible than the gauntlet and the stake of the Iroquois? What seemed to horrify Jogues as much as the torture itself was that it was practised not by official executioners but by women and children. But this was as much a part of Indian tradition as the public slaughter for sport of bulls in Spain.

By 1639 there were ten priests in Huronia as well as a number of French workmen, some engaged in building a central mission,

Sainte-Marie (near the modern town of Midland, Ontario) which would be independent of the Indian villages. Father Jérôme Lalemant had replaced Brébeuf as superintendent at the latter's request; Brébeuf felt (quite correctly) that his own abrasive temperament was not conducive to treating with the Indians. A new epidemic, smallpox, was sweeping the country and again the Hurons were blaming the priests – and why not? They seemed to pay attention only to the cabins of the sick, ignoring the living; it seemed obvious that they had a close connection with the disease.

At this time Jogues and a colleague, Father Garnier, were sent on a dangerous evangelical mission to the Tobacco Nation, or Petuns, who derived from the same stock as the Hurons and the Iroquois. These people lived forty miles from Sainte-Marie in the modern day counties of Simcoe, Grey, and Bruce. The two priests went alone, without any idea of the route they were travelling, because no Huron was willing to guide them. The hardships they suffered – they slept out in howling blizzards with only blankets for covering and no fire to warm them – were mild compared to the tensions engendered by their arrival in the Tobacco country. The Petuns turned ugly when a group of Hurons arrived to report that their nation was being ravaged by the white man's disease. The newcomers urged the Petuns to kill the priests. Jogues wrote:

"This whole country is filled with evil reports which are current about us. The children, when they see us arrive at any place, cry out that famine and disease are coming. Some women flee. Others hide their children from us. Almost all refuse us the hospitality which they grant even to the most unknown tribes. We have not been able to find a house for our Lord, nor any place where we can say Mass . . . . They treat us wretchedly in order to oblige us to leave. Truly we have nothing more than what suffices to keep us alive; our hunger usually accompanies us from morning till night. But these poor people do not understand that what keeps us here is more precious than all they can conceive in the way of [the] pleasures of this world . . . "

As they moved deeper into Petun country, the reception became more hostile. Every cabin was closed to them. A screaming, threatening mob followed them from door to door. The chiefs announced that anyone who killed a Blackrobe would be doing a service to his people. The wonder is that they were not murdered; the Indians, who thought nothing of torturing the captives of battle to death, seemed to shrink from cold-blooded assassination.

The two priests toughed it out for three months and then departed, pronouncing the mission a triumph. Why? Mostly because they had suffered so: suffering was their index of success;

suffering was noble; suffering was joy; the path of suffering led directly to the gates of paradise: "This mission to the Petuns has been the richest of all, since the crosses and the sufferings have been most abundant in it."

That spring – the year was 1640 – the missionaries gathered at their new base at Sainte-Marie to calculate their achievements. On paper, they were impressive. They had succeeded in baptizing one thousand Hurons, although more than a third of these were children under the age of seven. The victory was illusory. The smallpox had so terrified the Indians that by early summer fewer than thirty still called themselves Christians. Most of these were traders who saw substantial benefits in professing the white man's religion because it was noticed that those who were baptized got higher prices for their furs in addition to presents. The Hurons were pragmatic; they judged all charms and rites by their effectiveness. Theological argument did not interest them; they considered the French an inferior race intellectually. If they could benefit from their magic, fine; if not, they would seek to neutralize it.

In the summer of 1641, Jogues was put in charge of turning Sainte-Marie into a redoubt against both the Hurons and the marauding Iroquois, who had launched another violent offensive. The work was interrupted by an apostolic mission to one of the Algonkin nations far to the west. Jogues and another priest, Father Charles Raymbaut, made the three-hundred-and-fifty-mile journey in seventeen days, travelling as far as Lake Superior – farther west than any white man had ventured.

Jogues should have been ecstatic; everything he had worked for seemed to be coming true. The Hurons, freed at last from epidemics, were more friendly. New France stood behind the Jesuits. The governor of New France, Charles Huault de Montmagny, who was as pragmatic as the Indians, showered their emissaries with gifts, explaining that these were tokens of the Blackrobes' truths. By Easter of 1642, the missionaries had baptized one hundred and twenty Hurons, all adults in good health – a significant advance.

Yet these successes did nothing to hearten the little priest. He grew impatient, restless, out of sorts. It was almost as if things were going *too* well. The long voyages, the harsh conditions seemed no longer a sacrifice for he had been toughened by the environment. He was now a seasoned woodsman, a veteran of wilderness travel, his muscles as hard as iron, able to digest any kind of food and capable also of bearing up under long fasts. Life had become, well, *normal*, and blessed martyrdom seemed further away than ever! He longed to suffer for his faith, to do battle physically with Satan, but Satan seemed to have been routed or, at least, slowed down. Jogues could not sleep for the agony of it. While his fellow priests slumbered in the smoky cabin, he would rise from his mattress, fall on his knees, prostrate himself before his Maker, and plead for a chance to suffer, to endure pain and fatigue, to face dangers, to be subjected to extraordinary tribulations. He wanted nothing so much as to be "sacrificed as a victim of Divine Love."

Then one afternoon, while on his knees on the hard boards of the chapel, he heard, or thought he heard, God speak: "Thy prayer is heard. Be it done to thee as thou hast asked. Be comforted, be of strong heart." At that moment, Isaac Jogues knew that the martyrdom he longed for would eventually be his.

His prayers were answered with miraculous speed. Lalemant asked him to undertake a journey so hazardous that it came close to being a death mission. Each year it was necessary for a priest to accompany Huron traders down the St. Lawrence to the heart of New France to deliver letters and to fetch reports and supplies. Now, with the Iroquois in full cry against the Algonkins, the Hurons, and the French, this hazardous journey seemed certain to be fatal. Lalemant made it clear to Jogues that the request was not a command; Jogues was free to refuse. *Refuse*! It was exactly the test for which he had been hoping – the beginning of the fulfilment of his prayers.

Father Raymbaut, who was ill, was to accompany him to seek medical attention in Québec. Jogues would have three other white companions – two workmen and a *donné* or lay helper, a carpenter named Guillaume Couture. Eighteen Christian Hurons completed the party.

Even without the threat of Iroquois attacks it was a dangerous journey. Eight hundred miles of wilderness separated Sainte-Marie from Québec, yet the party arrived some forty days later, in the midsummer of 1642, without incident. Ten days later, Jogues, with Couture and another *donné*, René Goupil, headed back, their twelve canoes loaded with a variety of goods ranging from blankets and seeds to chalices and dried fruit. There were more than forty in the group, including some Huron children whom the priests had sent to school in Québec.

The brigade reached the western end of Lake St. Peter, a maze of small islands. The current was stiff, and the canoes held close to shore. To their right, the dense mattress of the forest reached to the water's edge; ahead, in the shallows, the bulrushes grew tall. Suddenly, there arose from the rushes the dread war whoops of the Iroquois. Thirty painted Indians sprang from the weeds and turned their muskets on the flotilla; the Hurons replied with a volley of arrows. Jogues, rising to his knees, made the sign of the cross and shouted words of absolution. When the pilot of his canoe, a non-Christian, was shot through the hand, the priest baptized him on the spot. Then, as more shots rattled around them, the canoe was smashed against the shore and Jogues was thrown into the weeds.

The Hurons in the following canoes turned and fled. Those left to fight were outnumbered two to one: forty more of the enemy appeared; the fighting was hand to hand. It is difficult not to admire Jogues at this moment; hidden in the weeds, he could have made his escape, for the fighting had moved more than one hundred yards away. But he could not abandon his people, especially those that had not been baptized. He stood up and asked to be taken prisoner.

What followed was pure horror. Jogues was knocked down, stripped, and beaten. Goupil, the *donné*, who had also been captured, was tied so tightly with leather thongs that he could not move. The two comforted themselves with the thought that their misfortunes were the will of God, but that did not make the coming torment easier to bear. Couture meanwhile had fought off the Iroquois, killing one of their chiefs, and had fled to the protection of the forest. He, too, decided that he could not abandon his comrades. He was captured, stripped, beaten senseless, and then revived by having his fingernails torn out and a knife jammed through his hand. Jogues did not at first recognize the blood-smeared *donné*, but when he did he threw his arms around him and kissed him. The action bewildered the Iroquois, who thought that the priest was congratulating Couture for killing their chief. Infuriated, they beat Jogues unconscious with clubs, muskets, and kicks. Two grasped his arms, clenched the nails of his forefingers with their teeth, and tore the nails from their roots. They then took each forefinger in their teeth and crushed them to a jelly. This grisly performance, common among all Iroquoian tribes, had a practical origin: it was designed to make escape difficult and to prevent the victim from using any weapon, from musket to bow, against his captors.

Jogues was desolated, not because of his physical condition but because he realized that, with one blow, the Iroquois had devastated the Huron Christian church. Almost all of its leaders had been captured. Paradoxically, his spirit was at peace. The torment that he had sought to suffer for his faith had begun. It would continue unabated for weeks.

The horror began eight days after the battle when the party came upon a camp of two hundred Mohawks. These warriors, armed with clubs and thorn switches, formed two parallel columns, a few feet apart, upon a slope. The prisoners, naked, were formed into a file, the older men at the head to keep the pace slow, and forced to run the gauntlet. Jogues was placed last so that his punishment would be the greatest. Before he had gone a hundred paces he was tripped, beaten unconscious, dragged to the top, revived, and beaten again. The Indians dug into his flesh with their fingernails and thrust burning faggots against his arms and thighs. One bit and crunched into his thumb until the bone was exposed, causing the priest to faint. He regained consciousness but did not rise, for he expected to die. He was exalted; the God "for whose love and sake it is delightful and glorious thus to suffer" had fulfilled his most cherished hopes.

The Iroquois, however, intended to keep him alive. Jogues was hauled to his feet and forced to witness the torture of his comrades, including Eustache Ahatsistari, a Huron warrior who had become a Christian. The priest, tears streaming down his cheeks, tried to intervene but was thrust away. The torture continued into the evening until, at last, the captives were left to sleep on the ground, their bodies a mass of festering flesh, caked with blood, dirt, and cinders.

The following day, the Indians and their prisoners moved off, heading for their home villages. Jogues might now have escaped. He was unfettered; he was at the end of the column; there was no guard; he could easily have slipped into the protection of the forest. But he could not: "I wished rather to suffer the most extreme tortures than to abandon the French and Christian Hurons in their death and to deprive them of that consolation which a priest is able to impart." In Jogues's creed, his comrades would be consigned to the eternal fires if they did not receive the last rites of the church while suffering the temporal flames of the Iroquois.

A march of thirteen days followed. "By the favour of God our sufferings on that march . . . were indeed great," Jogues wrote; "hunger and heat and menaces, the savage fury of the Indians, the intense pain of our untended and always putrefying wounds, which actually swarmed with worms . . . " On their arrival, the tortures grew more hideous. At one point a Christianized Algonkin woman was forced on pain of death to cut off Jogues's thumb. She took the knife in a trembling hand and slashed and tore until she had cut the tendon and pulled the thumb free. Throughout the ordeal, the priest remained silent. He looked at the thumb, which lay at his feet where the woman had dropped it and came to the odd conclusion that his Maker was punishing him for not loving him enough, a divine vengeance for which, as he later wrote, he was profoundly grateful:

"Picking up the severed thumb with my right hand, I offered it to You, my living and true God, for I remembered the Holy Sacrifice which I had offered to you on the altar of your Church through seven years. I accepted this torture, O my God, as a loving vengeance for the want of love and respect that I had shown in touching your Holy Body. You heard the cries of my soul."

Jogues was still struggling with this inverted reasoning when Couture called to him to throw the thumb away; if he didn't, he would be forced to eat it. God surely had not intended any act of cannibalism; Jogues did as he was bidden.

It would be pointless to detail the continued tortures to which these three devout and gentle men and their Huron comrades were subjected. But it is necessary to reiterate that they were scarcely more hideous than those visited upon heretics, traitors, and accused sorcerers in contemporary Europe. In each culture, religion was at the root of the savagery. The torment of captives by the Iroquoian tribes was a sacred ritual, the eating of parts of their bodies an act of religious significance. In Europe, heretics were disembowelled, broken on wheel or rack, roasted over slow fires, confined in iron maidens, gnawed to death by rats or torn to pieces by swine, all in the name of religion. The Iroquois were not the only people who mangled fingers; the Inquisition's thumbscrew was just as painful and mechanically more efficient.

The Mohawks who tortured Jogues and who seem in the Jesuit accounts to be little removed from animals were, in fact, among the most sagacious and civilized of the North American Indians. They belonged to the Five Nations Confederacy, the most sophisticated political alliance on the continent, stretching from the valley of the Hudson to the western end of the Finger Lakes. This league of mutual peace was a creation of genuine political genius. It survived the advent of white settlers and, centuries later, was used as one of the models on which the charter of the United Nations was based after the Second World War. Although the Iroquois often tortured captives, they spared far more, adopting them into their own culture, so that long after the Huron nation was decimated, many of its former members lived on as Iroquois.

Adoption was to be Jogues's fate and that of all but three of his fellow captives. He had been told that he was to die at the stake and had prepared himself, with his usual optimism, for the end: "Sooth to say, this last act was not without its horrors, yet the good pleasure of God, and the hope of a better life, where sin should have no place, rendered it rather one of joy." Again the delights of martyrdom were denied him. Conciliatory members of the Mohawk council argued for the life of the white men, hoping by that action to wean the French from their support of the Hurons and Algonkins.

But conciliation proved illusory. At Fort Richelieu on the St. Lawrence, three hundred Iroquois were driven away by the cannons of the French. The defeated natives returned, eager to put their captives to death. The Dutch, who lived peacefully among the Mohawks – and with reason, because they supplied them with the weapons to do battle with their trade rivals, the French – pleaded for the prisoners' release, offering gifts worth six hundred florins in exchange. The Indians vacillated.

Couture had been adopted by a family in another village. Jogues and Goupil, too weak to escape, were permitted to wander freely about Ossernenon, a community of some forty cabins and garden plots surrounded by a strong palisade. Jogues adapted easily; Goupil, unused to Indian life, was horrified by the filth and the savagery. The Mohawks despised him for his gentleness and feared his devotions, convinced that in making the sign of the cross he was weaving an evil spell. His death was foreordained.

It came one afternoon on a hillside above a brook, while he and Jogues were praying. Two Indians appeared; one produced a tomahawk from beneath his blanket and struck Goupil on the head. The *donné* called out the name of Jesus, staggered, and fell. Jogues knelt to give absolution, then presented himself for execution. The expected blow did not fall. The priest was later to learn that his friend's death had been ordered by an old chief who had seen him make the sign of the cross over his baby grandson.

For the next two months, Jogues was hidden in the home of the family that had adopted him. He was convinced he would soon die and made sure that he was never without a copy of St. Paul's Epistle to the Hebrews and a crude wooden cross he had made, so that when the end came he would have the cross and the scriptures in his hand and be spared damnation.

With autumn came the hunt. Jogues was lent to another family to help carry supplies. With winter approaching, his only clothing was a thin shirt, torn breeches, and a cloak. His stockings were in shreds, his moccasins almost worn through. In spite of his emaciated condition he was expected to carry a crushing load. Soon his legs were torn and bloodied by sword grass and rushes. He could scarcely walk with the pain, but he did not complain.

At first his new family treated him kindly: he was a novelty, docile and eager to help, amusing in his efforts to master the language. But once the hunt began, they lost interest. Jogues remained blind to Indian customs. He was offended when the choicest part of the first animal killed was offered to the Mohawk god. This was superstition: the priest would not, *could* not be a party to it. He was ravenous; his wasted body cried out for nourishment; there was plenty of venison, but he refused to eat a scrap of the heathen meat. His sole food would be corn.

After a week or two the game became scarce. The pagan Mohawks turned out to be as blind as the Christian priest. A sorcerer convinced them that Jogues, by his refusal to eat and his contempt for their god, had driven off the animals. They beat the Jesuit unmercifully, convinced that his prayers were demonic incantations.

The return trip to the village, in December, was an eight-day nightmare, first through tangled underbrush and thorny vines and then through bitter snowstorms. Jogues arrived back at Ossernenon, exhausted and frostbitten, his arms and legs cracked from the cold and running with blood. Now his adopted family, especially his master's wife, whom Jogues learned to call aunt, began to treat him with kindness, nursing him, feeding him, giving him two new deerskins, one to wear and another to use as a blanket. Her motive at the outset was pity; later she grew to like the priest, who was slowly becoming a second son. For the first time since his capture, Isaac Jogues no longer felt under sentence of death.

Forty miles to the east of Ossernenon, white civilization flourished after a fashion at Fort Orange and the surrounding settlement of Rensselaerswyck, the site of Albany, the present capital of New York. The Dutch existed among the Mohawks on sufferance; though they knew that white priests had been enslaved and tortured by the Indians, there was little they could do apart from offering money for their release. In May, Jogues and Couture actually appeared at the settlement but under heavy guard. In New France they were believed to be dead.

Once again the opportunity for escape arose. Jogues's "aunt" told him that if he slipped away during a trading expedition she would not sound a warning. But Jogues had no intention of escaping, for, as he asked himself, who in his absence would console the French captives, "who absolve the penitent? who remind the christened Huron of his duty? who instruct the prisoners constantly brought in? who baptize them dying, encourage them in their torments? who cleanse the infants in the saving water? who provide for the salvation of the dying adult?" Divine Providence had placed him in the hands of the savages for these specific purposes; who was he to shirk God's work? Without him, potential believers would be denied eternal life.

Arent Van Corlaer, the leader of the Dutch community, was irritated by the priest's attitude. Here he was, a Protestant, bending every effort, perhaps at the risk of his own safety, to ransom a Papist (or to connive at his escape), only to be met with a stubbornness he could not fathom. This wretched Jesuit in his tattered cassock seemed determined to remain among the very people who had mutilated him and who still spoke of killing him! Jogues, on his part, seemed to believe that any attempt to liberate him was the work, if not of Satan himself, then of some minor devil. Daily, he wrote, he bowed his knee to his Lord "that if it be for his glory, he may confound all the designs of the Europeans and savages for ransoming me and sending me back to the whites."

At Fort Orange, Jogues was able to pen a long and detailed letter to his superior in France, relating all that had happened. Written in Latin, the report ran to fifteen thousand words – a considerable feat for a man whose hands were so crippled he could hardly hold a pen and whose familiarity with that ancient language had been blurred by long disuse.

Then, once again, the Mohawks turned ugly, cursing him as an evil sorcerer and demanding his death. Some time before, Jogues had taken the risk of trying to smuggle a letter through to New France; a member of the Mohawk war party had taken it, thinking it might be used to entrap the French at Fort Richelieu. But on reading the letter the French had turned their cannon on the Mohawk warriors. The Indians were furious. It was clear now to everyone that Jogues's days were numbered.

Van Corlaer could not stand by and see a white man, albeit a Catholic, tortured to death. He sought out Jogues, who was being held in the Indian camp outside Fort Orange, and pleaded with him to try to escape. A Dutch ship, due to leave shortly for England, lay anchored in the harbour. If Jogues could reach it and hide in the hold until the ship sailed, he would be safe.

Jogues astounded the Dutch leader by asking for time to think the proposal over. Was he out of his mind to consider any other course? No; he was simply being true to his own concept of duty; with Jogues, personal comfort was never a consideration. All that night, surrounded by Indians in a stuffy barn, he wrestled with his conscience and came, at last, to the realization that there was no longer any compelling reason for him to stay. Couture, the only other white prisoner, was safe, adopted into a family. The best of the Huron Christians had managed to escape; the rest avoided his ministrations, believing that he was marked for death. On the other hand, he possessed a fund of Indian lore that would be extremely useful to his superiors in France. Again he weighed the pros and cons: what did the Lord want him to do? He concluded that the Lord "would be more pleased with my taking the opportunity to escape."

The following morning, he informed Van Corlaer of his decision. The Dutch leader called in the ship's captain, who assured the priest that he would be safe aboard ship. The plan was for Jogues to slip out of the barn during the night and to make his way to the river bank, where a rowboat would be concealed to get him to the ship.

The escape had all the elements of a scene from a suspense novel. The barn in which Jogues and his Indian captors were lodged was one hundred feet long, without partitions. It was owned by a Dutch farmer who kept his cattle at one end and slept with his Mohawk wife and children at the other. The Indians sprawled in the middle. When Jogues slipped out of the barn to reconnoitre his escape route, he was set upon by a watchdog that sank its teeth into his bare leg, all but crippling him. The outcry roused his captors, who brought him back, barred the door, and made him lie between two of them. There he remained until dawn, when a Dutch servant came to his rescue, tied the dog, and helped him to limp from the barn without waking the Mohawks. But when the priest reached the river bank, several hours after the appointed time, he discovered to his dismay the tide had gone out, leaving the rowboat stuck fast in the mud. He struggled but it would not budge. The sky had lightened, and he was now in full view of the Mohawk huts. He made one last superhuman effort to loose the rowboat and was successful. A short time later he reached the ship and was hidden in the hold.

The Indians were furious. They threatened to slaughter all the Dutch cattle and burn down the houses. Van Corlaer tried to calm them, offering a present of three hundred guilders; this they refused. The settlers were greatly alarmed. The natives were in a savage mood. Prudence won out over humanity. What was the life of one Catholic against those of a hundred Protestants? One man was deputized to go to the ship to persuade Jogues to return to prevent a massacre. The priest proved himself a more admirable human being than the wavering Dutch. Although in terrible pain from his leg wounds and nearly suffocated from the stench in the ship's hold, where he lay prostrate and half-conscious, he gave no thought to his condition. He was ready, he said, to return to captivity if it would save the Dutch settlement.

The ship's captain, however, had given his word that Jogues would be safe, and he did not intend to go back on it. Jogues remonstrated with him: "If this trouble has been caused by me, I am ready to appease it at the loss of my life." With that, he fainted and fell to the deck.

The Dutch delegate argued with the captain: the settlement did not want to surrender the priest and would do so only in the last extremity. He would be hidden among the Dutch and handed over only if the Indians threatened a massacre. The captain allowed himself to be persuaded. Jogues was rowed to land and hidden for twelve days in Van Corlaer's house. His condition was pathetic; one of the wounds inflicted by the watchdog turned gangrenous. The local surgeon prepared to amputate his leg but fortunately this proved unnecessary. Jogues was moved to another house owned by a miserly old trader who hid him in his attic. While accepting food and drink for the priest, he appropriated most of it, leaving the fugitive half-starved and cramped, crouched among a pile of barrels for hours while, on the floor below, the Mohawks traded with his host.

Meanwhile the Queen Regent of France, Anne of Austria, acting for the new child-king, Louis XIV, heard of Jogues's imprisonment and appealed to the Netherlands government to secure his release. The order came to Van Corlaer: Jogues was to be freed at once and sent to New Amsterdam. The Dutch leader stopped his vacillation. He bluntly told the Mohawks that Jogues was under his protection; if they refused his present of three hundred guilders, all trading would cease.

Why had he not used that threat before? Trade was the key to the matter. The Dutch had temporized because they dreaded the loss of trade as much as they feared the savage tomahawks. But the Indians, too, were unwilling to put an end to barter. On both sides trade was seen to be more important than a human life. That, of course, was not new. Trade was at the root of the bloody war between the Iroquois and the Hurons who were surrogates for the two commercial rivals, the Dutch and the French. It could not be helped that white Europeans were sometimes caught in the middle and condemned to agonizing death.

After much haggling, the Indians capitulated, and the priest was taken aboard a schooner bound for New Amsterdam. He was thirty-six years old but looked closer to fifty, his face drawn and deeply lined, his skin as rough and dark as an Indian's, his beard greying, his hair sparse. He waited until November 5 in the tiny settlement of New Amsterdam on the island of Manhattan until a small barque was ready to take him to England. The Atlantic crossing was stormy, but it did not matter to Jogues that his bed was a coil of rope on the top deck and that he was nightly drenched by the salt waves that rolled across him. He was inured to hardship.

His reception in England was anything but friendly. Civil war was raging between Oliver Cromwell's Roundheads and the Cavaliers of Charles I. Four Roman Catholic priests had already been executed. Jogues was forced to discard his cassock and to travel incognito until he secured passage to Brittany on a collier. It put him ashore on Christmas Day, 1643. The local inhabitants must have found him grotesque, a scarecrow of a man in a sailor's battered cap and an oversize greatcoat, speaking French with a strange accent as he asked the way to the nearest church. But for Jogues it was a moment to be savoured. He lost no time in confessing all the sins he could remember since the previous July – it is intriguing to wonder what these were – and then, on receiving communion, he "tasted the sweetness of . . . deliverance."

He made his way to Rennes and presented himself at the Jesuit college as a traveller from Canada. The rector hurried to greet the stranger. Did he happen to know Father Jogues?

"I know him well," came the reply.

"We have heard of his capture by the Iroquois and his horrible sufferings. What has become of him? Is he still alive?"

"He is alive," cried Jogues, "he is free, he is now speaking to you!" and he threw himself at the feet of his astonished superior, asking his blessing.

He became an instant celebrity. The *Jesuit Relations*, read throughout the nation, had announced his capture and probable death; now he had miraculously reappeared. His fellow Jesuits treated him with awe and reverence, but this was the last thing that Father Jogues wanted. He disliked talking about his adventures; he resisted showing his mutilated hands and his scars; he was concerned that people might think him a martyr, for he knew that he was not. That fate, he was convinced, was yet to come.

He did not want praise and recoiled from recognition but could escape neither. The next edition of the *Relations*, telling the full story of his experiences, was read eagerly. The Queen Regent commanded him to visit her. Alarmed, he tried to avoid the audience but of course could not. Feeling ill at ease, he was presented in the hall of the Palais Royal, where the Queen, examining his mangled hands, kissed them and wept. The publicity made him quail. He had only one ambition: to return to the frontier of New France and to the glory of martyrdom.

His contemporaries in France thought him mad to go back. Surely, it was said, he had done enough. Why expose his mutilated body to further hardships and almost certain death? But perhaps, having come to know something of Jogues's character, we can understand how he felt. For one thing, he felt guilty. Was he truly serving his God in the mirrored, marble halls of Paris? For another, he was genuinely homesick – homesick for the pine forests, the leaping cataracts, the winding trails of New France; homesick for the Indians with whom he had lived, for the smoky, suffocating lodges, and for those magic moments when, often with nothing more than a few drops of dew, he was able to dispatch a dying child to paradise; homesick even for Ossernenon and the verdant valley of the Mohawk, the scene of his greatest trials. Jogues had become a creature of the frontier. But there was something more: this humble and dedicated man had another frontier to cross – the frontier of the soul. He would not rest until he had conquered it.

He was faced with one obstacle – his mutilated hands could no longer hold the sacrament; how could he officiate at the Mass? The reigning pope, Urban VIII, was noted for his strict observance of ritual; would this stickler for rules grant a dispensation? The pope would and did – with dispatch. Jogues left France on the first ship to cross the Atlantic in the new year of 1644, a vessel so old and leaky that the passengers threatened to mutiny until the priest placated them.

At Quebec, Jogues learned that the Five Nations were again on the warpath, rapidly destroying their enemies, the Hurons and Algonkins, already ravaged by disease and famine. To the astonishment and admiration of his superiors, the priest begged to be allowed to work among the Iroquois should the opportunity arise; meanwhile he was sent to the far outpost of Ville-Marie on the island of Montreal, a settlement of fifty colonists then only two years old. Jogues was satisfied: the new community offered an ideal base from which to evangelize the Iroquois, should peace come.

All parties wanted peace, or said they did. Between July and the following May, the French, the Hurons, the Algonkins, and the Iroquois held three councils at which they all pledged themselves to end hostilities. Jogues attended the first of these, at Trois-Rivières, where the brilliant Iroquois orator, Kiotseaeton, spoke with such eloquence that the French suspected he was being more than a little devious. And so he was: officially peace would reign, but at a private meeting with the governor, Huault de Montmagny, Kiotseaeton shifted ground. The Iroquois would make peace with the French and the Hurons but not with their traditional enemies, the hated Algonkins. A compromise was reached, also in secret: there would be two kinds of Algonkins: Christian and non-Christian. The peace would apply to the Christians only; open season would prevail on the heathen. Nobody bothered to ask how an Iroquois war party, falling on an unsuspecting enemy, would be able to separate believers from infidels.

The shakiness of the peace was further demonstrated at council in September. The governor was vaguely disturbed by the fact that the Iroquois spoke only for the Mohawks and not for the other nations of the confederacy; he had indicated, in fact, that the Oneidas in particular were not satisfied. Further, as Jogues himself took pains to explain, even the Mohawks were divided. The Wolf and Turtle clans wanted peace; the Bears were for war.

In spite of the danger Jogues was desperate to return to the land of his tormentors. In April, 1645, he undertook a retreat, praying that he be allowed to go while steeling himself against disappointment. No man, surely, ever sought his own destruction so tenaciously. At this juncture, a letter arrived from his superior, Lalemant. Jogues described his reaction:

" . . . would you believe me that when I first opened the letter of your reverence, my heart at first was seized as if with dread; for I feared that which I desired might actually come to pass. My poor nature, which remembered all that has gone, trembled. But Our Lord in his goodness bestowed calm on it, and will calm it some more . . . . Ah, with what regret should I be filled if I lost such a wonderful occasion, one on which it might depend only on me that some souls were not saved . . . ."

On May 7, the third peace council was held. Again, the Mohawks pledged peace but warned that the Oneidas had refused to join with them. Jogues was appointed to return to the Mohawk nation as an ambassador. The journey was expected to be a brief one, but the little priest had other ideas: he would be more than an ambassador; he would become a permanent missionary to the Iroquois. Accordingly he packed a large box with everything he would need for the task: chalice, candles, wafers, sacramental wine, together with winter clothing and gifts.

He took the advice of a friendly Algonkin and packed his cassock also; he would travel as a civilian, not as a priest. The Indian warned him not to speak too freely of Heaven and Hell for "there is nothing so repulsive to us at the beginning as is your doctrine. For your teaching seems to destroy completely everything that men hold dear. Your long robe preaches as well as your lips. Hence, it would be better for you to walk in clothes which are shorter." Accordingly, Jogues set off in high-topped boots, pantaloons, a cloak, and a broad-brimmed hat.

His task was to confirm the goodwill of the French toward the Iroquois. Arriving at Ossernenon after an uneventful trip, the new ambassador was welcomed by the same people who had once used him so badly. The Mohawks were impressed by the new Jogues: his authority and his bearing contrasted vividly with his former docility and mildness. The one-time slave had become a figure of power.

The Mohawks unanimously pledged peace with the French and, though with more restraint, with the Algonkins. But there was resistance to Jogues's demands that the other four nations make similar pledges. There was only one disturbing incident: the black box containing the priest's possessions – strongly bound and locked and kept in the cabin of his Indian aunt – was causing difficulties. The Mohawks were afraid that it might contain demons – malicious spirits known to live in such things as boxes, hollow trees, caves, and holes in the earth. Jogues did his best to allay these suspicions, opening the box, removing its contents, and explaining that these were only personal effects. The Indians appeared to accept the explanation but were not entirely convinced. Jogues left the box behind and set off for Trois-Rivières, where he was greeted with a salute of cannon and the congratulations of the French officials.

He wanted to return at once, but his superiors demurred. The peace was untried. He must remain at Trois-Rivières unless an exceptional opportunity arose. The exceptional opportunity presented itself in September when the Huron plenipotentiaries arrived. If they decided the time was ripe to treat with their enemies, Jogues could accompany them.

He prayed that he might be permitted to go, even though he had a premonition that the journey would be his last. "If I shall be employed on this mission," he wrote to a friend, "my heart tells me . . . I shall go but I shall not return. In very truth it will be well for me, it will be happiness for me, if God will be pleased to complete the sacrifice where he began it, if the little blood which I shed there in that land will be accepted by Him as a pledge that I would willingly shed all the blood which I bear in all the veins of my body and of my heart . . . ."

He was determined that this time he would go back to the Iroquois as a priest and missionary first and an ambassador second. When the Hurons formally requested that he accompany them on the peace mission, he decided that once again he would wear the black robe.

The party set off from Trois-Rivières on September 24, 1646, in three canoes. Jogues and a young lay assistant, Jean de La Lande together with the Huron ambassador, Otrihouré, and another brave, occupied the lead canoe; a group of Hurons followed in the second; the third carried Mohawks returning home for the winter.

From the start, a sense of uneasiness hung over the convoy. At the site of Fort Richelieu, now abandoned by the French as unnecessary, a tense discussion took place. The Hurons sensed that something was wrong; they were about to enter Mohawk territory and their intuition told them that danger lay ahead. Only Otrihouré could be persuaded to continue the journey; his comrades retreated to the St. Lawrence. Then, suddenly, all the Mohawks vanished.

The three men continued alone up the Richelieu to its source and then, leaving the canoes, followed the mountain trail to Ossernenon. On October 14, they spotted a file of Mohawks coming toward them. Jogues halted and called out a greeting, but the newcomers melted into the forest. Jogues called out again, identifying himself. At this the Indians sprang from the trees, uttering war whoops, and surrounded the little party. Jogues went rigid with shock. La Lande froze beside him. Otrihouré was terrified.

The priest could not grasp what was happening. This was supposed to be a peace mission, but the Indians, brandishing muskets and knives, fell upon the three men, knocking them to the ground, beating them and ripping off their clothes. At last Jogues understood: this was a war party; the Mohawks had repudiated the peace. Dragged to the village and lodged again in the cabin of his Mohawk aunt, he learned what had happened. The Bear clan, always in favour of war, had gained the support of the other four nations in the confederacy as the result of events that took place after Jogues left Ossernenon earlier that summer.

Following his departure several people had fallen ill. The sickness spread; the people grew frantic. Pestilence, the greatest of their enemies, was threatening again to destroy them. Who or what could have caused it? A group of Hurons, adopted into the Iroquois nation, remembered that six or seven years earlier, their people had been similarly affected. It was the Blackrobes who brought the disease, they said; the Blackrobes wished to destroy all native people and have the land for themselves.

To make matters worse, in September, the corn began to wither, eaten by worms. Suddenly somebody remembered the box that Jogues had left behind. *The black box!* Might it not contain a blacker demon, who by sorcery was killing both the people and the corn? Was not the priest himself, robed in black, a harbinger of death? Now everybody recalled how he had fashioned a cross and uttered strange words over people who had subsequently died. Clearly he was a man who worked evil spells. He had come to them that summer in disguise; obviously this was designed to deceive them. He did not really want peace – he wanted to exterminate them. He was a witch, a sorcerer.

They dared not smash that terrible box, for that would release the demon. Instead, they drowned it in the river. With the sorcerer's creature destroyed, all that remained to be done was to destroy the sorcerer.

The object of this witch hunt and his companion were considered public hostages until a council could decide their fate. The priest had friends in the village who advised him never to venture beyond the stockade. As long as he remained in the house of his Mohawk aunt, a member of the conciliatory Wolf clan, he was safe.

But events which could not be reversed were now set in motion. On the evening of October 18, a young brave came to the cabin and invited Jogues to visit another lodge where there were people who, he said, wished to talk to him and eat with him. Jogues was in a dilemma; what was he to do? The invitation was highly suspicious because it came from a member of the war party – the Bear clan. Yet to refuse would be considered a deadly insult; no matter which course he took, he would be in peril. He did not wish to appear cowardly; what, he asked his aunt, should he do? She, too, feared treachery, but felt that he had to respond to the invitation. He went, accompanied by her grandson, Honatteniaté.

The two followed their guide through the village to a longhouse with Bear symbols carved on the doorpost. Realizing that the slightest hesitation, the smallest sign of suspicion or fear would give the Indians advantage over him, Jogues moved on, casually pushing the skin covering aside and bending to pass through the low doorway. A warrior stood behind the door, tomahawk raised, and as the priest entered brought it down on his head. Honatteniaté thrust his arm forward to deflect the blow, but the tomahawk slashed through the young man's flesh and thudded into the priest's skull. The guide sent the youth reeling as, with a second blow, the murderer dispatched Isaac Jogues. Screaming curses, Honatteniaté roused the villagers, who flocked to the cabin as the members of the Bear clan dragged the corpse into the street, dancing and chanting in triumph. In spite of the protests of Jogues's aunt, they scalped the corpse, cut off the head, and after parading it through the streets, impaled it on a sharpened pole at the northeast corner of the palisade. Later that night, they also ambushed and beheaded young Jean de La Lande.

Thus abruptly ended the mission of Father Isaac Jogues to the Iroquoian peoples. But why did he leave the safety of his friends' house for what he must have known was almost certain death? Is the usual explanation, that he did not wish to insult the members of the Bear clan, really valid? Had he chosen not to go he would have been safe, for the council, meeting that very day in a neighbouring village, had decided that both men were to be returned alive to Trois-Rivières. The young Bear hotheads were roundly condemned (though not otherwise punished) for their impulsiveness and the Huron chief, Otrihouré, was sent back to governor Huault de Montmagny to explain what had happened – a mission he could not complete, for he was killed en route. Jogues's actions, then, seem incomprehensible unless one has regard for his absolute faith in an all-wise Deity. Jogues was convinced that God was guiding his steps; if he was meant to die that night, so be it. As we have seen, he expected and even welcomed his own doom.

In a sense – an ironic sense – it may be said that he was fortunate. It is probable that sooner or later a more brutal and painful martyrdom would have been his. The shaky peace was shattered by his murder, though it was not until the following June that the French learned of his death. By that time the Iroquois nation was on the warpath, massacring and ravaging Hurons, Algonkins, and French. Three years after Jogues's swift dispatch, his former comrades, Jean de Brébeuf and Gabriel Lalemant suffered at their hands the ghastly tortures that the little priest firmly believed had been in store for him.

The tomahawk of the Bear murderer may have saved Isaac Jogues from the long torment of the stake. There were those, no doubt, who believed that he had already suffered enough and that Divine Providence had dictated a sudden and painless end. But would Jogues have wanted it that way? Knowing something of the workings of that zealous and passionate mind, knowing, too, the constancy of his aspirations which, in a more worldly or self-seeking man could be dismissed as vaulting ambition, one may be permitted to speculate that Jogues himself might have felt that the ending of his life had been unnecessarily swift, unnecessarily anticlimactic, even a little – dare one say it? – disappointing. But if so, that, too, was God's will.

FIVE

The odyssey of Cariboo Cameron

British Columbia: 1864

". . . By summer, the wooded defile of Williams Creek had become a desert of stumps as four thousand newcomers built themselves log cabins. . . . Saws screeched, trees toppled, water wheels creaked, hammers clanged in smithies. At night the narrow valley flickered eerily in the glow of a hundred torches marking the heads of the shafts. In the makeshift saloons the newly arrived Hurdy Gurdy Girls smiled and capered. . . . The nights were raucous with music and song, with the scraping of fiddles and the rattle of the piano, with the baying of dogs made manic by the moon, and the groans and cries of men intoxicated by Forty Rod – but rarely with the sound of gunplay, for firearms were taboo. British justice ruled . . . ."

The scene, as it has often been described by popular writers, seems to have been lifted verbatim from a Victorian melodrama. One can almost see the asbestos curtain rising on the small stage to reveal the setting: a humble prospector's cabin lit only by a flickering candle; a simple cot in which there languishes a lovely woman, her features drawn and pale; two bearded men in mackinaws on their knees beside her; *sounds off*: a howling gale; *effects*: confetti snow, blowing through the window.

The woman opens her eyes. "John! John!" she cries. "Promise me, you'll take me home. Promise me you will not lay me to rest in this unkind country!"

The bulkier of the two men tries to soothe her: "Now, Sophia, you're not going to leave me."

He rises to prepare some medicine, but as he does the woman, half hysterical, struggles up and gasps one final word: "Promise!"

"I promise," comes the choked answer, and, almost on the instant as his partner raises the sick woman's head to receive the potion, she expires.

One questions the dialogue; it is a little too contrived, more than a touch theatrical. But one cannot doubt the incident. It occurred in the early morning of October 23, 1862, in the shack community of Richfield, a mining camp in the Cariboo country of British Columbia. We have Robert Stevenson's word for it; he was one of the men in the cabin. The other was his closest friend, John Alexander Cameron of Glengarry County, Canada West, soon to be known as "Cariboo" Cameron, the richest miner in British Columbia and perhaps also in the Canadas. But Cameron's fame derives less from his wealth than from the Gothic sequence of events that flowed out of that bedside promise. If the scene in the cabin belongs in a Grade B melodrama, those that follow belong on the wider canvas of a nineteenth-century novel. There was, in fact, such a novel, *The House of Cariboo*, published in 1898, and based in part on the incidents of Cameron's life; even his surname was used. But in this instance, fact could not be transposed into fiction. The novel omitted the real melodrama because the truth was too bizarre: a deathbed promise following on a fabulous gold strike; a coffin and a sack of gold dragged for four hundred miles through impassable snows; a body pickled in alcohol to preserve it from the furnace of the tropics; and to cap it all, a public disinterment twelve years later – a corpse uncovered before a crowd of shocked and disbelieving villagers.

Nonetheless, the record is unequivocal. These things happened; eyewitnesses recorded them; three generations of popular writers have profited from them. The wonder is that so many have felt it necessary to embellish a tale that needs no embroidery.

John Cameron was born in 1820 in Lancaster, near Cornwall, in the County of Glengarry, Upper Canada. His father, Angus, was an immigrant farmer, a Highlander who could trace his ancestry back in a direct line to Donald Cameron, Chieftain of Lochiel. Young Cameron worked as a hired hand on the farm of his uncle John, near Summerstown on the St. Lawrence, but farming was not for him. There was in his make-up a streak of that mysticism which seems to be part of the psychic baggage of born prospectors. He was a dreamer; he believed in dreams; he dreamed of finding a fortune, and when the news of the great gold strike in California filtered East he determined to leave for the West. His neighbours laughed at him when he announced that he would prospect for gold. "Typical John Cameron dreams," they said.

California was not an easy frontier to reach; Cameron did not arrive until 1852 after trudging on foot across the Isthmus of Panama, an appalling forty-mile struggle through dripping jungles, malarial swamps, and cholera-infested shack towns along the route of the uncompleted Panama Railroad. Two brothers, Roderick and Allan, followed in 1854, and all three worked in the goldfields until 1859, when John Cameron returned briefly to Glengarry to marry his fiancée, Sophia, the willowy daughter of Nathan Grove, a veteran of the battle of Lundy's Lane, who owned a farm in the nearby township of Cornwall.

Cameron was in his fortieth year; Sophia was twenty-seven. The difference in age was not unusual at a time when a man needed "prospects" in order to take a wife. Cameron's prospects were just that: reasonably good placer ground in California. The happy couple set off for the Pacific, this time crossing the isthmus in comfort on the newly completed railroad. Sketchy accounts exist of Cameron's success and then failure in the California diggings. He did well for a time but then fell victim to that optimism, which also tends to be an ingrained trait in goldseekers; he overextended his resources constructing a flume to bring water to a mine that was already played out. To add to the problem, a serious depression was at that time sweeping the continent. But this did not really concern Cameron because reports were beginning to seep out about new gold finds in the Crown colony of British Columbia, first on the Fraser River and then farther north in that hazy section of the map known as the Cariboo. Men with colourful nicknames were striking it rich in narrow willow-choked valleys. On Antler Creek in 1860, Doc Keithley was reporting pans of seventy-five and one hundred dollars; by the spring of '61, the entire creek was solidly staked. By then Dutch Bill Dietz had given his name to Williams Creek, a fairy-tale stream so rich that one man took twelve thousand dollars from a fraction of ground between two claims, thus earning himself the title of Twelve-Foot Davis.

Creek after creek in the Cariboo yielded similar dividends, and the rush was on. On October 25, 1861, the little hamlet of Victoria was treated to a singular spectacle: a group of miners from Williams Creek arrived with eighty thousand dollars in gold dust, all from a single claim. An awestruck crowd at the Hudson's Bay wharf followed them as they headed for the Wells Fargo office, the heavy canvas bags of gold slung over their shoulders. The crowd squeezed into the office to watch the gold being placed in the Wells Fargo safe. The safe slammed shut, but the members of the crowd did not disperse; they stood as if mesmerized, gazing at the strongbox as though it were an icon, trying to pierce the door with X-ray vision, seeing the gold in their minds' eyes. Every man in the throng that day, it was said, announced his intention of going to the Cariboo the following spring.

Gold fever raged across the continent and leaped the ocean. In England, young men thirsting for adventure and sudden wealth in an unimaginable wilderness swallowed the fiction of the transport companies and laid out hard cash for what was billed as a joy-ride across the empty plains and through the mountain passes. A handful actually made it.

Crews deserted vessels; clerks left their posts. Hundreds poured off the ships into the tiny colonial backwater of Victoria, transforming it into a bustling city of tents. City men in top hats and boiled shirts, who didn't know a Long Tom from a sluice box, rubbed shoulders with kilted Scots and California miners in high, hobnailed boots, armed with bowie knives, derringers, and six-guns. Up from California by way of Portland on February 27, 1862, came the creaky side-wheeler *Brother Jonathan*, bursting with seven hundred and fifty passengers. The list included the names of John Cameron, his wife Sophia, and their fourteen-month-old daughter, Mary Isabella Alice. The family's circumstances were desperate. Cameron had forty dollars to his name. The child, wrapped in a blanket, was critically ill.

She died five days later in the Royal Hotel, a blow that all but prostrated her parents. But almost at the same moment fortune turned up in the guise of a young man named Robert Stevenson, a fellow Glengarrian. The two men – one twenty-four, the other forty-two – formed a remarkable if somewhat one-sided friendship that would last, off and on, until Cameron's death.

Of the two, Cameron had the more commanding presence – a massive Scot with a high forehead, clear eyes, straight nose, and vast beard. It was the eyes that everybody noticed: chill blue, they seemed to bore right through you. Stevenson was slighter then and neater, with a short clipped beard, a thin moustache, and the kind of pageboy hairstyle fashionable at the time and favoured by such romantic figures as the actor and future assassin, John Wilkes Booth. A number of portraits exist of both men at various ages. All are alike in one aspect: Cameron stares soberly at the camera; it is not too much to say that he glowers. Stevenson seems always good humoured: his eyes twinkle and in the later, less stiff-necked portraits, when the developments in photography encouraged subjects to be more casual, he smiles. This was his nature. Where Cameron was morose, stubborn, and often temperamental, Stevenson was obliging, constant, and cheerful. We do not know what it was that drew him almost instantly to the older man – a neighbour but a stranger; it is possible that he saw in him a substitute father because his own father, who had originally accompanied him to the West, had returned to Glengarry; but the attraction must have been powerful, for it never really faded. By Cameron's standards, his new friend was well-to-do. Cameron was nearly destitute. Stevenson set about making him rich.

Stevenson had left Glengarry at twenty-one, when news of the Fraser strike first reached Canada West. He was too late – or thought he was – and joined a new stampede to the Similkameen country in southern British Columbia, where he survived a series of adventures including, it is said, a volley of poison arrows from the bows of hostile Indians. He found little gold but secured a government job – customs officer at Osoyoos – which he quit when news of the bigger strikes in the Cariboo reached him in the spring of '61. Learning that pack horses were in great demand in the gold country, the shrewd young man bought one hundred head, drove them to Lillooet, and sold them at a profit of ten thousand dollars. On he went to Antler Creek, acquired a gold claim, and bought a building from which to launch a supply business.

Few miners were prepared to brave a Cariboo winter. In December, some two thousand, Stevenson among them, made the long trek out to the coast – four hundred miles of it on snowshoes – and then by boat across the strait to Victoria, where a tent city blossomed. Stevenson planned to return to Antler Creek the following year with a pack train of supplies. To do that, however, he would have to delay his departure until late spring when the trails were passable for horses. In Cameron he saw a solution to that problem. Cameron was sturdy; Cameron was dependable; Cameron could wait behind to supervise the pack train while Stevenson went on ahead with the first wave of returning miners.

He took the older man over to the Hudson's Bay store, introduced him to the chief trader, and, after an hour's parley, went security for two thousand dollars' worth of goods, which were placed in Cameron's name. Then, on April 2, he left for Antler Creek on a twenty-one-day journey through snows often seven feet deep. There he opened a store and in less than four months cleared eleven thousand dollars – more than most prospectors made from their gold claims.

Cameron and his wife arrived on July 25, but without the pack train. Something had happened. We do not know the details, but there had been a quarrel between Cameron and the freighter, Alan McDonald – a quarrel so bitter that the two were now deadly enemies. It was the first hint Stevenson had of Cameron's stubbornness and irascibility, a quality that would contribute to the bizarre events of a later decade. Again, Stevenson proved a friend in need. Cameron owed McDonald fourteen hundred dollars in freight money; Stevenson settled the account and had the goods delivered to the new boomtown of Richfield on Williams Creek where the latest strike had taken place. The supplies included a ton of candles of inferior quality, now badly broken after being carried on the backs of animals for some four hundred miles. Broken or not, they fetched five dollars a pound in a land of sky-high prices, where a pound of butter went for five dollars, a pound of salt for $1.50, and wax matches for $1.50 a box. By any standard the prices were incredible; in Toronto that year, a pound of candles sold for fifteen cents, a pound of butter for twelve cents, and and a box of matches for about fifteen cents. You could buy an entire barrel of salt for four dollars.

That summer, Billy Barker, a bow-legged English merchant seaman who had jumped ship at Victoria the previous year, decided to move into virgin territory below the Williams Creek canyon. Barker, a complete amateur, had decided to sink a shaft some distance from the rimrock above the creek in the belief that the prehistoric creek bed, where the gold lay, had been turned aside at that point. His story – the story of a naïve newcomer who strikes it rich as old-timers snicker – was to be re-enacted many times in this and future gold stampedes. While prospecting veterans made sport of him, Billy kept digging. On August 22, at fifty-five feet, he struck paydirt: five dollars to the pan. At eighty feet he took out one thousand dollars in gold in two days. The camp went wild.

Stevenson had already moved his business to Williams Creek. According to his own account he was tipped off by a Dr. Crane that there was good ground vacant about a half-mile below Barker's diggings. Crane wanted to stake immediately, but Stevenson was to recall that he held out for organizing a company of six friends, including Cameron and his wife. His solicitude for Cameron at this point is remarkable. He was forced to wait, he wrote, for more than a day before Cameron would come with the group to stake; the superstitious Scotsman had a prejudice against taking any action on a Friday.

There followed a disagreement between the two friends, which came close to being a quarrel. Again Stevenson backed down. He had wanted to stake on the right bank; Cameron insisted on the left. As it turned out, the right bank was richer; Henry Beatty of Toronto, who had an interest in that property, became a millionaire shipowner as a result of the booty he obtained from it; his son, Edward, rose to be president of the CPR.

Stevenson not only gave in to Cameron but he said he also insisted, over Dr. Crane's objections, that the claim be named the Cameron and not the Stevenson claim. As for Crane, he was swiftly eliminated as a partner by reason of some gunplay in a local saloon, an incident that got him thirty days in jail and a heavy fine. "We did not wish this kind of man in the same company with us," Stevenson later wrote. In his long account of the saga of Cariboo Cameron this is the only remark that might be described as uncharitable; if Crane had steered the others to riches, surely he deserved something.

Yet one must pause to consider the evidence. All tales of placer mining locations are notoriously tangled, especially in the minds of the participants. When a strike is made, the breathless scramble for land becomes confusing. Who can remember who told whom to stake what, and where? There is the further complication of mining law, which was in this instance especially rigid, holding that no man could own more than two properties; as a result, many claims were held by proxies. Stevenson's memory does not jibe with the record, which shows that six men, including Cameron – but neither Stevenson nor Crane – recorded claims on Williams Creek on August 25, three days after Billy Barker struck his first pay; and that on September 15, Stevenson recorded an adjoining claim to be worked with the Cameron claims. After that the chronology becomes more complicated: Stevenson, Cameron, and the others are frequently shown to be buying bits of their interest from each other or selling fractions to outsiders. One fact, however, is indisputable. One way or another, Stevenson was responsible for steering Cameron to one of the richest pieces of ground in the Cariboo.

The riches were yet to be proved. Until a shaft was sunk, the Cameron company's property was nothing more than a seven-hundred-foot strip of moss-covered clay and gravel. Cameron had other matters to concern him: a few days after the claims were registered, his wife, grief-stricken over the death of their child and weakened by the hardships of the trek into the interior, was struck down by typhoid fever. Cameron and Stevenson took turns nursing her, the latter tramping at midnight through the heavy brush and later through snow to the cabin at Richfield to make sure she took regular doses of the medicine that the pioneer doctor, Charles Wilkinson, had prescribed.

On September 26, with the shaft at twenty-two feet, bedrock was reached on the Cameron property. There was no gold. All work ceased. Two of the partners, discouraged, gave up and left for Victoria.

Sophia Cameron's condition grew worse until, at three o'clock in the morning of October 23, with the wind howling at sixty miles an hour and the thermometer at thirty degrees below, Fahrenheit, she exacted that memorable promise from her husband and expired – the first white woman to die in the Cariboo. A local miner was engaged to prepare a double coffin, the interior of tin or galvanized iron, the outer case of wood. Thus protected, the body was placed in an empty cabin on the outskirts of Richfield. There was no need to embalm it; the corpse was already frozen solid.

By this time, all but ninety of the several thousand miners working in the Cariboo region had fled to the outside world. Almost everyone who remained attended Sophia Cameron's funeral – the first of four that would be held. Two days later work began again on the Cameron claim and a new shaft was started; on December 22, again at twenty-two feet, Cameron and his partners struck it rich.

It was a chillingly cold afternoon. Cameron and Stevenson were working at the mouth of the shaft when they heard a cry from Richard Rivers, one of the original stakers, working at the bottom. "Come down here at once – the place is yellow with gold. Look here, boys!" and he held up a flat rock "the size of a dinner pail." Stevenson, lying flat on the platform and peering down, could see the gold sticking out of the rock. It was an electric moment; that one piece of rock, as it turned out, was worth sixteen dollars. Cameron scrambled down the shaft while Stevenson hacked away at some frozen muck that had been sent up that morning. From three twelve-gallon kegs of gravel he panned $155 in gold.

Cameron realized that he had one of the richest claims – if not *the* richest – in the Cariboo. But most of the gold was in the ground and could not be realized until it was washed after the spring thaw. Moreover, he was haunted by that deathbed promise. How could he scrabble for material treasure while his wife's corpse lay unburied? And of what use was gold anyway, when his happiness had been taken from him? Something was gnawing at Cameron, disturbing his sleep, bedevilling his waking hours, and that something was guilt. He blamed himself for his wife's death; greed for gold, he now felt, had caused him to push her beyond her resources, to drive her, in the midst of her grief, to a long wilderness struggle on an unkind frontier. Gold or no gold, he must get her body out of the Cariboo. But how? Between Williams Creek and Port Douglas, where the steamboats docked, was a four-hundred-mile wilderness of slippery mountain slopes, tangled trails, dense forest, and endlessly drifting snow. To transport her coffin through that complexity of natural barriers would require manpower as well as horsepower, and *that* would require money. The only answer was to sell part of his interest in the Cameron claim at a sacrifice.

He approached Charles Hankin, a shareholder in the Barker company, and revealed his secret. Hankin was allowed to climb down the Cameron shaft; what he saw caused him immediately to offer a fifty-pound sack of gold for a part interest. Thus enriched, Cameron made an offer to the ninety men left in the mining camp. He would pay twelve dollars a day and a bonus of two thousand dollars to any one of them who would agree to make the round trip with him to Victoria, where he intended to bury his wife's body temporarily. It was a fantastic offer at a time when a dollar a day was good pay for a workman, but after some consideration, every one backed away. Fifty miles to the south and all the way along the trails to the coast, smallpox was epidemic. It was the most virulent kind, the kind that killed or at least left pockmarks on its victims. Cameron was desolated. Even with the help of horses, he could not haul that sleigh alone, with all his supplies, the heavy double casket, and the fifty pounds of gold. What was he to do? At this point young Stevenson, ever the friend in need, volunteered. In vain Cameron protested that Stevenson had never had smallpox and so was not immune; Stevenson said he did not fear the disease, was willing to chance the journey. But, Cameron asked, who would run the mine in their absence? The enterprising Stevenson already had a substitute.

"Well," said Cameron at last, "if you'll go, I'd rather have you than any man in the Cariboo."

"I'll go and I'll pay my own expenses," his friend replied.

Stevenson's sparse diary still exists in the public archives of British Columbia, and it records that on Saturday, January 31, 1863, he "left Williams Creek in company with J. A. Cameron bound for Victoria with the remains of his wife." That blunt statement in no way conveys the immensity of the task the two men had set themselves.

In 1863, British Columbia was an unmapped wilderness, especially in winter – a realm without people. It had been a Crown colony for less than five years; before that it was the fiefdom of the Hudson's Bay Company, populated only by Indians and a handful of fur traders. Apart from a few hundred souls in the new stump-filled capital of New Westminster, the only real congregation of people was along the goldfields of the Fraser River and the Cariboo, and most of these vanished at the onset of winter. Even in summer there were as many people living in the sister colony of Vancouver Island as there were on the mainland.

To reach the Cariboo in summer was strain enough. The succession of routes that led into the interior from the head of Harrison Lake, where the steamer traffic from New Westminster ended, could scarcely be called trails, let alone roads, being nothing but "mud, stones [and] trees fallen in every direction" in the words of one traveller. The goldseekers were forced to flounder hip-deep through glacial streams or trudge for miles in muck to the knees, often in pouring rain, all the while vainly battling hordes of mosquitoes and flies.

In winter, the route was all but impassable, especially at the northern end, where a tentative trail some seventy miles long connected the main wagon road at 150 Mile House to Williams Creek. It was this first seventy miles that would be the most difficult, for in winter there was no semblance of a trail. When Cameron set out, the pathway was under seven feet of packed snow with another two feet of freshly fallen powder above. Behind

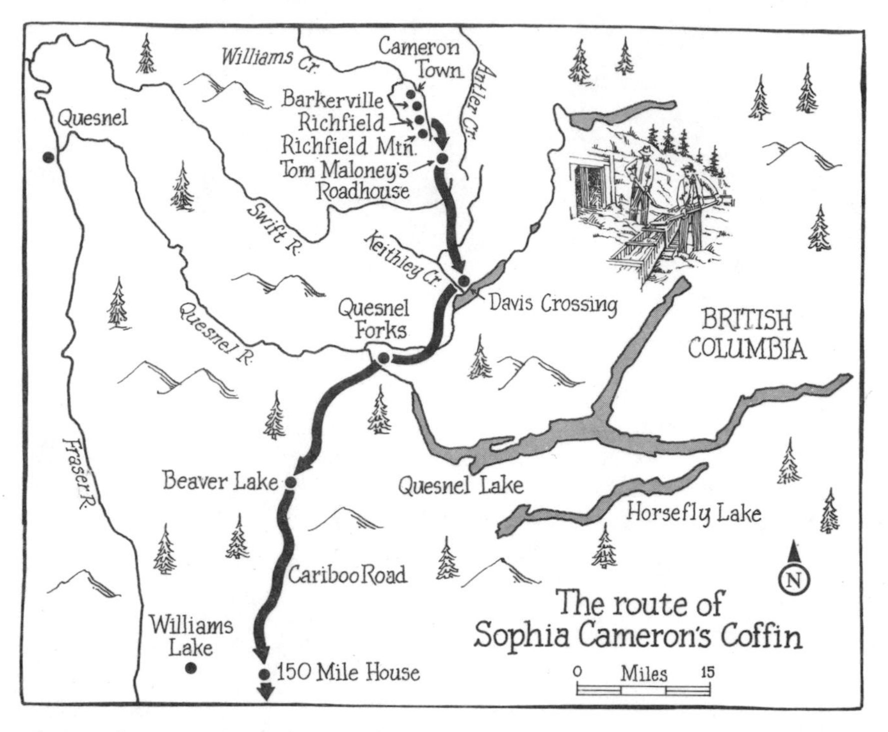

them, the two men dragged an awkward burden: the casket, fastened to a narrow toboggan scarcely more than a foot wide, on top of which were lashed blankets, food, and then fifty pounds of gold. With this preposterously top-heavy load the two friends faced the barrier of Richfield Mountain. Fortunately, twenty members of the mining community offered to accompany the cortège for the first few miles to help hoist the coffin and its burden over that rampart. These men, all of them on snowshoes, hitched themselves to a long rope, with Stevenson as guide, taking the head of the line. There was no trail to follow, "not even the mark of a dog's foot."

The climb was treacherous and slippery. The absurd load kept turning turtle. By noon, the party had managed to move the toboggan a scant three and a half miles. Many of the men lost their bearings and were worried that Stevenson, who suddenly turned off into a maze of green timber, was also lost. But he found what he was after: the faint furrow of Grouse Creek, whose frozen path would lead them to Tom Maloney's roadhouse. They reached it long after nightfall, with the thermometer at minus thirty-five, the wind blowing at gale force, and the snow piling into immense drifts on a treeless plain. The next morning, fourteen of the party returned to Richfield.

The remaining eight pushed on in the stinging cold, following Antler Creek and Swift River. It was hard going. The snow was dry and loose; the top-heavy toboggan was constantly turning over, spilling its load into the drifts; there was no shelter, and the men were forced to sleep in the open. The weather grew colder; one night Cameron glanced up at the spirit thermometer he had hung on the limb of a tree and saw that it read fifty below.

Their food ran out. Worse, a two-gallon keg of rum, rolling down a hill after one of the upsets, smashed into a tree and spilled its contents into the snow. Worse still, the party discovered one day that all its matches had been lost. It was late afternoon and the sun was already commencing to dip below the level of the trees; the situation was desperate. There they were, in the midst of a spruce forest with no sign of a trail, somewhere between Swift River and Snowshoe Creek. Their only hope was to find the road-house at Davis Crossing on Keithley Creek. But who would go in search of this oasis? They were all exhausted; none was prepared to move an inch further; a dangerous lethargy was settling over the group. At last Cameron and Dr. Wilkinson – the same Charles Wilkinson who had attended the dead Sophia – asked "with almost imploring looks" that Stevenson make the effort. He was reluctant but finally agreed. "Don't be afraid," he said, "I'll not make the least mistake." The doctor looked at him soberly. "If you do," he said, "we are all dead men."

He made no mistake. He seems to have had an uncanny sense of direction. He reached the roadhouse some hours after dark and immediately turned back, taking with him a quantity of bread, meat, and matches. Hours later he encountered the rest of the party who had been laboriously following his snowshoe tracks in the dark. Two of them – French Joe and Indian Jim – were carrying the blankets and the gold; the toboggan and the coffin had been abandoned in the forest. It took a day to retrieve it, after which four more men turned back to Williams Creek. Only French Joe and Indian Jim remained to push on with the two friends to the forks of the Quesnel, where they sought shelter in a hotel run by a mysterious Irishwoman known as Mrs. Lawless. She was, in actuality, Johanna McGuire, the "lost" daughter of Dan O'Connell, known as the Liberator, the first of the great nineteenth-century Irish leaders in the British House of Commons – or so Stevenson believed, and with some reason, for she had been identified by the brother of an Irish peer who had known her well in Dublin. Stevenson described her as "rather a wild creature [who] consumed a large amount of liquor" and steadfastly refused to reveal anything about her background. Gold rush camps attract such exotics. Mrs. Lawless tried to persuade the party to go back to Williams Creek because of the smallpox raging a few miles farther south, but all four men pushed on as far as Beaver Lake, at which point French Joe and Indian Jim departed. The date was February 10; it had taken eleven days to haul the coffin seventy-two miles.

A single Indian greeted them at Beaver Lake; the rest were dead of smallpox. It was not possible to inter the corpses in the frozen earth; they were concealed instead under hummocks of hardened snow. Stevenson counted ninety of these snow graves in the vicinity. More lay ahead, for the disease was raging all down the Lac La Hache valley. Cameron had bought a horse for three hundred dollars, which he hitched to the toboggan. Stevenson led the animal through the drifts while the older man, shoving and pushing and trying to keep the load upright, brought up the rear. There were snow graves everywhere: Stevenson recorded one hundred and twenty at Williams Lake.

The going grew easier on the newly improved Cariboo wagon road that led south to Clinton and on to Lillooet. Everywhere they encountered grisly reminders of the disease that had swept all of southern British Columbia that year. When the first horse died of exhaustion, Cameron purchased a second; it died also; he purchased a third for the last leg of the journey along the Lillooet-Port Douglas portage. Before the trip was finished, it, too, was worn out and useless. Jim Cummings, who joined the pair at Pemberton, described their slow progress along a slippery hillside:

"Cameron went ahead with the axe and cut out brush and stakes. Stevenson led the horse and I was trying to keep the toboggan on the road. My boots were nearly worn out and very slippery. We would all go down, the toboggan, coffin and gold dust, and get up before the horse. The horse got on to the job. He would turn his head to the mountain, then the whole thing would stop. It took a long time to get it back on the road – over four hundred pounds. I said to Cameron that I would take the gold dust off the coffin and pack it . . . . After that I could keep the toboggan from turning over . . . ."

At last the party reached the end of the trail at Port Douglas at the head of Harrison Lake. The little steamer *Henrietta* lay ahead – a welcome sight – but en route to embark the three men had to endure a grim gauntlet, passing down a road lined on each side with tents in which Indians lay stricken with smallpox. The flaps were raised sufficiently so that the dying, some of them turned black by the disease, could be clearly seen; and over the trail, like an unwholesome fog, hung the stench of death.

At New Westminster, the two men moved their burden onto a seagoing vessel, the *Enterprise*. On March 7, they reached Victoria after a journey of six hundred miles, four hundred of it through deep snow – a journey that Stevenson was to call "the most severe and trying I have ever experienced."

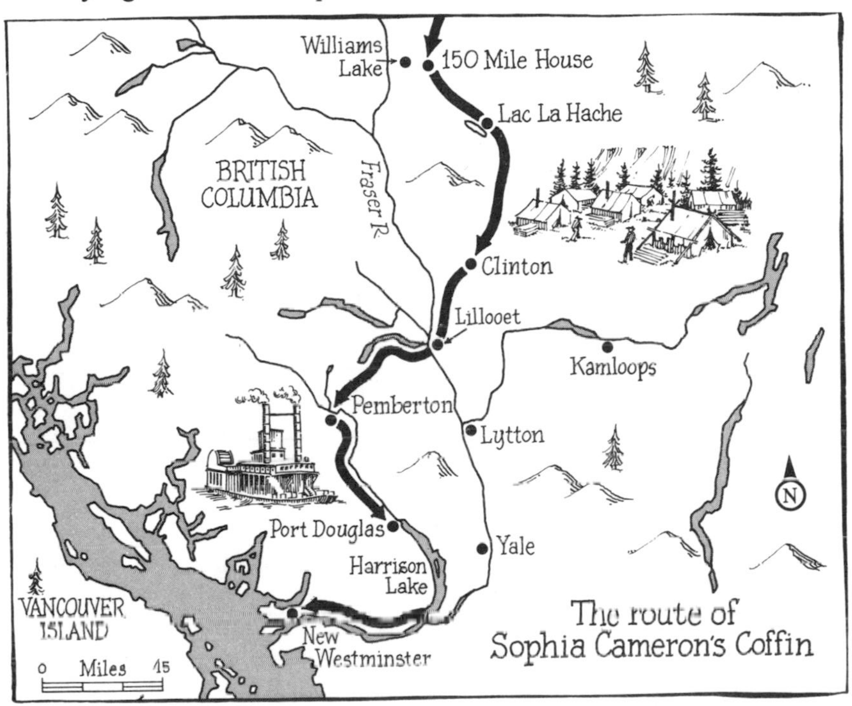

Cameron's intention was to leave the coffin interred in a local cemetery long enough for him to realize the fortune in his claim on Williams Creek: that achieved, he would set out on the long voyage home. Meanwhile, Sophia must be given a second funeral. The *British Colonist*, in its report on that melancholy rite, noted that the "arrangements here were conducted by Mr. Richard Lewis, undertaker, very creditably." That bland phrase scarcely did the matter justice, nor did it reveal any of the fascinating details. Cameron decreed that his wife's frozen body should be preserved in alcohol to prepare it for the future day when he would transport it across the cauldron of the isthmus of Panama. Lewis, who was also the mayor of Victoria, was equal to the task. He had a tinsmith drill a one-inch hole through the wooden and metal coverings. Into this small aperture he poured, over a period of three hours, twenty-five gallons of ninety-five proof alcohol. When the job was done, both Stevenson and Cameron stuck a finger into the hole to make sure the spirits had reached the top. The hole in the metal was soldered shut and the opening in the wood filled. The funeral cortège that wound its way to the Quadra Street cemetery that Sunday, March 8, was "the largest and most respectable . . . ever witnessed in the city." Eight hundred mourners, most of them Cariboo miners wintering in the capital, followed Sophia Cameron to the grave.

With Cameron's arrival in Victoria word of the big new strike, which had been seeping out of the Cariboo since late February, was confirmed. Whisper became rumour; rumour became fact; fact became published news. When gold was first found on the Cameron claim, the partners had agreed to keep it a secret, but there can be few secrets in a mining camp. Hankin's purchase of a single share for eight thousand dollars was already known and published, and now, as miners moved from tent to tent, wheeling and dealing in shares, half-interests, fractions and slivers of property, the law of supply and demand took over. The results made headlines. On March 15, Cameron himself bought an additional share in the Cameron company for six thousand dollars. In three days the price doubled. A man named Cunningham bought a share from Stevenson for twelve thousand dollars. Still the price rose. A fortnight later Stevenson decided he wanted back in; Cameron sold him a share for fifteen thousand dollars. As it turned out, these were all bargains. From this point on, the name of John Alexander Cameron would be linked permanently with the Cariboo goldfields. For the rest of his life and long after death he would be Cariboo Cameron.

The two men wasted no time in returning to British Columbia. They left Victoria on March 19 and arrived at Richfield on April 4, making most of the journey on horseback. Cameron, meanwhile, had written home that he had struck it rich. That summer, with the mine in full operation, his brothers Roderick and Allan joined him.

This was the Cariboo's bumper year, a year in which at least four million dollars in gold was sluiced out of the gravels of the creekbeds. (In 1978 that gold would be worth forty-four millions.) By summer, the wooded defile of Williams Creek had become a desert of stumps as four thousand newcomers built themselves log cabins. Two new communities sprang up downstream from Richfield – Barkerville, opposite Billy Barker's rich ground and Cameron's town – later contracted to Camerontown – opposite the company's diggings. Saws screeched, trees toppled, water wheels creaked, hammers clanged in smithies. At night the narrow valley flickered eerily in the glow of a hundred torches marking the heads of the shafts. In the makeshift saloons the newly arrived Hurdy Gurdy Girls smiled and capered. These were German dancers, *fraülein*s brought originally to California and now, following the trail of gold, to the dark heart of the new colony, accompanied by a French upright piano, the first in the district, lugged on the backs of four men for sixty miles from Quesnel to Barkerville.

The Cariboo was no longer a male preserve: sixty orphan girls from England had been imported to Victoria by the British Columbia Emigration Society; many of these, newly married to wintering miners, began to drift into town with their husbands. The nights were raucous with music and song, with the scraping of fiddles and the rattle of the piano, with the baying of dogs made manic by the moon, and the groans and cries of men intoxicated by Forty Rod – but rarely with the sound of gunplay, for firearms were taboo. British justice ruled in the gigantic and bearded person of Matthew Baillie Begbie, the legendary Cariboo judge. The old mulatto fur trader, James Douglas, now governor of the colony, had seen to that. Without the presence of Begbie, an intimidating imperial symbol with his fierce waxed mustachios and his piratical black slouch hat, the whole of the interior might have drifted by default to the Americans. Douglas had no intention of letting it slip away, as the Oregon Territory had once slipped away. His incredible wagon road, an extraordinary engineering feat designed as an umbilical cord to secure the goldfields to the seacoast, was already being blasted from the granite and quartz of the Fraser canyon. Here, in the heart of the empty colony, the seeds of a new civilization were being cultivated. Union in the Canadian confederation was less than eight years away.

Cameron was blind to all this hustle and clamour. It is doubtful if he even heard the music; his claim occupied all his energies. He worked it all that summer, a man urged on by inner furies: hired a dozen men to help him; built a double sluice box to wash the gold at a faster rate; drove himself with all the impatience of a man desperate to get the job done and be off. Guilt obsessed him. He could not rest until he had fulfilled his promise.

The richness of his claim is legendary. One anecdote gives a graphic idea of its value. When, in October, the Cameron brothers were preparing to leave, Roderick announced that he would take one last pan and make a ring for his wife out of whatever gold it contained. "No," said John Cameron, "I'll pan the final round." He did so and washed out close to a pound of gold, then valued at one hundred and twenty dollars.

Stevenson estimated that Cameron took $350,000 out of the

Cariboo, a sum whose value is difficult to comprehend in an inflationary era, especially when one remembers that interest was untaxed. It was easily the equivalent of three million dollars in 1978 terms. Nor is it likely that Stevenson's estimate included Cameron's take from an adjoining piece of ground purchased during his trip to Victoria. Since he could not legally hold more than two claims, he asked Jim Cummings, whom he had met on the trail, to stand proxy for him. Cummings worked the claim all summer and as Cameron prepared to leave, handed him the key to a strongbox containing one hundred thousand dollars in gold. Cameron had come into this additional fortune as the result of a dream in which he saw the pay streak of his own property running into the next. He was a believer in such portents. He sought out the owner of the adjoining claim and bought it for three hundred dollars. That happy windfall did nothing to weaken the mystical streak in his make-up.

Cameron tendered a thousand-dollar banquet to the men who worked for him and then, on October 6, 1863, he and his brothers and Stevenson left the Cariboo. It took some time to get underway; there was so much gold dust that eight horses had to be engaged to carry it. Cameron hired twenty men to guard this treasure, each armed with a Colt revolver. It was later said that if anyone had had the misfortune to emerge from the bush when the pack train went by, he would have been riddled with bullets, Begbie or no Begbie.

At New Westminster, the gold was melted into bars. Cameron went on to Victoria where he ordered his wife's coffin exhumed and a new outer covering constructed. On November 8, he and Stevenson embarked for San Francisco on the old steamer *Pacific*. At the California port the gold was converted into coin while the coffin, now weighing 450 pounds, was hoisted aboard the *Constitution* bound for Panama City. There it was transferred to the freight car of the world's most expensive railroad, where the fare for a jungle journey of forty-seven and a half miles was twenty-five dollars in gold. At Colon, on the Atlantic, they boarded another steamer, *Champion*, for New York. They would complete the journey to Glengarry by rail.

Cameron had encountered no trouble in San Francisco, but in New York he ran hard against a series of obstacles. The customs officials refused to believe that the coffin contained a body. Why did it weigh so much? What else was inside? If it actually contained a corpse preserved in alcohol why did it not gurgle, slosh, or splash? In vain Cameron tried to explain that besides filling it to the brim, he had surrounded the body carefully with old clothes so that it would not be battered during the trek to the coast. The dead woman's head lay pillowed on her favourite Paisley shawl, a wedding present from her mother.

The red tape in New York was serpentine. The two men were shuttled in a hired hack from office to office where each time Stevenson was required to swear that the casket contained a corpse and nothing more; that the corpse was that of Cameron's wife; that he had personally been present and seen the occupant expire; that the extra weight consisted of metal and alcohol. In each office – Stevenson insisted later that he must have been to a hundred – Cameron was required to pay a fee of two dollars. It is doubtful that the customs men were as sceptical or the Manhattan bureaucracy as muddled as this implied. Simple corruption is a more likely explanation. Tammany was at its height; the infamous "ring" of Boss William Marcy Tweed, which milked the city of at least thirty million dollars, was solidly entrenched. The town was riddled with graft. Cameron was an incidental victim.

At last the customs men declared themselves satisfied; one story has it that Cameron convinced them by offering to pay the way of one of them to watch the coffin buried at Cornwall. The two men had been bouncing around lower New York since eight that morning. Dusk was falling. But a further difficulty now presented itself; the overweight casket, lying deep in the hold of the *Champion*, had to be unloaded. It would require Herculean efforts to haul it free, for there was no winch aboard. The customs men secured a two-hundred-foot length of rope; they corralled seamen from the *Champion* and from neighbouring vessels and they even conscripted passersby into service – all at two dollars a head. This nondescript crew – some hundred men in all – leaned on the rope, heaved, tugged, wheezed, gasped, and finally yanked their burden out of the hold. Cameron set off at last for Glengarry County with his cargo, some hundreds of dollars poorer.

He arrived on December 22. The eight-thousand-mile journey around the continent from Victoria had taken forty-four days. As far as Cameron was concerned, the frontier was behind him; now he could forget the hardships, the struggle, and the tragedy and indulge himself with the wealth that the wilderness had provided.

It was not to be that simple. The frontier had changed Cameron, as it changed so many others. His experiences on the trail had contributed to his self-confidence but also increased his stubbornness. The seemingly magical fulfilment of his dreams had strengthened his mysticism. He had conquered the wild; he felt he was invincible; no one could tell him what to do.

After Christmas, he made arrangements for his wife's third funeral at her family's plot at Cornwall. It was assumed that he would have the casket opened so that her parents might gaze for the last time upon her face, but he had no such intention. Instead, he ordered the coffin further enclosed in a casing of sheet lead. This led to a painful scene at the cemetery. Stevenson reminded Cameron of a promise to open the coffin, which he claimed had been made in Victoria. Cameron refused. The younger man, now thoroughly angry, could be heard by every mourner in the graveyard.

"Cameron," he shouted, "the day will come when you will have to show her face. The people are not satisfied, and never will be, until you do show it. This is an awful mistake you are making. You made a distinct promise to me that you would do so, or I would never have left the Cariboo with her body and you!"

Again, Cameron refused. Instead, he asked Stevenson to sign an affidavit attesting to his wife's death. Stevenson, still highly irate, turned him down. He asserted that even Cameron's father-in-law had doubts that his daughter's body was in the coffin. The old farmer, pointing at the box, had remarked in a dubious tone: "Yes, they *tell* me she is there." This angered Cameron further; he refused to believe the story until a corroborating witness was produced. "That settles it," said Cariboo Cameron. "I will never show her face now to any person." And the coffin, unopened, was consigned to the earth.

His intransigence remains a mystery. Why was he so insistent on keeping the coffin closed? It was common practice for mourners to view the remains of the dead: corpses were often displayed in front parlours. It would have been a simple matter to satisfy the customs men in New York and the suspicions of his in-laws in Cornwall; yet even when his closest friend requested it, Cameron refused to comply. Was it because he shrank from looking again on the face of the woman whose death he believed he had caused by his own avarice? Or was it simply pride – a bitter pique against intimates who refused to accept his word? We do not know. But had he heeded Stevenson's advice, John Cameron would have saved himself a decade of grief.

The night of the funeral Stevenson stayed at the old Cameron homestead, and here the two old friends quarrelled again. Cameron's brothers and sisters tried to smooth matters, but, as Stevenson put it, "neither of us was satisfied." Early in February, the younger man left for the Cariboo. It would be a quarter of a century before they would meet again.

Now Cameron set about spending his money. He paid fifty-six thousand dollars for his uncle's farm at Summerstown – the same farm on which he had worked and dreamed as a youth. On it he built a cavernous mansion in the pompous but then popular style known as Italianate, complete with belvedere, projecting frontispieces, and stained-glass windows. Stone was imported from Scotland, marble from Italy, mahogany and other rare woods from the Philippines. He adopted a style to match his estate, driving about in a gold-trimmed carriage behind four dappled grey horses imported from Europe. He held flamboyant parties at the mansion, Fairfield, to which prominent citizens of the day were invited. He rode to hounds and nurtured political ambitions. A staunch Conservative, he sat on the platform when the member from Kingston, John A. Macdonald, visited the area.

He seemed obsessed by his wealth. He coveted a team of matched blacks owned by a neighbour, Donald McLennan. McLennan had no intention of selling, but when Cameron called, he invited him in for a drink. Cameron sat down, produced a leather pouch and, as he sipped his drink, began to fill the pouch with five-dollar gold pieces. He left with the team; he had made an offer McLennan could not refuse.

If he was indulgent with himself, Cameron was more than generous with others. When he dropped in for a drink at the local tavern, he would tip the man who held his horses five dollars, almost a week's pay. He bought all four of his brothers three-hundred-acre farms on the best available land on the banks of the St. Lawrence. On each farm he built a house, completely furnished with custom-built sideboards, matching chairs, expansion dining tables, and small pieces of mahogany, not to mention complete sets of silverware. Other gifts followed such as the eighteen carat gold belt, studded with diamonds, he gave his sister Mary.

Still brooding over Sophia's death, he married Emma Woods, the daughter of a well-to-do neighbour, described by a grand nephew as "a somewhat flighty wench whose giddiness must have contrasted sharply with the gentleness of his first spouse." The bride was twenty-two years his junior.

His temperament became unpredictable. He was often rude to the very relatives who were the objects of his generosity, perhaps because he felt they were more interested in his wealth than in his welfare. His fits of temper could be frightening: a physically powerful man, he was known to throw guests out of his mansion by picking them up and tossing them bodily through the ornate front door. He became a controversial figure in a community that distrusted lavish displays of wealth as much as it was suspicious of its sudden acquisition.

Rumours and gossip, mere whispers at first, then hoarser and more strident, echoed about the community. How was it possible for any man to have accumulated such a fortune in a single year? Nobody had ever done such a thing – at least, not honestly. How could anybody dig up that much gold in one summer? A working man would have to toil for . . . what ? One hundred years? No . . . far longer, at a dollar a day, to earn as much as John Cameron was said to have stored away. Why had he refused to open that coffin? What was the secret? What had he *really* buried in that churchyard: the body of his wife, as he claimed, or, more likely, a vast hoard of treasure? That would explain its weight; that would explain Cameron's adamant refusal to open it. Was his wife really dead? They had only Cameron's word for that, and his friend Stevenson had pointedly refused to sign a paper swearing to it. Did he in fact have a rich claim in the Cariboo? Again, they had only the word of a man who was behaving in a most eccentric fashion, flaunting his wealth, engaging in quarrels, flinging his gold about in a most un-Scotslike manner. *Could* it be that Sophia Cameron was still alive, perhaps held in thrall by some exotic native prince in that faraway wilderness, as distant and unknown as the moon, where white women were so rare that they might be worth their weight in gold? The whispers spread, grew louder, were half-believed, until they became a kind of Greek chorus, haunting the master of Fairfield.

Then, in the autumn of 1865, the rumours were given voice by a political opponent, a Lancaster physician, Dr. Alex Macpherson, who was heard to say that Cameron had not come by his money honestly and had, in fact, served a term in jail in the Cariboo. Macpherson had an axe to grind: Cameron had taken his brother to court, where he was fined for discharging a firearm on the Cameron estate. The doctor's accusation stung Cameron; enraged, he travelled all the way to Montreal to purchase a rawhide whip with which he intended to flay his accuser unless he recanted in writing.

The confrontation took place in a hotel sitting room. Several witnesses were present. Macpherson refused to sign anything; Cameron brandished his whip; cooler heads restrained him. Macpherson, however, charged his would-be attacker with assault. The results of the court case were inconclusive: Cameron was found guilty but was granted a new trial, which never took place.

The incident did nothing to halt the rumours; indeed, to many it seemed to confirm their truth. The Cornwall *Freeholder* attacked Cameron as a "shameless rowdy" and declared that "his conduct for the last year or two has been such as to incur the displeasure and contempt of his neighbours." Then it gave substance to the gossip by adding that "his conduct during his absence from the country probably does not reflect much credit upon him, and we must say that his mode of treating the author here of the rumour as to his imprisonment in British Columbia is not such as would be expected of a man who was conscious of its untruthfulness."

The newspaper went on to needle Cameron for his open display of his gold:

"It is all very well for Mr. Cameron to exhibit about his person a large quantity of the precious metal. No one needs complain about his 'cutting a swell,' as the popular phrase goes. He may drive his coach-and-four where ever he has the disposition to put on airs, and not excite the displeasure, although he may not avoid the ridicule of his neighbours . . . . But when Mr. C. assumes to introduce Lynch law into the community . . . he need not be surprised at the indignation which such dastardly conduct has in this instance created. To Mr. C. as a dandy we have nothing to say; but we can assure him that he will not be tolerated here as a ruffian . . . . Mr. Cameron has been away from home and like many other weak-minded persons has contracted some bad habits; let him relinquish them and the sooner the better."

The conviction grew that Cameron had something to hide. But he refused to clear the air. When one of his brothers suggested that some sort of explanation was in order, Cameron tossed him through a stained-glass window. When his wife urged him to make some sort of announcement to still the wagging tongues, he roared out: "I'm feeding most of the people who are doing the talking. I won't be pushed around by them." Nothing, it seemed, could move him. Again the question nags: *why?* Was it pride alone? Or was it something more arcane, the by-product of the mystic streak that persuaded him of the efficacy of dreams, convinced him that he was born under a lucky star, and now caused him to shrink from a deed that would disturb the ghost of the woman of whose death, he felt, he himself had been the instrument? A clue to this inner torment lies in the answer he flung back at a local judge who pleaded with him to still the outcry.

"My wife rests in peace," said Cariboo Cameron. "She will continue to rest in peace. If anyone disturbs her grave, I'll kill him."

Cameron lived with the calumny for more than nine years and kept his silence. Then, in the summer of 1873, an extraordinary story appeared in the *Sunday Times* of Syracuse, New York.

A Romance in Real Life. A Feast for a Novel Writer. Ten Years with an Indian Chief. Just Retribution.

Fifteen years ago there lived on the banks of the St. Lawrence, near the village of Cornwall, a man named Cameron of near Scotch descent. He dwelt until after maturity, with his parents in their rugged homestead in a poor log-house, and then he married from among his associates, a good girl, who afterwards did her best to help her husband on in the world. But somehow fortune always frowned, and the couple found life an uphill road.

At last, seemingly convinced that they could barely make a living on a farm, Mr. Cameron bestirred himself among his acquaintances and relatives and picked up money enough to purchase a passage for himself and his wife to Australia, which was then in a fever of excitement over the gold discovery. Nothing more was heard from the wanderers for five years, when all at once Mr. Cameron returned, and bearing with him

A STRANGE BURDEN!

It comprised, first, a coffin with the embalmed remains of his dear wife, and second, unbounded sums of money, all in glittering gold!

His report was that instead of going to Australia as they had contemplated, they had finally brought up in the Fraser River region, at a point called Cariboo. That he there got possession of a claim, which he had worked so successfully, and yielded so well, that he was the possessor of untold wealth, and he was in constant receipt of more. These facts were proven by the after events. Moreover, he said, with tears in his eyes, that his poor wife had died in that inhospitable country, and that his fortunate wealth and his love for her had prompted him to have her body embalmed that he might bring her home and bury her among friends. This was done; and then commenced a series of lavish expenditures on his part. First, he bought the old homestead and erected thereon, a grand and princely mansion, of Milwaukee brick, surrounded the ample grounds with a unique and costly wall, purchased his parents and other relations comfortable homes, and seemed bent on the most lavish hospitality and generous use of his wealth in every direction. And still his store never seemed to diminish, and the people all blessed him, and copied him and united in calling him

CARIBOO CAMERON.

Everybody in the northern part of our state knows Cariboo Cameron, and he had not an enemy. But look at the sequel. After ten years of uninterrupted prosperity, during which he had risen to the very top of the social scale,

THERE CAME A CRASH!

And it came in an unthought of manner. One dreary night, late in the evening, a rap was heard on the door of the Cameron mansion, and a poor weak woman was admitted, who begged for shelter for the night, and it was granted. Nothing special was thought of her, until next morning, as the family – the jovial husband, the happy wife whom he had married a year after his return, were seated at the breakfast table, the strange woman came from her room, walked straight in front of Cameron, and asked in an agonized tone,

"Do you know me?"

"My God, yes, I do!" was the reply, and Cariboo Cameron fell senseless to the floor.

The woman was thrust hastily aside, and Cameron was restored to consciousness, but the moment he escaped from the house he left the country, and has not been heard of since then. That was last week.

And now comes a most horrible tale from this first sad wife, for the poor woman was none other than Cameron's wife, whom he had taken away so many years before. For the past ten years she has been the unwilling prisoner and wife of an Indian chief near Cariboo, to whom Cameron had

TRADED HER

for the claim that yielded him all his wealth.

That claim contained unbounded stores of gold, and its wealth was known to none but the Indian. After the bargain was struck Cameron supplied himself with great quantities of it, put the rest in the hands of a partner, who has worked it since, and sent Cameron's share to him.

THE COFFIN WAS TAKEN UP

and found to contain a mass of clay!

Of course the poor woman who has been so foully dealt with, will step into the possession of the valuable property left on the St. Lawrence.

Who ever read a chapter more replete with incidents than this, and it has all the additional interest of being fact.

It is hoped that the guilty fleeing wretch will be caught, and dealt with as he deserves.

This astonishing tale says a good deal about the standards of journalism, the laws of libel, and the gullibility of the public in nineteenth-century North America. That it should be published at all is incredible; that it should be believed is staggering. Yet it must be understood that British Columbia a century ago was scarcely known to the outside world. Who really knew what weird rites were practised among the savage tribes who roamed that dark labyrinth of forest and canyon behind the bulwark of the Rockies? Just as the Elizabethans believed that strange creatures with flat heads and single eyes lurked beyond the unexplored rim of the world, so credulous Easterners were prepared to accept the fantasy of a native chieftain exchanging a golden hoard for the body of a white maiden.

With the rumours out in the open, Cameron realized that finally he must act. He published an advertisement in the Cornwall *Freeholder* announcing that on Tuesday, August 19, 1873, he would have the coffin raised from the family plot at Cornwall and cut open so that all present might look upon the face of his dead wife. The entire population was invited to the opening, to take place at another burial ground, the Salem Cemetery, nine miles east of Cornwall, only a few hundred yards from Fairfield.

Here before a crowd of hundreds of the curious and the morbid, the outer casing of the casket was removed. Then the tinsmith began his work.

Cameron stood at the new graveside, head bowed, his late wife's family beside him. His brother Duncan, standing directly behind him as the coffin was opened, noticed red and white streaks on the back of the bereaved man's neck and thought he was about to suffer a stroke. Later he learned what was in John Cameron's mind: what if some vandal, in search of rumoured treasure, had opened the coffin? What if the body had been disposed of and the box sealed again? If there was no corpse, Cameron was convinced he would not leave the cemetery alive.

His fears were unfounded. As the metal was worked open, the face of the dead woman appeared, almost perfectly preserved; only the eyes were sunken. A cry rent the air; it was the dead woman's mother. "*It's Sophie!*" she cried. She had recognized her daughter and the Paisley shawl beneath her head, its colours faded by the alcohol.

Hundreds now filed soberly past the opened casket. That done, Cameron asked if they were satisfied that the remains were those of his first wife. All agreed that they were.

"Dust to dust," said Cariboo Cameron. "Pour off the alcohol."

Twenty-five gallons splashed on to the ground, burning the turf; months later visitors to the cemetery would point out the spot where no grass grew and repeat the story.

Sophia Cameron was given that day her fourth and final funeral, her last resting place marked by a marble memorial four feet high, running the full length of the grave and surrounded by an ornamental fence fixed in a base of cut stone.

The episode, in his nephew's phrase, "did something" to Cameron. He stepped up the pace of his living and spending. On the first day of each month he held court in the front hall of Fairfield, seated behind an ornate carved desk, listening to the appeals of neighbours, relatives, and complete strangers, and dispensing largess.

His standards of judgment were uncomplicated. He would fix his ice-blue eyes upon each petitioner and ask: "Are you an honest man?"

If the answer was a flat yes, he was inclined to refuse. But if the answer was "I try to be," the request was usually granted. Cameron's loans were generally in the range of one hundred dollars, a considerable sum at the time.

If he was trying to buy respect, he did not succeed. The very people who grovelled in that pillared hall were later to jeer at the "crazy old prospector" who went through a fortune in less than a generation. What *was* Cameron's motivation? His nephew believed he was trying to buy his way out of a self-inflicted purgatory.

His investments began to turn sour. He plunged into gold properties in Madoc, Ontario, and Beauce County, Quebec. He built a lighthouse at Port Magdalen. He took a contract to dredge the Lachine Canal. None of these ventures paid off. But the real financial blow came when he bought a working sawmill with two million feet of dressed lumber and a timber limit on Lake Superior. Cameron, the man who had squandered hundred-dollar bills on strangers, quarrelled with an employee over the sum of $3.50. The disgruntled worker set fire to the mill. Cameron had no insurance. Shortly afterwards he lost the timber limit in a law suit. In 1884, he tried to recoup by investing in yet another gold mine, this one in Nova Scotia. But Nova Scotia was not the Cariboo, and Cameron lost the remnants of his fortune.

The Cariboo! It haunted his mind and obsessed his dreams. Some of his relatives had banded together to mortgage their properties and raise a few thousand dollars for the man who had been their benefactor; others with shorter memories refused to join. Cameron went through it all in a few months. What did it matter when he had already resolved to make a new fortune in British Columbia? All of the old optimism returned; he, John Alexander Cameron, would go back to the frontier and, he promised, within three years come back in triumph. Had he not done it before? Had he not followed his dreams and seen them come true? It would all come true again.

No need now to make that exhausting journey across Panama. The newly completed Pacific railroad would speed him and his wife to the coast in a few days. On May 11, 1886, the *Colonist* noted his arrival: "Old British Columbians experienced a genuine and agreeable surprise yesterday when the once familiar form of John A. Cameron appeared on the streets." The paper also noted that Cameron "looks as young as he did 23 years ago." That was journalistic licence. Cameron's hair and beard were white, his massive figure shrunken. He left his wife in the capital and set out for the Big Bend of the Fraser River, where he staked a claim on Carne Creek. He did his best to work the ground, but heavy rains in the summer of 1887 broke not only his dam but also his health. Reluctantly he abandoned the claim, returned to Victoria in November, and, enfeebled by a haemorrhage of a lung, spent the next ten months in convalescence.

But he would not give up, for the Cariboo still called. Surely there must yet be gold in those golden valleys! His old friend Robert Stevenson, now a prosperous farmer in the Fraser Valley, came to Victoria to renew a long-dormant friendship. In vain he tried to persuade Cameron to give up his dream of the Cariboo; it was not possible to make a second fortune in a worked-out mining camp. Cameron stubbornly refused to heed his advice. Off he went to the Cariboo, wearing his $150 Persian lamb coat, a relic of his former wealth, "an emaciated old man . . . a wreck of his former self," to quote the *Colonist*'s later obituary (journalistic licence works both ways), "but with the fires of his enterprising spirit unquenched."

The Camerons put up at Mason's Hotel in Barkerville, but this was not the Barkerville that Cameron had known. As for Camerontown, it was a ghost community, its shacks crumbling before the invading forest. There are few sights more depressing than a dying mining camp. The roofs of log cabins untended cannot withstand the weight of the winter snows and are soon crushed. Doors hang open, creaking and banging in the wind. The panes in the saloon windows are quickly shattered. Rust and rot take over. Willow and alder creep through the plank sidewalks, blurring the perimeter of the community. Trudging up the familiar length of Williams Creek, Cameron came face to face with decay: old lengths of cable tangled in the gravels; crumbling mineshafts; the skeletons of wheelbarrows; and the valley floors washed down to bed rock, scoured clean of gold.

The dream was shattered. He returned to the hotel and took to his bed. His wife tried with little success to rouse him. On Wednesday, November 7, 1888, he turned his face to the wall and died. The doctors diagnosed the cause as "paralysis of the brain," but the handful of old-timers in Barkerville had a different explanation: they said that Cariboo Cameron, at the age of sixty-eight, had died of a broken heart.

Nobody struggled this time to take the coffin back to Summerstown, although the task would have been immeasurably easier. He was buried, instead, in the frontier community that briefly bore his name, almost on that site where his dreams had come true and far, far away from that other grave whose occupant could now be truly said to rest in everlasting peace.

SIX

The revenge of Mina Hubbard

Ungava: 1903

". . . The interior plateau, a jigsaw puzzle of schist and granite, quartzite and basalt, rises steeply from the coast to a height of two thousand feet. This rolling wasteland of timeless rock and ragged scrub is pockmarked by innumerable lakes and marshes from which swift rivers pour off to every compass point, descending through a constant succession of cataracts and rapids. In Hubbard's day, the only means of travel was by canoe, and even that was considered dangerous . . . there were scores of instances of Indians dying of starvation among those riven crags and skeletal larches . . . ."

On June 27, 1905, two oddly similar expeditions were launched from trading posts on opposite sides of the North West River to map and explore the interior of what was then called, with considerable validity, "darkest Labrador."

One expedition made its headquarters at the Hudson's Bay post on one side of the water; in charge was a stocky lawyer and outdoorsman from New York City named Dillon Wallace. The other expedition was located on the opposite shore at the French trading post run by one M. Duclos. It was headed by a small, neat, and determined widow of thirty-five, Mina Hubbard.

Both expeditions had identical objectives. Each was intent on completing the work of Mrs. Hubbard's late husband, Leonidas, who had starved to death on the Susan River two years before during an abortive attempt to travel across the unmapped heart of Labrador to Ungava Bay.

Dillon Wallace and Mina Hubbard had once been friends, drawn together by a mutual attraction to the dead man. Wallace, Hubbard's closest male crony, had almost died with him on the previous expedition. Now he and Mrs. Hubbard were no longer speaking, the estrangement made embarrassing by their proximity. It was not easy to avoid one another, for they had no option but to travel from Rigolet at the head of the Hamilton Inlet aboard the same boat. Wallace, who was nervous and uncomfortable in Mrs. Hubbard's presence, did his best to keep his distance. As for Mina Hubbard, she loathed Dillon Wallace – despised him, hated him, detested him. When she learned of his presence aboard the *Harlow*, the ship that would take her from Rigolet to North West River, she "trembled like a leaf for an hour." She was determined that if anyone completed her dead husband's work it would be she. For the two expeditions were engaged in more than simple exploration: they were bitter rivals in a race across the broken surface of an inhospitable plateau that no white man had yet conquered. They were racing not only against each other but also against the calendar. If they did not reach Ungava Bay by the end of August, they would miss the season's only steamer and be forced to spend the entire winter in each other's company in the cramped quarters of the George River trading post. It was a prospect that neither wished to contemplate.

To understand the reasons for the contest, it is necessary to meet the main characters and follow the singular chain of events that led to the tragedy of 1903 and its extraordinary aftermath.

Mina Hubbard was born Mina Benson in April, 1870, on a farm near Bewdley, Ontario, not far from Rice Lake. She studied nursing in New York and after graduation was assigned to Leonidas Hubbard, Jr., a young journalist convalescing after a bout of typhoid fever. Hubbard was the son of a Forty-Niner who had left the California goldfields for a more prosaic life as a farmer in Michigan. The younger Hubbard, "high strung and sensitive" in Mina's phrase, had developed a romantic love of the outdoors, an attachment nurtured by the stories of his grandfather, a frontiersman and an Indian fighter. The young man, possessed of "a driving energy to have a part in the larger work of the world," was graduated from university at Ann Arbor in 1897, wangled a job on a Detroit newspaper, moved to New York to the staff of the *Daily News*, wrote editorials for the *Saturday Evening Post*, lost his job as a result of his illness and, on recovery, decided to free-lance. His first article was accepted by *Outing*, and from that point on he did most of his work for that magazine.

In January, 1901, he married his nurse. Although she was two years older (thirty-one to his twenty-nine), he called her "my girl." She called him "Laddie," and as far as she was concerned he was perfection itself, "utterly fearless, resolute, persistent," possessed of "a beautiful simplicity, a gentleness and interest that rarely failed to disarm and win admission where he desired to enter." There was more: "Added to this equipment were a fine sense of humour, a subtle sympathy and a passionate tenderness for anyone or anything, lonely or neglected or in trouble. . . ." In short, a paragon without fault or blemish; in Mina Hubbard's eyes he would never be anything else.

Hubbard's closest friend, Wallace, was nine years his senior. The two had been drawn together by a mutual, if somewhat unrealistic attachment to the outdoors; they yearned for the frontier life, for the thrill of crossing unknown country, of walking where none had walked before. They saw only romance; the hardships they ignored or brushed aside.

Dillon Wallace was a self-made man with a remarkable background. At the age of thirteen, with his mother dead and his father's legal business a failure, he had taken over and single-handedly run the family farm in Orange County, New York. When the farm was lost, he worked first in a grist mill and later mastered the art of telegraphy as a Morse operator while saving all the time for a future education. He put himself through law school and, in 1897, entered private practice in New York. Clearly, Dillon Wallace was a man who felt he was capable of anything he attempted, but when Hubbard first met him, around 1900, he was at the end of his tether, lonely and disconsolate over the death of his young wife of three years, a victim of tuberculosis, the ravaging disease of the day. Legal work failed to stimulate him; he found his therapy was the outdoors. In November of 1901, while he and Hubbard were on a camping trip on Shawangunk Mountain in New York, the younger man suggested as a distraction an expedition into the heart of Labrador.

Wallace was puzzled. "Now where in the earth is Labrador?" he asked. He had a vague idea of it being "a sort of Arctic wilderness" – nothing more.

But Hubbard was bubbling with excitement: "Man, don't you realize it's about the only part of the continent that hasn't been explored? As a matter of fact, there isn't much more known of the interior of Labrador than when Cabot discovered the coast more than four hundred years ago. Think of it, Wallace! A great unknown land near home, as wild and primitive today as it always has been. I want to see it. I want to get into a really wild country and have some of the experiences of the old fellows who explored and opened up the country where we are now."

Wallace was caught up in Hubbard's enthusiasm; yes, he would go with him to that unknown domain! It was, however, more than a year before Hubbard dropped into his law office to announce that the trip was on. "It will be a big thing, Wallace. It ought to make my reputation." Hubbard now saw himself as another Stanley, probing a frontier as dark and as mysterious as Africa.

At this time – February, 1903 – Hubbard was assistant editor of *Outing* and not without camping experience. The previous February he had gone on a snowshoeing journey with the Montagnais Indians of northern Quebec, and that summer he and his wife had camped around the north shore of Lake Superior, mainly in the interests of journalism. His editor, Caspar Whitney, did not share his enthusiasm for the Labrador excursion. "It was a trip with which I was frankly not in sympathy and from which I sought to dissuade Hubbard," he was to write. He bluntly told his assistant that he did not think it worth the money; however, because of his regard for Hubbard, he agreed to help finance him.

Hubbard insisted on planning the entire expedition himself. Through his magazine he had access to a rich store of wilderness experience, but he disdained it. He "neither took *Outing* nor its editor into his confidence," Whitney wrote. He asked no help or advice from anyone in selecting his equipment or the members of his party; this was to be his expedition and his alone; the glory would be his also. He had determined to travel lightly: too many provisions would slow down the expedition. It would be a small party: himself, Wallace, and a woodsman.

He wrote to the Hudson's Bay agent at Rigolet asking if he knew anyone who could be hired for such a journey. The agent was discouraging: everyone feared to venture too far inland. Finally, Hubbard engaged a Cree named Jerry from Missanabie, Ontario, but at the last minute the Indian backed out, not because he feared the wilds of Labrador but because he was terrified of the jungle of Manhattan. As he put it to Hubbard, he didn't "want to die so soon." Hubbard was fortunate in his replacement. From Eastmain, Quebec, on the shores of James Bay, he engaged a remarkable half-breed, George Elson, a solid, rangy, God-fearing outdoorsman, difficult to ruffle, easy to live with. Though Elson was half Cree, he looked more like a white man, with his black moustache and his pipe. And *he* was not in the least inhibited by the menace of the metropolis.

He had never travelled on a train and had never been in a city; it did not faze him. Hubbard and Wallace were supposed to meet him when he arrived at Grand Central; they missed the appointment. That did not faze Elson either. He had never travelled by cab, but he found a stand, rented a hack, and was trotted off to the office of *Outing* where Hubbard finally caught up with him, seated in the waiting room quite unconcerned.

Elson, in Wallace's later description, was "something more than a woodsman – he was a hero. Under the most trying circumstances he was calm, cheerful, companionable, faithful. Not only did he turn out to be a man of intelligence, quick of perception and resourceful, but he turned out to be a man of character."

It tells us something of Hubbard's misplaced self-confidence that at no time did he ask Elson for advice about equipment or other arrangements for the expedition. Elson had expected to plan the provisions and set the travel schedule, but he found, to his surprise and chagrin, that Hubbard intended to use him only in a minor capacity. With all the optimism and arrogance of the amateur, Hubbard decided he alone would plan the details and make the decisions.

The three men, with Mrs. Hubbard, left New York on June 20, 1903. On July 5, they reached the Grenfell Mission at Battle Harbour. Here Mrs. Hubbard debarked to return by another steamer to her home at Congers, New York. The idea that a woman might take part in a journey of exploration was then inconceivable; it was adventurous enough merely to express a desire to be a telephone operator. Mina Hubbard parted from her husband at 6.00 a.m. in a cold, drizzling rain, stepping into a small boat in which she was rowed to that bleak and rocky shore, still mottled by a patchwork of old snow. She had been married for just thirty months, and she did not know when she would see her husband again. She cried. He tried not to. As yet there was no hint of a breach with Wallace, who wrote: "She was very brave. . . . Poor little woman! . . . I stood aside with a lump in my throat as they said their farewell." It was to be their last.

There exists a pencil sketch of Hubbard, made in New York about the time of his marriage. It shows a rather ascetic-looking man, finger to forehead, hair in a prim part, pince-nez centred on a thin, sensitive face, looking very much the man of letters. A stylish rendering. The photograph taken at Rigolet shows a different figure: a bantam cock of a man, dressed for the trail, legs astride, feet planted on the ground, jaw set. Wallace, in the companion photograph, looks a little more nondescript, a little less self-assured, with a large moon face, slashed in the middle by the downward curve of a dark moustache, the eyes also drooping as if in concert.

Hubbard's objective was to explore the eastern and northern areas of the Labrador peninsula, these being the least known. The interior plateau, a jigsaw puzzle of schist and granite, quartzite and basalt, rises steeply from the coast to a height of two thousand feet. This rolling wasteland of timeless rock and ragged scrub is pockmarked by innumerable lakes and marshes from which swift rivers pour off to every compass point, descending through a constant succession of cataracts and rapids. In Hubbard's day, the only means of travel was by canoe, and even that was considered dangerous. Because the condition of the rivers made it impossible to transport sufficient food for any considerable period, the plateau was shunned by white men. Game was not always plentiful, and there were scores of instances of Indians dying of starvation among those riven rocks and skeletal larches.

The plan was to follow the North West or the Naskaupi River

(there was some confusion as to whether these were the same) to Lake Michikamau and, from the northern end of that body of water, to strike across the height of land to the headwaters of the unmapped George River and perhaps, if time allowed, to follow that river to Ungava Bay. En route the party expected to witness the great caribou migration across the Labrador interior – something no white man had seen – and to spend some time observing the habits of the Naskapi Indians, then the most primitive on the continent. Hubbard's plans for returning were a little vague: these would depend on how far the season had advanced. They could go across country to the St. Lawrence; they could retrace their own route; or they could go down to Ungava Bay and pick up a boat for Newfoundland. Hubbard's view of the Labrador interior was blithely optimistic; his plans to cut across the peninsula, as he outlined them to Wallace, seemed to envisage nothing more fearsome than an excursion across Manhattan Island on roller skates.

It was not to be that easy. The only useful map of the peninsula was that of the Geological Survey of Canada, based on information gathered by that remarkable wilderness traveller, A.P. Low. Much of Low's material came from hearsay. His map showed only

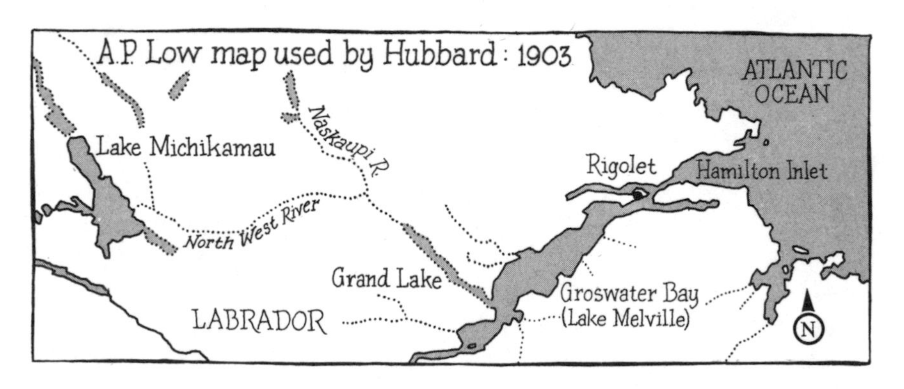

one major river, which he called the North West River, rising at Lake Michikamau and flowing into Grand Lake. There were five. At Rigolet on Hamilton Inlet, Hubbard and Wallace talked to several natives who convinced them that Low's North West River was actually the Naskaupi. Nobody bothered to tell either man that there were other rivers as well; it did not occur to the natives – who knew this part of the country as intimately as Hubbard knew his home village of Congers – that anybody could miss the obvious. But miss it they did.

At Rigolet almost everybody predicted that the expedition would never return. Hubbard brushed these prophecies aside;

indeed, he welcomed them, for he said it would make his work seem more important in the end. "He could do it and he *would*." At the North West River Post at the south end of Grand Lake, the Hudson's Bay agent was the only man to show any enthusiasm for the venture. When the party left, at nine on the morning of July 15, the others were "grave and sceptical and shook their heads at our persistency in going into a country we had been so frequently warned against."

They set off on one of those marvellous northern days that remain in the mind long after the hardships of the trail have been blurred and softened by the cumulus of memory. The air was crisp and heady with the incense of the evergreens; the sky was a clear robin's-egg blue; sunlight danced on the dark waters of the lake. The prospect was pleasing: all they needed to do was paddle to the head of the lake, find Low's river, and follow it to Lake Michikamau at the top of the Labrador plateau.

They found it – or thought they did – the next day, just after noon, a swift stream about 125 feet wide. It never entered their heads that they could be wrong. But they had made a tragic error. The mouth of the river they sought, the Naskaupi, was five miles behind, its mouth divided by a wooded island that concealed the opening. The river they entered was the Susan, "a river which was to introduce us promptly to heart breaking hardships," a forbidding tangle of rocks and cataracts that forced them to struggle knee-deep in the icy water as they tracked their loaded canoe around rocks and through eddies. The portages, which seemed endless, were worse; day after day they manhandled their craft and their supplies through gullies and swamps, hands, faces, and wrists swollen by the bites of blackflies, clouds of which often filled their nostrils and caused their eyelids to puff up so badly they could scarcely see. The cheesecloth and ointment purchased in New York against such an eventuality proved useless.

They were lost but did not know it, persisting in the belief that this was Low's North West River. Tom Blake, a half-breed at Rigolet who trapped at the upper end of Grand Lake, had told them they would encounter close to twenty miles of good paddling. Hubbard concluded that Blake was wrong; it did not occur to him that he might be himself. Nor did he listen to Elson. To lighten the load on the portages he began to discard supplies – clothing, a five-pound pail of lard, coffee, several pounds of flour, a box of milk powder. In vain Elson argued that these would be needed. Fifteen days and eighty miles out of the North West River Post, Hubbard still believed himself on the right route. The river forked and the three men followed the south branch, believing it

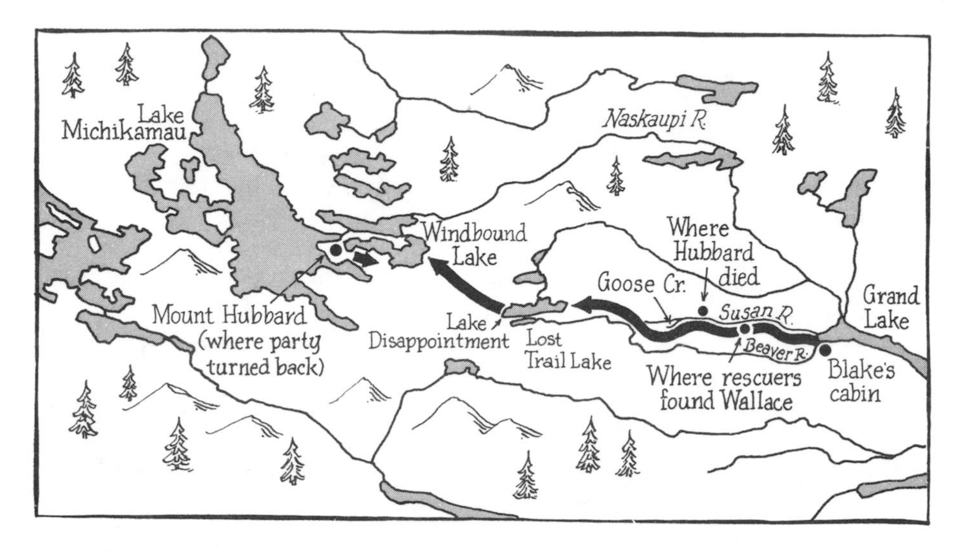

would lead to Lake Michikamau. Actually, they had turned up Goose Creek, a tributary of the Susan. Eventually, in the course of a portage, they lost it and crossed to a different river, the Beaver. They had no way of knowing that they were now following an old Indian trail to Michikamau. Then they wandered off that, too. As they moved westward they named some of the features along the route, and these tell their own story: Lost Trail Lake . . . Windbound Lake . . . Lake Disappointment.

Hubbard's diary, which has been preserved, reads very like all diaries of abortive wilderness excursions. It begins with enormous zest: "Pancakes, bread and melted sugar at 3 o'clock. Bully. Dried apple sauce and hot bread, bacon, coffee . . . for supper . . . Bully. Apples and abundant sugar great comfort. Keep us feeling good and sweet and well fed." Then, as the insects did their work, as the supplies diminished with alarming swiftness, as the portages grew wearier and limbs weaker, the diary becomes a record of slow disillusionment. Within three weeks the trio had run out of lard, sugar, bacon, salt, and flour. The trout they managed to catch and the geese and the single caribou they shot were not enough to maintain their strength, for they lacked fat, the one resource absolutely necessary for men struggling with heavy loads. When the caribou skin turned rotten and was crawling with maggots, Hubbard and Wallace were persuaded by George Elson not to throw it away. Keep it, Elson told the astonished pair, "we may want to eat it some day." That day was not far off.

Both Hubbard and Wallace quickly wore holes in their moccasins; they had not thought, as Elson had, to bring an extra pair. Hubbard lost two of his toenails and cracked the skin on his heel;

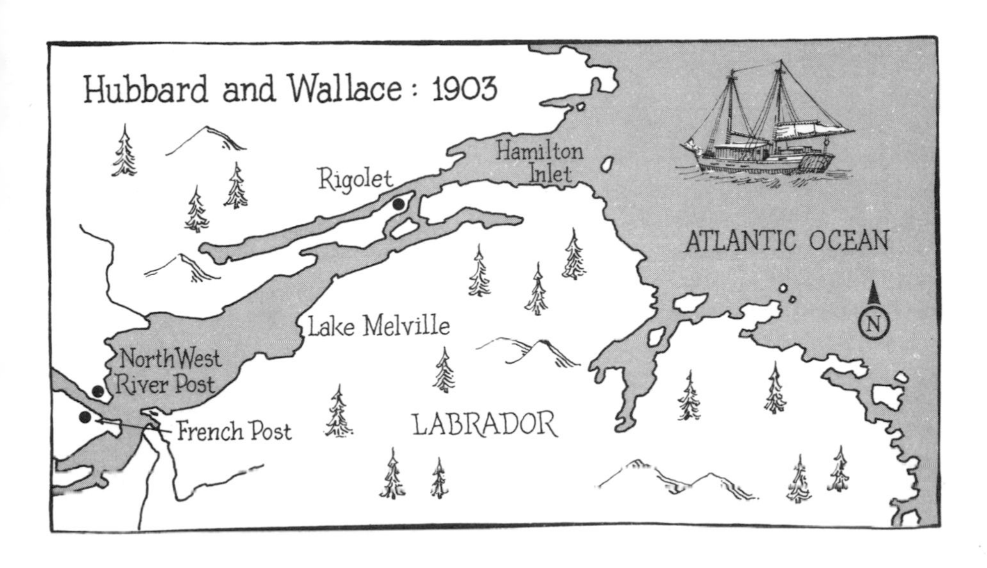

he had not thought to bring adhesive plaster, either. By early August, his clothes were in dreadful condition, his trousers ripped clear down the leg from the waist. "Don't know how to patch them" he confided to his diary, "no stuff." He had not foreseen that eventuality, either. Yet he was able to add: "Spirits high."

He refused to entertain any thought of turning back, and the other two dared not suggest it. "Failure makes me shudder," he wrote in his diary on September 6. By that date he was a grotesque sight. He refused to take a bath, not because of the cold – the first snow fell that day – but because he was "ashamed of my bones . . . I'm a walking skeleton." Two days later he wrote: "Moccasins in tatters, socks and duffle hang out at every angle and catch on every bush. Pants in rags from knees down – could trade pants and footwear with the raggedest tramp I ever saw and be better off. It is depressing, so is grub lack. Hard to keep up courage when hungry – but we do it. . . ."

The following day, September 9, Elson and Hubbard crossed a small lake, climbed a mountain (later to be called Mount Hubbard), and saw in the distance, at last, the lonely sheet of water for which they had been searching.

"It's there! It's there!" Hubbard shouted to Wallace on his return. "Michikamau is there, just behind the ridge. We saw the big water! We saw it!"

They saw it but could not reach it. A storm on the lake – which they named Windbound – held them in camp. Then lassitude gripped them. Wallace began to notice a change in Hubbard. To this point he had been full of the work at hand, of the mountains and rivers to be conquered, of the tales he would tell, and, above all, of the stories he would write. Now he "craved companionship" and began to talk intimately about his early life, his relatives, his home. Hubbard's diary entries make it clear that he was obsessed by two subjects – home and food. Like so many other wilderness journals, his contains long descriptions of meals he has had or meals he hopes to have:

"W & I talk of restaurants and what we would do if we were in New York. We would take bread and pie and chocolate mainly. Never dreamed one could want bread so. . . ." And again: "How we will appreciate home and grub when we get out. Coffee, chocolate, bread, pie, fried cakes, puddings – these are what W. and I talk about. . . . We tell of good dinners we have had, dwelling on the minutest details. I like to think best of those dinners at Congers where M. sat opposite and poured coffee. What dinners they were!" And on September 14: " Wallace and I . . . made a list of restaurants we are going to visit when we hit New York. Our tastes are decidedly plebeian. I would delight to enter a mission restaurant on the Bowery and eat flour and bread at 2 cents a plate. . . . I would like now best of all big slices of boiled pork, bread . . . and sorghum or New Orleans molasses. . . ." And so on and on for page after page, listing all the food he *should* have taken and would take on another trip or even on a picnic in the Hudson Highlands: oatmeal, rice, flour, bacon, fat pork, beans, baking powder, salt, sweet biscuit, sugar, marmalade, onions, potatoes, raisins, figs, dried fruit, tomatoes, chicken – the very words seemed to intoxicate him, as if the act of putting them down on paper nourished him – "then some good stews, soups, French toast, syrup, pancakes, omelettes, sweet biscuits and jam with a broiled steak and chicken roast . . . canned pork and canned plum pudding must also go in the menu. . . . Mina and I must study delightful camp dinners now and carry out the nice little woods dinners we started. . . ." The scribbles continued on, and then these glum words: "Hard to keep off depression . . . . All hungry."

The day after Hubbard composed that extended gastronomic fantasy, George Elson, sitting around the campfire with the other two, began to tell stories of Indians who had starved to death in the bush. That was scarcely tactful. Hubbard stood up, pushed some partially burned sticks into the flames, turned his back on the fire and, deep in thought, walked down to the lakeshore, staring out into the windswept waters – a gaunt, haggard figure in rags, dashed by the spray. Finally he wheeled about and walked briskly back.

"Boys," he said, "what do you say to turning back?" Wallace was stunned, Elson relieved. They ate their last bacon and rice and talked feverishly of home and food. But the storm held them on the lakeside for five more days.

During this period of waiting Hubbard held long conversations about his wife with Wallace. He felt guilty because he believed he had not given her or their life together the attention they deserved. "That's real happiness, Wallace – a good wife and a cheerful fireside. What does glory and all that amount to, after all? I've let my work and my ambition bother me too much. I've hardly taken time for my meals . . . ."

They had been more than two months on the trail. Winter was setting in. By September 24, six inches of snow covered the ground. How could they hope to get back to North West River in their weakened condition? "We were almost as thin and almost the colour of the mummies one sees in the museums," Wallace wrote. The talk turned less to food now – they were subsisting almost entirely on berries, the occasional grouse, and sporadic feasts of fish – and more to their childhood memories. Hubbard, suffering from the recurrent diarrhoea that had plagued him almost from the outset, was too weak to do his share of work. By October 4, he was staggering as he walked and suffering lapses of memory. "On this last day of our long portage he came near to going to pieces nervously," Wallace wrote. "When he started to tell me something about his wife's sister, he could not recall her name. . . . For a long time he sat very still, his face buried in his hands, doubtless striving to rally his forces. And the most pitiable part of it was his fear that George and I should notice his weakness and lose courage."

On October 11, with the weather bitterly cold, the three men tried to lift the canoe and carry it the thirty yards to the water's edge. They could not raise it onto their heads and it crashed to the ground. For the first time each was forced to admit to the others that they were weaker than they had dared acknowledge and that "if we ever got out of the wilderness it would be only by the grace of God."

Still they staggered on, dragging the canoe over the portages and finally abandoning it, leaving everything behind that was not strictly needed, so that their passing was marked by a trail of discarded paraphernalia; sextant, axe, waterproof camp bag, film, blankets – everything that could be shucked off save a Bible, comforting passages from which they read aloud to each other every night.

They reached a river. It was, as Wallace later discovered, the Beaver. Elson wanted to follow it, but Hubbard insisted that they keep to their original trail. Elson did not argue; Hubbard was leader. Their only hope would be to find the lard, flour, and milk powder they had discarded early in the journey. They were ready to eat anything, and when they came upon an old flour bag, they scraped the residue into a pot of water with some leftover bones and devoured the result. Then they found a box of baking powder and ate that, and another box, half full, of mustard, which they also ate. When Hubbard came upon this last item, he could not control himself. Tears trickled down his cheeks as he said, "That box came from . . . my home in Congers. Mina has had this very box in her hand. It came from the little grocery store where I've been so often. Mina handed it to me before I left home. She said the mustard might be useful for plasters. We've eaten it instead. I wonder where my girl is now? I wonder when I'll see her again? Yes, she had that very box in her hands – in *her* hands. She's been such a good wife to me."

He could go no further. Instead, he insisted that Wallace and Elson try to reach the abandoned flour and lard. Elson would then continue on to seek help while Wallace would return with the provisions.

The following day all three made their wills, and Hubbard urged that if he died Wallace should write the story of the expedition and give his diary to Mina.

In his own diary, George Elson described the moment of parting:

"Just before starting, Mr. Wallace says that he is going to read the 13th chapter, First Corinthians, and so he did.

"It was time to start.

"Mr. Wallace went to Mr. Hubbard and said, 'Goodbye, I'll try and come back soon.'

"Then I went to him and tried to be as brave as Wallace.

"When I took his hand he said, 'God bless you, George,' and held my hand for some time.

"I said, 'The Lord help us Hubbard. With His help I save you if I can get out.' Then I cried like a child.

"Hubbard said, 'If it was your father, George, you couldn't try harder to save.'

"Wallace came back to Hubbard again, and cried like a child and kissed him; and again I went to him and kissed him and he kissed me, and said again, 'The Lord help you George.'

"He was then so weak he could hardly speak.

"We came away."

That scene haunted George Elson for the rest of his life. Almost thirty years later, in the winter of 1932-33, when he was living in Moosonee, Ontario he would come to the station of the Temiskaming and Northern Ontario Railway to reminisce with the agent, W.G. Brittain, about his days in Labrador. Elson's visits were regular; Brittain could predict to the minute the time at which he would walk down the pathway. The routine was always the same: Elson would walk in, say hello, and then tell the story of his trip with Leonidas Hubbard. He told it in great detail – it took two hours – and always in exactly the same way. On each occasion, when he reached the point in his narrative where he left Hubbard behind to look for help, George Elson would begin to cry; tears would stream down his face and he would take from his pocket a clean red handkerchief to wipe them away. Then he would continue with the tale.

Elson and Wallace came upon the discarded flour the following evening – several pounds of it, black with mould. They divided it. Elson headed down the valley toward Grand Lake, twenty-five miles away, while Wallace was to retrace his steps to the point fifteen miles back where he had left Hubbard.

A blizzard sprang up; it would last ten days. Elson warned Wallace to stick to the river – never to leave it for any reason – and then he plunged off into the snow, walking only in his socks, making slow time in the drifts. He had no mitts and was forced to make some from the sleeves of his undershirt to keep his hands from freezing. He found the abandoned coffee, milk, and lard, and these, with a partridge and a porcupine, gave him enough strength to continue. In the evening, to keep up his spirits, he read a chapter from his Bible and sang a hymn, "Lead, Kindly Light." He reached Grand Lake on October 26, followed the shore, came to another river (it was the Beaver, which, had they taken it as Elson urged, would have led all three to safety), decided to swim across in the floating ice, suffered terrible cramps, and turned back just in time. The following day he built a crude raft, which took him to a small island before it collapsed beneath him.He made a larger raft and, talking to himself all the while ("telling myself what a fine raft it was"), managed to reach the far shore and make camp. That night he went to explore a nearby point and, as he rounded it, saw a sight he would never forget. Just a hundred yards away lay a small boat, the first sign of civilization he had seen since he left Wallace. A moment later, a human sound broke the silence – harsh and grating, yet immensely comforting – the scream of a small child.

"I cannot tell how I felt. I just run the direction I heard the sound. The next, the roof of a house I saw. Then I came on a trail. I saw a girl with a child outside of the door. As soon as she saw me she run in and a woman came out. I sung out to her before I came to her. Meeting me she looked so scared. Then I shook hands with her and told her where I come from. She took me in the house and told me to sit down. But I was – well I could not say how I was and how glad I was."

The woman was the wife of Tom Blake, the Grand Lake trapper. Her presence was fortuitous: the cabin had just been built; the family had moved in only the week before. Blake and his brother plunged off at once to fetch two more men; the four then set out to rescue Wallace and Hubbard. Elson gamely offered to accompany them, but they convinced him that he could not stand the pace.

Wallace, meanwhile, struggling in knee-deep snow, had become hopelessly lost. In his delirium, he thought he heard his dead wife calling to him through the storm, a phantom whisper, sighing in the wind. He lost count of the days; actually he was travelling in a circle. One night, building fires more by instinct than by conscious effort, he boiled his moccasins and ate them. He was prostrate in the snow, half dozing, when four swarthy men on snowshoes loomed out of the blizzard. He gazed at them stupidly as in a trance; it was some time before he realized that they were not apparitions. He must have presented a bizarre appearance – a tattered, bony wraith "standing in drawers and stocking feet with the remnants of a pair of trousers about his hips, there in the midst of the snow covered forest."

Two of the rescue team stayed with Wallace; the others set off in search of Hubbard. His tent was only a short distance away, his corpse inside, wrapped in blankets. He had died soon after the others had left him after writing a long passage in his diary, which ended with these words: "I am not suffering. The acute pangs of hunger have given away to indifference. I am sleepy. I think death from starvation is not so bad. But let no one suppose that I expect it. I am prepared, that is all. I think the boys will be able with the Lord's help to save me."

Wallace's rescuers turned over to him all of Hubbard's effects. They were prepared to bury him where he perished, but Wallace insisted that the body be taken to New York. Because of the weather, that took some time. It was not removed from the tent until mid-March and did not arrive at Battle Harbour until mid-May where, still frozen, it was sealed in a lead-lined coffin to be buried later that month at the cemetery in Haverstraw on the Hudson.

Wallace accompanied the body back to New York. His own recovery had been slow; he had, in fact, almost lost a leg from gangrene. Ironically, the young medical student who saved it,

George Albert Hardy, a tubercular convalescent, caught a chill and died on the trip out from North West River.

Mina Hubbard learned of her husband's death in a brief telegram sent in January, 1904: "Mr. Hubbard died October 18 in the interior of Labrador." In March, she received the letter he had written to her before his death and also his diary but not his maps and field notes, which Wallace considered his property. To say that she was prostrated by the news of the tragedy scarcely describes the depth of Mrs. Hubbard's despair; her husband had been the very centre of her existence, the orb around which she, a minor planet, had revolved. She could not conceive of life without him. All that remained for her was to erect a monument – not some stark and useless pillar but a living document, a testimony to his wisdom, his courage, his selflessness, his . . . *perfection*.

She turned to Wallace: Wallace would create the monument. Wallace would tell the world about her Laddie's remarkable struggle with the wilderness – his explorations, his sacrifices, his heroic death. She was prepared to pay handsomely: one thousand dollars, a substantial sum in the fall of 1904. Wallace agreed, signed a contract, and in his turn engaged a ghost-writer, Frank Barkley Copley, to help with the task. The result, constructed from Wallace's and Hubbard's diaries – with many purple patches by Copley – became an enormous best-seller entitled *The Lure of the Labrador Wild*. It pleased the public; it pleased Hubbard's parents and his sister; but it did not please Mrs. Hubbard.

The book, written in the breathless, exclamatory style popular at the time, scarcely made Hubbard out to be a saint. Wallace yielded to no one in his admiration and love for his friend but he did not try to omit from the narrative those moments on the trail when the younger man was discouraged and depressed; when he had worried aloud that he had led his comrades into a tight spot; when, with tears in his eyes, he had talked of home and Mina. Such evidences of human frailty Mrs. Hubbard could not abide; she wanted them excised from the manuscript. It was far too sensational, far too, well, *popular*; she had asked, or thought she had asked, for a eulogy; she had received instead a parcel of Sunday supplement prose. She demanded changes; Wallace refused. The book, which eventually went into twenty-three editions, was published exactly as he wanted it.

It contained passages that must have cut her to the quick: "Undoubtedly the boy was beginning to suffer from homesickness – he was only a young fellow, you know. . . ."

The *boy*! How dare Wallace use that word to describe someone who was to her a man in every sense, and more than that, a man above all other men – a saint! And here was Wallace, in his subtle way, attempting to put the blame for the failure of the expedition on him. On August 30, so Wallace wrote, he had seriously considered whether or not he should "strongly insist" that the party turn back, but had decided against it, knowing so well Hubbard's determination to do what he set out to do. Wallace had treated Hubbard's stubbornness with some delicacy, but not delicately enough for Hubbard's widow. On October 14, he portrayed Hubbard as adamantly insisting on retracing their steps along the old trail rather than taking the Beaver River, as Elson suggested. "The question was settled," Wallace wrote. "Hubbard was the leader." Really, it was too much! In Mina Hubbard's view, the mean-spirited Wallace was absolving himself of all blame for her Laddie's sacrifice and death – her Laddie, who was "oh, so brave and glad hearted and beautiful," so noble that she felt "wretched and mean and unbeautiful . . . when I compare myself to him." Those excerpts from her later diary suggest that Mrs. Hubbard became a little unhinged by the growing realization that her Laddie was lost to her forever. Her worship of him took on a mystical, almost religious quality. In her diary she expresses herself as awestruck that a man of his calibre could "honour with his love" a mere mortal such as she – and a wretched, mean, unbeautiful mortal at that; "and yet *he loved me*!" she wrote, underlining her amazement at that miracle. And this was the man whom Wallace saw merely as a homesick boy!

There was, perhaps, more to it than that. For Wallace had cheated her out of the last six months of her husband's life. Wallace had experienced that intimacy, which she could never know, that draws men together in moments of crisis. It may well be that, subconsciously, she had from the beginning been jealous of the man-to-man palship that had seen the two of them go off together into the mountains of New York State without her – cutting her off from her husband in the first year of their marriage.

In Mrs. Hubbard's eyes, her Laddie could do no wrong. Then what *had* gone wrong? Slowly she came to believe – and her diary reveals it – that the villain in the piece must have been Wallace. Why had he not got back to her husband with the flour? She refused to believe that he had been weak, lost, and close to death. No: he was more concerned about himself; he had, in fact, by his cowardice and weakness let her husband die alone of starvation, when he might easily have been saved. Now here he was, publicly announcing that he, Wallace, would finish her husband's work; he would not even return to her the maps and field notes. "The work must be done," Wallace quoted Hubbard as saying, "and if one of us falls before it is complete, the other must finish it. . . ." "His words," Wallace wrote, at the conclusion of the manuscript, "ring in my ear as a call to duty . . . perhaps it is God's will that I finish the work of exploration that Hubbard began."

Mrs. Hubbard first read those words in January, 1905, when Wallace submitted the manuscript to her. She was repelled. Wallace was about to snatch all the glory, all the honour, that rightfully belonged to her Laddie. *No!* It could not be permitted. One can almost see Mrs. Hubbard's eyes glisten, her jaw set. If anyone completed the work it would be a Hubbard. Without delay she announced that in order to vindicate her husband's name, she would undertake to complete "his work." She would write her own book, and in it, as she was to confide to her diary, she would "let all the world know that he was loved and honoured, almost worshipped, by the one whom he honoured with his love."

All of which explains how it came about that Mrs. Hubbard and Dillon Wallace arrived at the twin trading posts at North West River on the same boat but did not speak. The two books that were published as a result of their subsequent adventures are notable as much for what they leave out as for what they recount. In Dillon Wallace's *The Long Labrador Trail*, there is no mention of Mrs. Hubbard. In Mrs. Hubbard's *A Woman's Way Through Unknown Labrador*, there is no mention of Dillon Wallace, only an oblique reference in the preface expressing the hope that the inclusions, as appendices, of her husband's diary and that of George Elson "may go some way towards correcting misleading accounts of Mr. Hubbard's expedition, which have appeared elsewhere." But the diary of Leonidas Hubbard, Jr., as she published it, was not complete. Most of those obsessive, mouthwatering visions of food, which suggest a certain derangement, a growing weakness of mind and spirit, were stricken out; so were most of the references to tattered clothing, worn-out moccasins, Hubbard's attacks of diarrhoea and vomiting, and his more desperate references to homesickness. So also were many of the references to Wallace.

In her version of the tragedy, Mrs. Hubbard did her best to remove all blame for faulty planning from her husband's shoulders. In spite of contradictory evidence from the editor, she insisted that the Labrador journey was an assignment for *Outing* magazine. Again, in spite of evidence to the contrary, she insisted that her husband did not plan his own inadequate outfit; the impression she left was that the planning was Wallace's. Finally, she placed the responsibility for the expedition's tragic ending on the weather. It was, she pointed out, correctly, "a season of unprecedented severity." Had the winter been normal, she wrote, "he would still have returned safe and triumphant."

No doubt she believed it. Her own remarkable journey through the lonely heart of Labrador reads like a pleasant Sunday jaunt in comparison with the horrors suffered by her husband's party. She was sensible enough to hire George Elson as her guide and to follow his instructions carefully. In addition to Elson, she had three other sturdy and experienced woodsmen to shepherd her across the Labrador plateau: Joseph Iserhoff, a Russian half-breed; Job Chapies, a James Bay Cree who spoke little English; and a fifteen-year-old Montagnais boy, Gilbert Blake, who Mrs. Hubbard persisted in believing (to his annoyance) was an Eskimo. The party planned to travel in two canoes – and in comfort: besides the stove, the balloon-silk tents, the waterproof bags, and a vast amount of food, there were also, for Mrs. Hubbard, an air mattress, a feather pillow, and a hot-water bottle.

She did not look like an explorer. A small slender woman with delicate features, she is best described as comely rather than beautiful – her hair piled high in the Gibson Girl fashion of the day, her nose small and pert, her chin receding but determined. In the artist's rendering of her profile that accompanies her book, she appears remarkably bland and passive; there is no hint of the passions revealed by her diary, of the elation she felt in following in her husband's footsteps, of the anguish that gnawed at her when she contemplated a future without him. Ten days out of North West River, she confided to her journal:

"Very tired, very sad, very glad to be here and getting on with our work. Two years ago last night, Laddie asked me: 'Will you miss me, sweetheart?' Two years ago this morning we said: 'Goodbye.' Sometimes it seems too much to bear. This work keeps me from being utterly desperate. Wonder what I shall do when this is done?"

For Mina Hubbard, the long trek across the peninsula had a justification apart from the one to which she publicly admitted: for her it was an escape, a postponement of reality, a therapy. By planning and organizing, by moving ceaselessly, by keeping busy, she shored herself up against the contemplation of what seemed an empty future.

She dressed for the adventure with a practicality that did not detract from her femininity: a short skirt over knickerbockers, high boots, a sweater with a belt (adorned with a knife and a revolver), and a felt hat with a mosquito veil. She did not make her husband's mistake of taking one pair of footgear; she had knee-length leather moccasins, high sealskin boots, a pair of low seal sneakers, three pairs of socks, five pairs of stockings, to say nothing of three suits of underwear, two pairs of gloves (one of wool, one of leather), a rubber automobile shirt, a long Swedish dogskin coat and – a feminine touch – a blouse for Sundays. In the contemporary photographs she always looks as if she were the guest of honour at a fashionable picnic. The factor at the Hudson's Bay post, who originally believed that Mrs. Hubbard had set herself a fool's errand, took one look at her and quickly changed his mind. "You can do it," he said, as she stepped nimbly into one of the canoes, "and without any trouble, too."

She was relieved to be on her way, guided by George Elson, "the trusty hero, whose courage and honour and fidelity made my venture possible." Elson was determined to see her through to a successful conclusion. He felt that somehow he had failed her husband, that his abilities as a woodsman were in question, that his honour, too, must be vindicated. The task would not be easy: he must guide her across five hundred and fifty miles of wilderness, much of it unknown, and he must do it within two months; the Hudson's Bay supply steamer, *Pelican*, was due to arrive at the George River post on Ungava Bay during the last week in August; there would be no other until the following summer. Also there was the race with Wallace; Mrs. Hubbard wanted to be the first to reach Ungava Bay and to be able to write that she was first. She watched anxiously for signs of Wallace's passing and, to her satisfaction saw none. She slept that first night out "as if in a most luxurious apartment."

The Hubbard Labrador Expedition was more properly the Elson Labrador Expedition. George Elson watched over Mrs. Hubbard as a mother cat watches over its kitten. On June 30, she left her knife behind; Elson would not let her go back for it; he went himself. She lost the tube for her mattress pump and realized that she could not sleep properly on the ground without growing very tired, "when I lose my nerve and am afraid to do anything." George solved the problem by blowing up the mattress himself each night. Once he found her standing on a rock gazing hypnotized, at the rapids below: "They grew more and more fascinating . . . so strong, so irresistible. . . ." He was quite firm with her: she might grow dizzy and fall; she must not stare into the rapids again, otherwise "we will just turn around and go back to North West River."

She grew fond of her guardians. "How easy I feel in the midst of them all," she told her diary. "Could not feel more so if they were my brothers. And no one except Laddie was ever as thoughtful and kind to me than they have been." At night she and George Elson had long talks beside the campfire. He told her of his childhood, of how he had learned to keep a diary, even though he had never seen anyone do it, and did not even know the word, but had wanted to learn to write and so made little books out of pieces of paper and then learned from other books his father bought him. She was charmed by this account. She suggested that he try to write about his experiences, perhaps a book for boys. A bond was growing between them.

One Friday late in July, while the men were making a portage, she asked permission to climb a hill. After some thought, Elson agreed to let her go. He urged her to take her rubber coat in case of rain, but, loaded down with two cameras, revolver, knife, barometer, and compass, she objected, and he did not insist. She was excited as a schoolgirl at being allowed to go off on her own. When a storm did come up she decided to push on farther than agreed upon because she was already wet to the skin. She set off through the rain for a ridge on the far side of a lake "with something of the feeling of a child who has run away from home, for it had been constantly impressed upon me that I must never go away alone. . . ." At the top of the ridge she looked down and saw the men on the edge of the bay, canoes drawn up on shore, brewing tea. She fired two shots to let them know where she was and noticed that they seemed to panic. They scurried up the ridge to meet her; but she had moved on, and it was some time before they caught up. Somewhat to her surprise she discovered that they were extremely upset: "Their faces were covered with perspiration and rare expressions, which were a funny mixture of anger, distress and relief and much more. They had been thoroughly frightened. I smiled at them but there was no answering smile from George."

"You have just had us about crazy." Elson told her, declaring that she should never have climbed the ridge in the storm. They would never again trust her to go off on her own; whenever she wanted to wander, one of them would go with her.

She tended to laugh off the experience, but Elson explained why they had been in such a state: "What would we do if you got lost and fell in the rapid? Just what *could* we do? Why, I could never go back again. How could any of us go back without you? We can't ever let you go any place alone after this."

She was truly sorry. She had not meant to frighten them, but their faces were still pale and their hands trembling so much she decided she must pass around her bottle of medicinal brandy. To her dismay, they drank it all.

The contrast between Leonidas Hubbard's struggle toward Lake Michikamau and that of his widow is so stark that the two accounts seem to be describing a different realm; and so, in some ways they were, for that earlier trip up the Susan to its headwaters

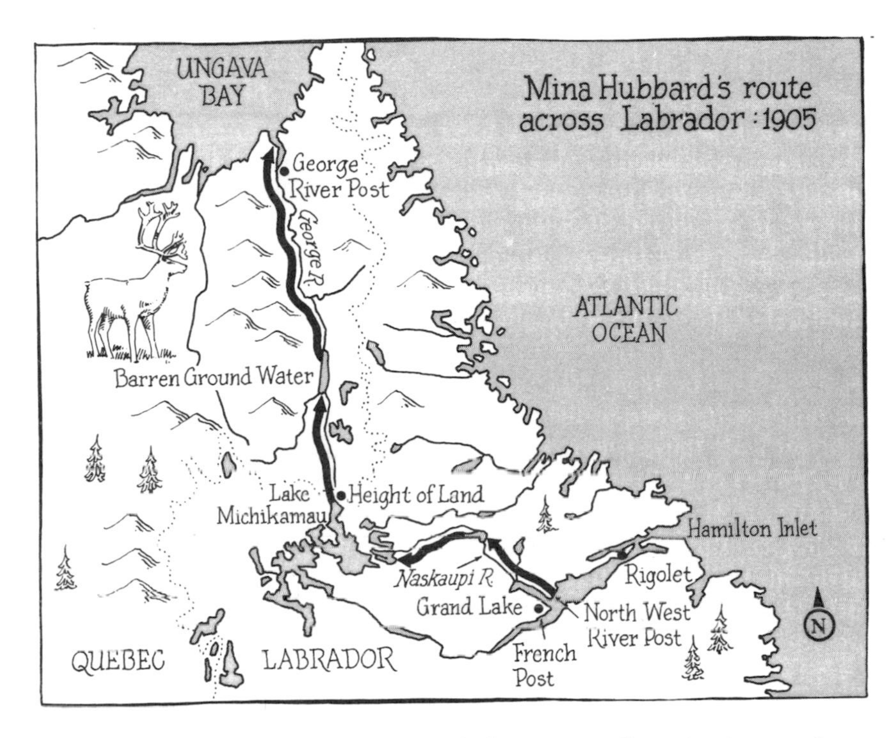

and then overland – a journey of almost unrelieved misery – bore no relation to the much easier voyage up the broad Naskaupi. Hubbard had neither time nor energy to wonder at the scenery; it represented only a barrier to his ambitions. His widow revelled in it: the torrents and cataracts of the upper river, "where water [was] pouring over ledges, flowing in a foaming, roaring torrent round little rocky islands or rushed madly down a chute," and the colours! – rocks a rich chocolate brown and in places almost purple, garlanded with mosses, grey-green and vermilion.

Ahead lay the first of their objectives, the great lake, the sight of which Mrs. Hubbard half dreaded because she knew it would bring back memories. Her husband's presence haunted her, and in her diary she gave vent to her emotions:

July 7: "Had a fine fire and I thought of Laddie's proverb 'On a wet day build a big fire.' It often seemed as if he must be standing just near and that if I turn I must see him. *Strange part* of all this experience *it seems* perfectly natural. . . ."

July 10: "How my heart aches with hunger and longing for him. It would be so perfect if he were here. How he would revel in it all. . . . It is all so wild and grand and mysterious and how his heart would beat with pride and joy in it all if he could be here. . . . So very, very beautiful and yet lacking that which completes and perfects. I have not his spirit, not that of the true explorer. I have to keep reminding myself all the time that I am the first of my kind to see it and I don't get any thrill out of it except only as I can make it honour him. . . ."

July 16: "Oh, what this trip would be if he were here. I have to keep reminding myself that the hills he is climbing now must be so much grander and more beautiful to escape an ever-recurring feeling that it is wicked for me to be here when he is not and Oh how desperately hungry and desolate and sad. . . . I never dreamed it could be so splendid. And the grander and more beautiful it grows, the more I hunger for the one who made all things beautiful, so much more beautiful by the spirit he breathed into them."

July 26: "Very, very hungry and lonely for my Laddie. His life and the spirit in which he lived in seem to grow more and more beautiful all the time as I look back to them. My own inability to measure up to them makes me feel so desolate. Wonder so much what I shall do without him. It will be the best I can but it seems such a poor best compared to his. . . ."

In the words she directed to the public, Mrs. Hubbard did not allow herself the luxury of such emotions. Only occasionally did she permit her private feelings to encroach upon the narrative, as in her description of that moment when, scouting from a hilltop, she was able to see in the blue distance the daisy chain of lakes through which that earlier party had made its way en route to Michikamau. "So much of life and pain can crowd into a few minutes," she wrote guardedly. "The whole desperate picture stood out with dread vividness. . . ."

By this time, as his diary entries reveal, George Elson had become greatly attached to her. At first his attitude was reserved, but as the journey progressed his remarks grew warmer:

July 1: "Mrs. Hubbard enjoying the trip very much. . . ."

July 8: "Mrs. Hubbard doing very well indeed in her travelling through such rough country. . . ."

July 17: "Mrs. Hubbard is enjoying her trip. She is so nice to me and a bright little woman she is. We are getting on fine."

July 23: "When I shot the caribou Mrs. Hubbard was after shading [*sic*] tears. I suppose it must remind her of the one Mr. Hubbard killed on our trip we had out here in Labrador. I feel very sorry for her."

By the end of July, the two had become close companions. She was genuinely interested in George Elson in a way her husband and Wallace had not been. He was more than her guide: he was her protector, her guardian, her big brother. Leonidas Hubbard had tended to think of him as an employee, a "woodsman"; Wallace had invariably referred to him as an Indian. But in those long talks around the glowing fire she showed an interest not only in his past but also in his future. He *must* write a book; she would help him. "Mrs. Hubbard, she is really so good and a really kind hearted woman she is," Elson wrote in his diary. "She is more than good to me. My sister could not be kinder to me as she is. How glad and proud my sisters would be if they knew how kind and what a good friend I have. Still I don't want to say she is only a friend to me, but that she is my sister. God will help her and bring her again to her good friends home to where she came from. She is so brite and smart and I am glad she does trust me. . . ."

This was one of Elson's longest entries and one of the most personal, but it was not quite enough. The following day he felt the need to repeat those sentiments: "I like her so much. She is really nice to us. I cannot speak enough good things about her. Oh I do wish I will be able to bring her out safe again. . . . I trust in the Lord. . . ."

On August 2, they reached Lake Michikamau. A wild demonstration followed, the men "jumping and waving their hats and yelling like demons." On a flat stone Mina Hubbard carved the words "HUBBARD EXPEDITION ARRIVED HERE AUGUST 2ND, 1905," adding the names of the members of the party. That afternoon they crossed the lake, with the call of the loons echoing down the empty waters. "It was weird and beautiful beyond words; the big, shining lake with its distant blue islands; the sky with its wonderful blue clouds and colour; two little canoes so deep in the wilderness and those wild, reverberant voices coming from invisible beings away in the long light which lay across the water." It was a scene no white human had encountered before and one that none will ever see again, for Lake Michikamau has vanished, lost in the vaster waters of the manmade Smallwood Reservoir that feeds the power project at Churchill Falls.

Other unique experiences followed. The great Labrador caribou herd, which no white man had ever encountered, was flowing east like a brown river toward the highlands between the George River and the Atlantic. On August 8, after leaving Michikamau, the party came upon it, "a solid mass" draped across a hillside. Shortly afterward, Mrs. Hubbard watched the herd plunge into a lake, forming an unbroken bridge of animals three-quarters of a mile long between the shoreline and a barren island far out in the water. For the next fifty miles they encountered thousands of caribou ("the country was literally alive with the beautiful creatures") and Mrs. Hubbard was able to report that "so far as I can learn, I alone, save the Indians, have witnessed the great migration. . . ."

On August 10, she added another record to her accomplishments. The party had portaged to a small lake. To the north lay a bog. Beyond that was a second lake, from which the water flowed in the opposite direction – north. At five that afternoon after travelling three hundred miles through the wilderness, she stepped out of her canoe "to stand at last on the summit of the Divide – the first of the white race to trace the Nascaupee river to its source." The canoes were portaged across the height and in less than an hour of paddling they came upon the outlet from the second lake – a tiny stream, which they identified as the George. By the time they reached its mouth, at Ungava Bay, it would be three miles wide.

In her diary, she allowed herself some moments of reflection:

"I wish I need never go back. I suppose I will never be taken care of in the gentle *careful* way I have been since we left N.W.R. I came away expecting to have all sorts of hardships to endure and have had none. . . . Labrador skies have so far been kind to us. Oh if they had only been so kind two years ago. . . . It has been a wonderfully interesting day for me. It has interested me in a way I did not suppose I should ever be interested again and in my heart tonight a touch of gladness that our work has prospered so far. It has not been perfectly done. I have felt my lack of training . . . deeply and keenly. . . . Yet even so we have opened the way. . . . And I can bring a tribute to the memory of my husband which he at least would think worthwhile. . . ."

There were worries. Could they cover the three hundred miles to Ungava Bay in time to meet the boat, due in little more than a fortnight? And where was Wallace? His name, if we believe Mrs. Hubbard's diary, evoked amusement and disdain from the other members of the party:

"Always there is much talk of the other party and their probable doings, esp. the probability of their getting lost. All are familiar with the story of W.'s prowess in wilderness travel. Geo. and Gil both know Stanton [a member of the Wallace party]. Gil says: If Stanton falls off of his seat in the canoe, he'll get lost. Geo: 'Well, W. won't make much progress on Mich. today.' Gil: 'I think it's blowing pretty hard on Seal Lake too, don't you?' Then his boy's merry laughter in which everybody joins."

The other worry was the mood of the Indians – the Montagnais and the little known Naskapi – who lived along the banks of the George River. Mrs. Hubbard detected some uneasiness among the men as they sat around the campfire. One evening she was made to realize what was bothering them. The Indians would not kill *her*. "No," said Gil Blake, "they wouldn't hurt a woman, I don't think. They want the women for themselves." It had not occurred to Mrs. Hubbard that she might be the prize in a bloody struggle. That night she lay awake in her tent "turning over in my mind plans of battle in case we should meet with treachery."

But the Indians were not treacherous, merely curious. On August 17, a cold and misty morning, the party espied on a hillside a dark, shapeless mass, which they took to be caribou until the glint of metal and the crack of a rifle dispelled the illusion. The men approached the Montagnais camp with some uneasiness until they discovered it was populated almost exclusively by women and children; the men were away trading at Davis Inlet. The women told the party that they would meet the Barren Ground People – the Naskapi – farther down the river and that they would receive a friendly reception. They also said that it would take two months to reach Ungava Bay.

Mrs. Hubbard was sick with disappointment. Should she turn back? For some days this worry had disturbed her sleep. She held a long palaver with her guides. The argument continued for some time, but finally the decision was made to continue down the George River and try to discover from the Naskapi Indians what their chances were of reaching its mouth in time to catch the *Pelican*.

Three days later they came upon the Naskapi camp. These Indians, dressed mainly in skins and hides, had little contact with civilization. No white man or woman had yet encountered them on their home ground. Mrs. Hubbard's photographs and observations would be unique. Over the objections of George Elson she insisted on visiting the camp and would have stayed longer had he not been impatient to move on. But from the Naskapi they received heartening news: Ungava Bay, they were told, was only five days down river.

Now Mrs. Hubbard became intensely aware that sweet victory lay in her grasp. They had seen no evidence that Wallace and his party had passed this way; *she* would be the one to complete her husband's work. Yet the slightest mistake could mean disaster; and potential disaster loomed ahead. As they hoisted sail on the canoes and slid across the surface of the slender lake known then as Barren Ground Water, they could hear in the distance the roar of the rapids. An almost unbroken stretch of angry white water, one hundred and thirty miles long, lay before them.

They were all worried. Job Chapies dreamed that night of danger; each man had a spare paddle ready beside him in case his should snap at a crucial moment. The river exceeded Mrs.

Hubbard's wildest nightmares; it was like a gigantic toboggan slide, a chute down which the canoes raced pell mell, past sharp rocks, around perilous curves, over slippery ledges, through boulder-strewn shallows, and under spray-soaked cliffs. The strain was intense on passenger and paddlers. Mrs. Hubbard, trembling with excitement after a night rendered sleepless by those insects whose continual patter on the tent "sounded like gentle rain," was never permitted an instant's relaxation in the canoe. She could not even allow herself to slap at mosquitoes "each bite of which was like the touch of a live coal. . . . It was most difficult to resist the impulse to grasp the sides of the canoe and to compel myself instead to sit with hands clasped about my knees and muscles relaxed so that my body might lend itself to the motion of the canoe."

The ordeal continued for the best part of a week. On August 23, George Elson and Job Chapies were nearly wrecked when their craft whirled about in the torrent and slammed against a cliff. The bottom caught on a rock but fortunately the canoe did not tip. The men leaped out, clambered to a perilous perch, and with ropes on either end succeeded in freeing it. Elson worried less about himself than about his charge. That night he wrote: " . . . what makes me so scared of the rapids is on account of having a woman in my canoe . . . because I don't want to get Mrs. Hubbard in any trouble. . . . Such a dear little lady and a sister to me."

On her part it was "almost unbelievable" that they had nearly reached their goal. "I begin to realize that I have never actually counted on being able to get there." Now, with Ungava Bay almost in sight, the strain became more intense. What if the *Pelican* had been and gone? The suspense was too much, the pace too slow.

"I did wish that the men would not chat and laugh in the unconcerned way they were doing, and they paddled as leisurely as if I were not in a hurry at all. If only I could reach the post and ask about the ship! If only I might fly over the water and not wait for these leisurely paddles! And now, from being in an agony of fear for their lives, my strong desire was to take them by their collars and knock their heads together hard. . . ."

In her diary entry of August 25, there appears a curiously obscure remark:

"Full of thought we are reaching the Geo. R. Post. It grows more and more wonderful and oh if Laddie were only here. . . . It has been another day of running down rapids, some of them have been particularly trying and hard to run. I have walked over several and once I thought we were certainly going to destruction.

Now that the work [is] so nearly done I don't want to though I dread going back. . . ."

If that passage means anything, it means that, at the back of Mina Hubbard's mind as she planned her trip to Labrador and later, as she struggled across the plateau, was the thought – almost the conviction – that she was going to perish. It is not too much to conjecture that she welcomed the prospect, for she believed devoutly in an afterlife. Her husband – that unbelievably noble man – had not been able to survive; what chance, then, did she, an inferior mortal, have? And what better death than one that would unite her with him under the same circumstances that had originally claimed his life?

But it was not to be, and now she must face that which she had not yet composed herself to face: the reality of a life without him. It is clear from her words that she had never for an instant been able to look beyond the day when she would reach the little fort on Ungava Bay. "What am I going to do?" she asked her diary and then answered, "I don't know."

Yet in retrospect she came to realize that she had found some measure of peace in this savage yet hauntingly beautiful land:

"Was thinking today how strange it is. I have not wanted to see anyone, I have been lonely for no one. We have come these months through this deserted wilderness and I have never felt as if I were far from home. I have felt more at home here than I have ever done any place since our home in Congers. But I mean to try to face the other life as bravely as I can and in a way that will honour the one I loved more than all the world and who loved me with such a beautiful, generous love. . . ."

On the final night of her journey she could not sleep, for she knew the race was not yet over. If she could make the ship in time, she could get her story and pictures out to the public before Wallace was heard from. "That would be the thing for me. If I am to be successful that would make it complete. Oh if it might only come out that way. How grateful I should be and how complete my victory and how completely it would make of no account W.'s reflection." She was convinced that, in this bitter contest, God was on her side, for she believed, with all the fervency of a Gordon or a Kitchener, that her cause was just. How could the Deity do anything to further the fortunes of the despised Wallace? "I believe His hand is with me," she wrote.

On August 27, exactly two months from the date in June when they had left North West River, they spotted deep in a cove a small huddle of buildings, nestling at the foot of a mountain of solid rock. They paddled up a little stream and poled their way over a mudbank. The agent, John Ford, came down to meet them, followed by a retinue of Inuit. There is extant a photograph of Mrs. Hubbard alighting from the canoe, a man at each arm to steady her. She looks perfectly composed in her hat and long skirt as if she were stepping off some royal barge. She inquired about the *Pelican*; had it left? No; it had not yet arrived nor would it arrive until the middle of September at the earliest. She was surprised at her reaction to this unexpected news: "There are times when that which constitutes one's inner self seems to cease. So it was with me when Mr. Ford uttered those words. My heart should have swelled with emotion but it did not. I cannot remember any time in my life when I had less feeling."

Rummaging about in one of the bags, George Elson found Mrs. Hubbard's sealskin boots, into which she changed for her walk across the mud flats. The agent's wife greeted her with the words: "You are welcome, Mrs. Hubbard. Yours is the first white woman's face I have seen for two years." Looking back, she was puzzled to discover that the men were still sitting in the canoes. Only then did she realize that the positions were reversed: "They were my charges now." A certain ceremony was obviously required. Back she went down the hill to meet them and thank them, "and Heaven knows how inadequate were the words." Later that day, from the window of her room in the post, she watched them setting up camp and, with a little pang, became aware of the gap already widening between them. "It was with a feeling of genuine loneliness that I realized that I should not again be one of the little party."

George Elson was more than a little in love with her. She had given him ambitions – to go to school, to set himself up as a trader on James Bay, perhaps even to become a writer.

"I am very sure [I] could write a nice little story. I am sure someone would be good enough to help me in doing so. Another thing is in my mind. I would like now to get married this fall, if I was lucky enough – if I could strak [*sic*] luck and could get a white girl that would marry me and especially if she was well learnt we then could write some nice stories because she would know lots more than I would but not likely I will be so lucky. I think some way my chances are small in that way, but I know that I would be very happy, I am very sure it is a happy life anyway. So many nice girls in the world and yet – none for me. . . ."

And again, a week later, on September 7: "In the afternoon Mrs. Hubbard and I working and talking about some things [of] great importance. Great afternoon. . . . I could not sleep last night awake all night, thinking lots of new things. Was up at 3 a.m.

What a happy life it would be if it would really happen. New plans so good of her to think so kind thoughts of me. She is more than good and kind to me."

Yet, as the days went by and the *Pelican* did not arrive, Mina Hubbard, using the time to prepare her story for publication, was not quite so enamoured of George Elson. He had persuaded Gilbert Blake to make a map of Grand Lake, and this aroused her suspicions. Was George planning to write his own account of the journey? "Am wondering whether I had better ask him to sign a written agreement not to write anything about the trip without my written consent and approach [*sic*]. I almost think I had. There would be no question about the thing then."

Was there something more? "Am beginning to see through quite a few things I did not understand before. He [George] has been contradicting himself lately in a way which makes me sick at heart. Makes me feel depressed and then I try to persuade myself I am wrong in my thoughts but I always suffer for that kind of thing."

The entry is tantalizing in its ambiguity. What exactly was it that disturbed Mrs. Hubbard? Why did she find it necessary to ask her four male companions to sign a joint statement in her diary that "we at all times treated Mrs. Hubbard with respect and each also declares his belief that Mrs. Hubbard was also treated with respect by other men of this party" and that "each also here records his promise that he will never, by look or word or sign lead any human being to believe that during the trip there was anything in the conduct of Mrs. Hubbard and her party towards each other that was unbecoming honourable Christian men and women . . . "? At Mrs. Hubbard's suggestion, and also their request, she prepared and signed a similar statement, which appears in Elson's diary. Were such protestations really necessary? Perhaps. One must remember the atmosphere of the time: a pretty widow alone for two months with four woodsmen could really give rise to gossip.

Whatever Mrs. Hubbard's reservations were about George Elson – and it may only have been that she felt he was not resolute enough in the ambitions she had for him – they were soon dissipated. She read portions of her manuscript to him and, on October 15, recorded that she had had "a pretty good talk" with him that night and felt "encouraged about him more than I have ever done before. How I hope he may work up to his possibilities. They are great."

At this point, the *Pelican* was more than six weeks overdue, and there was still no sign of the Dillon Wallace party of five. Then, the following evening, he turned up with a single companion, Clifford Easton, a forestry student from North Carolina. "They both look strong and well," Mrs. Hubbard wrote. "Wallace a little more coarse and common than ordinary. Looks positively repulsive to me. Felt a little nervous about their coming and now it is an end to peace of mind for me. Awfully hard to know what to do."

In his book, *The Long Labrador Trail*, Wallace was to write that he had decided at the outset to sacrifice speed for thoroughness and that he took scientists with him to help in research. These remarks do not ring true. The only scientific figure in the party was George Richards, an American geologist, whom he sent back when his expedition reached Lake Michikamau along with two others: Leigh Stanton, a Boer War veteran, and Peter Stevens, an Ojibway from Minnesota. Nor was Wallace's work as thorough as that of his rival. For reasons that are again obscure he decided not to take Hubbard's planned route up the valley of the Naskaupi but to try to follow an old Indian trail overland to the big lake. The party went astray more than once and found the journey hard going. They did not reach Michikamau until September 3, long after Mrs. Hubbard had arrived at Ungava Bay. The Hubbard party had come down the George River in twenty-five days; it took Wallace and his companion forty-three, in part because of the lateness of the season. There is no evidence that he observed the caribou herd or visited the Naskapi Indians. In short, he did not do what he set out to do, which was to follow in his dead friend's footsteps and complete his work.

That Mrs. Hubbard had done. Certainly Wallace was able to supply new information for maps of the country to the north of the Naskaupi, but Mrs. Hubbard's accomplishments were greater and were so recognized by geographical authorities. She had produced the first usable maps of the Naskaupi and George River system, had shown for the first time that Seal Lake and Lake Michikamau were in the same drainage basin, had proved that what geographers had supposed to be two different rivers – the North West and the Naskaupi – were actually one, and had produced notes on the flora and fauna of the region together with written and photographic observations on the lifestyle of the Naskapi Indians. On the other hand, the public found Wallace's book more entertaining than Mrs. Hubbard's partly, perhaps, because he had more adventures and mishaps and employed a more colourful and racy style. His chapter headings certainly suggest adventure; they also suggest a certain amount of fumbling and bumbling: "We Go Astray" . . . "Scouting for the Trail" . . . "We Lose the Trail" . . . "Disaster in the Rapids" . . . "Caught in the Rapids" . . . "Caught in the Artic Ice." Wallace no longer had need of a ghost-writer; he quit his law practice and became a popular story-teller, producing twenty-four more books, most of them for boys, before his death in 1939.

He did not long embarrass Mrs. Hubbard by his presence at George River. To her intense relief, he and Easton decided not to embark on the *Pelican*, which turned up two days after their arrival, but instead headed off for Fort Chimo and further adventures. On October 22, the entire Hubbard party boarded the Hudson's Bay steamer in heavy snow. Ten days later they reached Rigolet, where Mrs. Hubbard picked up a second steamer bound for Quebec. En route, she knitted a pair of mittens for George Elson. "How sorry I will be when we part," he wrote, " . . . I do wish her in every good thing. May God bless her. Dear little woman my best friend in the world and will always be I know."

They had talked of going to England together, but this was only talk. Mrs. Hubbard returned to New York, saw her book serialized in *Harper's*, then published on both sides of the Atlantic. She went to England in 1908 on a lecture tour to promote it. There she met Harold Ellis, the son of a British Member of Parliament. The vision of Laddie was fading more swiftly, perhaps, than she would once have expected. Before the year was out, she and Ellis were married.

But the memory of that wilderness interlude never left her. Like many before her who had experienced the frontier – Jogues, Cameron, Grenfell – she felt its pull, even at a distance of three thousand miles. She longed to return, to experience again those oddly satisfying days when the Unknown unrolled before her in a succession of lonely ridges, blurred by the haze of summer; when the great caribou herd thundered out of the west, so close she could see the velvet of the horns; when the leaping canoes breasted the wild water and she felt the cold spray lashing her face; mornings when the lichens were grizzled with frost; afternoons when the valleys turned misty with the new green of the larches; evenings when the lakes became drops of quicksilver shining through the conifers.

There was, as well, the memory of a special comradeship. She did not lose touch with George Elson. They continued to correspond and to plan a return to the wilderness. It was a long time coming. First there were children – three of them to be raised and schooled in England. Then, in the 1920s, Mina and Harold Ellis were divorced. Another decade went by before she was able to set her plan in motion. By then she was sixty-six. Elson had also been married – not to the white girl of his dreams but to a James Bay

Cree. In 1936 Mina sought him out at Moosonee, and the two old friends set out on a canoe trip up the Moose River. We do not know the details; if she kept a diary it has been lost.

Accounts of her later life are sketchy. During the Second World War, as in the first, she welcomed into her English home a number of Canadian soldiers. One was her grandnephew Edgar Benson, of Kingston, who was to become finance minister in the first Trudeau cabinet. He remembers her as a pleasant old lady, serving tea and crumpets. They did not talk of Labrador.

In old age, her mind began to wander. Her relatives placed her in a nursing home, and there one day, at the age of eighty-six, she went for a stroll. It was half a century since she had walked the long portages of Labrador. Did she recall those days, so far behind her, when she had crossed that desolate, lovely land of rock and rapid, with the shade of her lost Laddie constantly at her side? Probably not; for her thoughts had grown furry, the past was a muddle, the present a confusion. She strayed onto a railway track as she had once strayed up a distant mountainside, but this time there were no strong woodsmen to guide her to safety. A locomotive thundered out of nowhere. She stood, confused, directly in its path, and in the next instant was carried to her rest.

SEVEN

The legend of Almighty Voice

Saskatchewan: 1895

". . . For a man of Almighty Voice's skills, the prairie was a boundless hiding place. To seek him was like searching for a small ketch in the infinity of the ocean. In spite of the coming of the railway, the prairie remained virtually empty of settlers . . . . Roads did not exist. Bridges across the ice-choked rivers were few. Deep coulées, wooded valleys, marshes, and those thick copses of poplars and tangled willows that the prairie people called bluffs provided cover. All this would change within a decade. The North West was about to experience one of history's phenomenal mass movements . . . . But that was still in the future. In 1895 the prairie was silent, as a heath is silent just before a thunderstorm . . . ."

The sorry, garbled story of Almighty Voice, the outlaw Indian, has long since assumed the proportions of a legend. In at least a dozen magazine articles, in several books, in an eloquent short story by Rudy Wiebe, in a play by Len Peterson, in a film by Claude Fournier he is depicted as a tragic hero, an inspiration to his race, the valiant symbol of a people dispossessed. Yet a careful examination of the record suggests that if symbols are needed, far worthier ones exist. It has taken some powerful myth making and a remarkably loose interpretation of the facts to raise Almighty Voice to a prairie pantheon. In their zeal to espouse the Indian's cause, two generations of romantic writers have unwittingly done the Plains Cree a disservice. For surely it is a libel on any race to suggest that a twenty-one-year-old punk is the best it can produce.

Almighty Voice murdered three Mounted Policeman in the performance of their duty, murdered a white civilian and maimed three others. He lured two teen-agers to their deaths – one a child of thirteen – and was the cause of a furious gun battle. If he had been a white kid from the city slums, he would have gone down in history as a mad-dog killer, venerated only by those who insist on making heroes out of people such as Bonnie and Clyde.

But he was an Indian – a "red man" – a romantic figure out of the last frontier, flitting through the prairie grasses, cornered finally in a poplar bluff, facing overwhelming odds not far from the spot where, only a decade before, Riel's ragged band had uttered its final, violent protest. In describing the last stand of Almighty Voice – the last battle between white men and Indians in all of North America – almost every white writer has had to wrestle with his own tribal guilt: the Mounted Police are the bad guys, the symbols of white oppression, while the cornered Indian is the last of a noble race, the champion of a vanished lifestyle. From the record, neither Police nor Indians come off very well; both were prisoners of a frontier image that belonged to an earlier decade. It was this notion – a form of role-playing that transcended reality and common sense – that touched off the tragedy.

One must also consider the role of the name: Kah-kee-say-mane-too-wayo (which some writers, nourished on Longfellow, have romanticized into Gitchie Manitouwayou), a rough, phonetic spelling of a Cree word meaning Voice of the Great Spirit, or simply, Almighty Voice. It was given to him, so it is said, by his grandfather, One Arrow, because he squalled so lustily at birth, but it suggests a mighty orator, a leader, a man to be reckoned with. Even the police were captivated by the name; on the agency rolls he was Jean Baptiste, but as the hunt intensified they reverted to calling him Almighty Voice. Would the legend have been as effective if he had been known as The Rump, as the father of one of his wives was called? The name has become the man, but the man was a tall skinny kid with a parrot's nose, a scarred cheek, and features that the police poster described as "feminine." Much has been made of the only photograph – the sensitive nostrils, the hard line of the mouth, and especially the eyes, burning into the camera. The problem is that no one can be sure that the photograph is authentic. The RCMP archivists are reasonably certain that it is not.

Almighty Voice had the misfortune to be born when the frontier was undergoing a fundamental change. Before he was six the buffalo had vanished and the railway was on its way. In the worst winters the Indians were reduced to eating field mice and grubbing for roots. Herded on to reserves, dependent on a meagre and grudging subsistence from the federal government, they were attempting to become farmers and herdsmen with the help of the Indian department.

Following a treaty in 1876, when Almighty Voice was two, the little band of Swampy Crees under Chief One Arrow retired to a reservation, just sixteen miles square, a few miles east of Batoche on the south side of the South Saskatchewan River. Most of the band fought, somewhat reluctantly, on Riel's side during the Rebellion of 1885 at Fish Creek and Batoche. One Arrow was sentenced to three years in the penitentiary for his part in the uprising. As to whether John Sounding Sky, Almighty Voice's father, actually took part the evidence is conflicting. But there is no doubt that the rebellion and its aftermath formed the backdrop of the boy's childhood and that in the mid-nineties, when he had his moment in history, it was fresh in the minds of both whites and

Indians. For years the Crees suffered the consequences; they were confined to their reservations and deprived of privileges such as selling wood to white settlers. By 1895, the band numbered 108 persons but only twenty were adult males. The families lived in small, flat-roofed shacks, raised cattle, planted hay, oats, wheat, barley, potatoes, and turnips, depending on a reluctant and parsimonious government to supply them with such staples as flour, sugar, beans, and tea. The Indians were considered an inconvenience; the prairie was being prepared for white settlement; that was where the money was to be spent.

Of the families at One Arrow's reserve, that of John Sounding Sky was the only one with a bad reputation at the Duck Lake Indian Agency. On October 18, 1895, Old John, as the police called him, was sentenced to six months hard labour for stealing a coat containing money and personal papers belonging to a white farmer named Couture. His son Almighty Voice, a restless and volatile youth, had several enemies on the reserve because of his consuming but transitory interest in young girls, whom he would purchase, marry Indian style, and subsequently abandon. By the summer of 1895, he had gone through three and was casting his eyes upon a fourth.

He was sixteen when he married the first, the thirteen-year-old daughter of an elder named Nepean; he kept her for one summer. The following year, he bought himself a second teen-ager, the daughter of Kapahoo, her price being a small steer. When, a year later, he tried to return her and get the steer back, he found that the child's shrewd old mother, knowing his fickle reputation, had reduced the animal to dried meat. His third marriage, in 1895, was to the daughter of The Rump, but that too was faltering. This flouting of white convention was too much for the Indian agent at Duck Lake, R.S. McKenzie, who tried to compel Almighty Voice to return to his first love, wed her in an orthodox manner, and remain monogamous. Almighty Voice, whose religion was recorded on the agency list as "pagan," retorted that he "wouldn't live with that offal." McKenzie warned that if he attempted to keep more women he would be arrested and punished. Almighty Voice rebelled. In the old days men had taken as many as six wives. Why should he not have two or more if he chose?

Almighty Voice threatened to kill McKenzie, but before he could make good that threat fate intervened in the person of an angry brother-in-law. Nepean's son Laroque, whose sister was the first of the jilted wives, went to the Mounted Police on Treaty Day, October 22, 1895 to inform on Almighty Voice, charging that he had broken the law the previous June by stealing and killing a steer.

The motive for this minor misdemeanour, which touched off the tragedy and led, obliquely, to ten deaths, has in the hands of the myth makers been used to justify much of what followed. It has been written again and again that the steer was a government-owned animal lent to Almighty Voice as breeding stock and that he had asked permission of the Indian agent to kill it in order to make broth for his brother's starving child. When the callous agent refused, so the legend has it, Almighty Voice took the law into his own hands to save his nephew's life. But, as the records of the Indian department make quite clear, Almighty Voice's action was anything but planned. The steer belonged not to the government but to a white settler named Parenteau who lived several miles away. Almighty Voice and his seventeen-year-old crony, Flying Sound, found it wandering in the woods near the Minichinas Hills, shot it, and shared it. The incident would have gone unnoticed had not Laroque used it to exact revenge.

McKenzie, the agent and justice of the peace, did not have time to dispose of the case on Treaty Day. The two Indians were held at the Mounted Police guardhouse at Duck Lake until the following morning, when a summary trial was scheduled. At worst, they could expect a few days in jail, at best a suspended sentence, which was, in fact, what Flying Sound received.

And that would have been that had it not been for the unfortunate dereliction of Constable R. Casimir Dickson.

Here begins the second myth on which the case for Almighty Voice rests. Dickson is cast as the villain of the legend – the vicious, racist Mountie taunting a poor savage into a state of panic. Certainly, Dickson's service record was abysmal. In just eighteen months on the Force he had collected ten infractions on his default sheet: making a false statement, absent from fatigue duty, dirty on church parade, loitering during stable duty, careless during riding, using threatening language, neglecting his horse and blaming others for it. A picture emerges of a slovenly, careless, somewhat lazy man. It is, however, belied by his appearance, for Constable Dickson was a muscular thirty-year-old who stood six feet five inches in his socks – the perfect image of the idealized Mountie, but one that does not match reality, for the police of the nineties were of medium size, their average height being five feet nine and a half inches. Nor were they all perfect examples of what Mounted Policemen were believed to be, as Dickson's record shows. But whatever he may have been, Dickson was not the tart-tongued bigot that legend has made of him.

This misconception is the basis of much of what has been written of Almighty Voice since the 1920s, when that singular journalist who called himself Chief Buffalo Child Long Lance first published the tale in *Maclean's*. Long Lance, who passed himself off as a Blackfoot chief, was actually Sylvester C. Long, a mixed-blood – part white, part Negro, and part Catawba – from the black ghetto of Winston-Salem, North Carolina. For more than half a century a succession of writers has swallowed whole his story of Almighty Voice's escape from prison, a story he claimed to have heard from the lips of the young man's mother, Spotted Calf. But the Long Lance narrative is studded with so many errors, easily established from the record, that it is not possible to give credence to his account.

The story he told was this: Dickson, as a joke, taunted Almighty Voice through an interpreter, telling him that he was going to hang for killing the steer. He did this, he said, to scare him. Almighty Voice, believing that his life was in jeopardy, made up his mind to escape. To forestall this the police had chained him to a heavy iron ball. Dickson was relieved at midnight by a constable who fell asleep, allowing the Indian to pick up the heavy ball, tiptoe to the table, reach across the sleeper, steal the keys, unlock the manacle, and make his escape.

The more easily verified errors here suggest the casualness of Long Lance's investigation. There were three Indians in the guardroom, not one, these being Flying Sound, charged with the same offence as Almighty Voice, and an Indian woman charged with the theft of some blankets and saucers from the police barracks (she was, by coincidence, the wife of the same Laroque who had informed on Almighty Voice). None of the three was shackled – in fact, the sergeant in charge, who did not believe any of the trio dangerous, was later disciplined for not shackling his prisoners. Dickson did not arrive in the guardroom for his two hour tour of duty until after midnight, when all three Indians were asleep. His own story was that he left the room at 2:00 a.m. and went upstairs to awaken his relief, Constable Andrew O'Kelly. He was absent, he said, for one minute and thirty seconds, during which time Almighty Voice picked up his keys, unlocked the door, and vanished. His superiors thought it more likely that the prisoner escaped when the notoriously careless Dickson was asleep on duty. Escape he did, no matter how, and Dickson was for it: he was subsequently sentenced to two months hard labour and dismissed from the Force.

The astonishing aspect of this trivial escapade is that Long Lance's tale of racist goading should be believed. And other writers have embellished it. Dickson is supposed to have pointed out the window to a place where workmen were building some scaffolding to repair the barracks (at *midnight*?) and told his prisoner that this was a gallows being constructed for him. Thus, in seeming to give Almighty Voice a motive for murder, the romantics succeeded in libelling him and, by implication, all of his fellow Crees. For only a moron or a naked savage plucked from the wilderness would have believed such a trumped-up tale. Almighty Voice was neither. Reckless he certainly was, and impulsive, but not stupid. Nor was he ignorant of the law; he knew that cattle killing was a minor offence; he had just that week seen his father given six months on a more serious charge. He walked out of the guardroom for the simplest of reasons: the key to the door lay on the table within easy reach; its guardian was either asleep or absent. It was an act of pure bravado, and Almighty Voice could not resist it. His companions could, however. He urged them to flee with him; they chose to stay. The following morning both were freed.

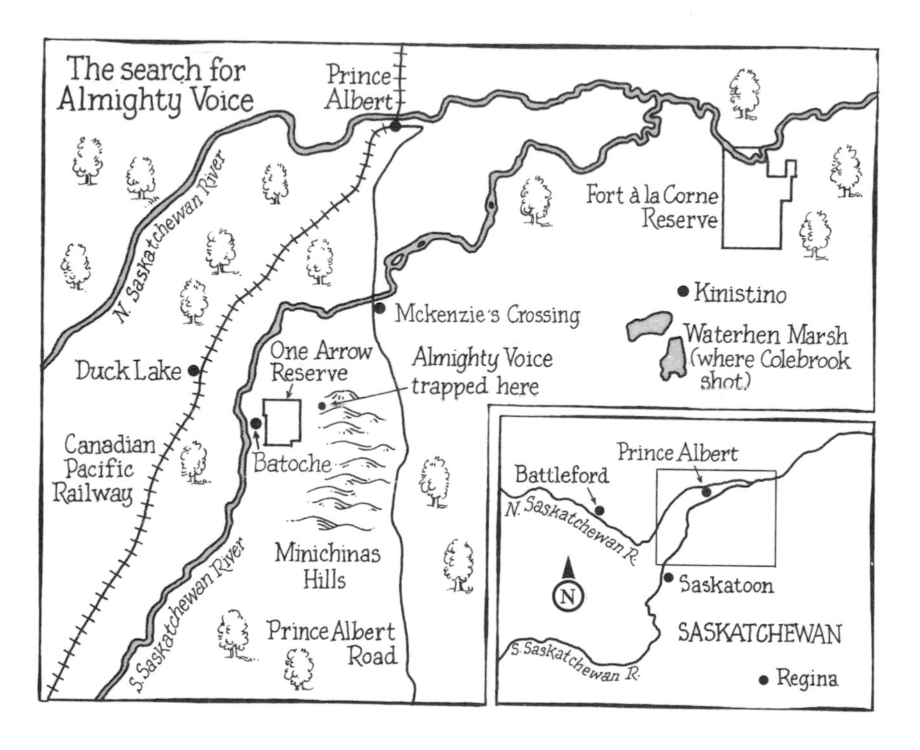

Almighty Voice, meanwhile, swam the South Saskatchewan, a considerable feat, for that broad river was a mass of floating ice. Then he headed for the La Corne Reservation to pick up his newest love, Small Face, the thirteen-year-old granddaughter of one of the tribal elders, Old Dust. Sgt. Colin Campbell Colebrook, a thirty-three-year-old Englishman, was dispatched to find the fugitive and bring him back.

It is important to note, in the light of what followed, that Sergeant Colebrook (whose given names suggest a parental reverence for the hero of the Indian Mutiny and the Crimean War) was a policeman by sufferance. A veteran of fourteen years on the Force, he had become accustomed to three-year tours of duty. But his latest re-engagement, beginning on October 16, 1895, just one week before he set out on the trail of Almighty Voice, was for twelve months only. There was a cloud over Colebrook; its presence is implicit in the letter that the commissioner, L.W. Herchmer, had written to Colebrook's commanding officer: "I have talked the matter over with Inspector Strickland and have concluded to re-engage him [Colebrook] for one year. He can remain at Batoche if you are satisfied but should be cautioned to attend to his duties."

There it was – the note of suspicion. Colebrook's record was checkered. Apart from a number of minor breaches of discipline, there were several major complaints against him. He was an aggressive policeman, a little too aggressive to suit the Mountie image. In August of 1888, a complaint had been lodged against him for using "unnecessary violence" in arresting four men in a private railway car on a gambling charge. A year or so later that aggressiveness paid off when he captured "in a very plucky manner" an American gunfighter wanted in Montana for the murder of six cowhands. Yet this, too, was to rebound against him. Urged on by a U.S. senator, Colebrook committed an unpardonable breach of Mounted Police etiquette by insistently demanding the five-hundred-dollar reward posted for the gunman's capture. It was explained to him that since the reward was good only if the arrest was made on American soil, he was not eligible. Whereupon Colebrook, "in a most impudent letter" (Herchmer's words), threatened to go to the U.S. president. The commissioner ordered him to headquarters and gave him a dressing down. In his view, Colebrook's actions were an example of his "gross insubordination and cussedness"; for months he had been "a perfectly worthless sergeant." Nevertheless he remained a sergeant until the fall of 1890, when he was broken to corporal as a result of a series of misdemeanours involving being absent without leave. He managed to rise again to sergeant and for the past three years had kept his name off the defaulters' sheet. At least one citizen had written to headquarters, praising him for his swift apprehension of two horse thieves. The picture that emerges is that of a career policeman, determined to make good in spite of his superiors' doubts and careful not to overstep the line.

Colebrook spent six days searching for Almighty Voice, mainly in the area of the One Arrow reserve. He did not lack informants among the embittered relatives of the escaped man's first wife. On Friday, October 25, Colebrook learned from one of them that his quarry had left the reservation and was heading east toward Kinistino. Colebrook hired a local Métis, François Dumont, as a guide and interpreter and set off to track his man. He did not catch up with him until early the following Tuesday, just as Almighty Voice and Small Face were breaking camp after breakfast.

The Indian had just shot a prairie chicken. Small Face was mounted on a pony nearby. At Colebrook's order, Dumont shouted to the pair in Cree not to run. Small Face stopped, but Almighty Voice said to her: "Come on, they are only trying to deceive us." As Dumont and Colebrook trotted toward the couple, Almighty Voice picked up a double-barrelled shotgun and told the interpreter to warn the policeman that he intended to shoot him. At this, Small Face began to cry, urging her lover not to fire.

Colebrook was some twenty feet from his man. The Indian was on his knees, attempting to load his gun. Colebrook hesitated, then moved forward. As the policeman came on, Almighty Voice backed away toward a small copse of poplars, dropping to one knee from time to time to finish capping his weapon, and calling out in Cree: "Go away! Go away!" Small Face had not budged. The policeman moved past her. Dumont sat his horse some yards to one side.

Several writers in describing this scene have reported that Colebrook, in true Mountie fashion, kept repeating to himself, "I've got to do my duty! I've got to do my duty!" But there are in existence the detailed and sworn statements of the only eyewitnesses present – the girl and Dumont – and they testify that what he actually said was "Come on, old boy . . . come on, old boy" – the master coaxing the errant spaniel.

Thus they faced each other, two men who seemed perfectly cast by fate for their roles: the policeman in his cloak – swarthy features, small moustache, drooping eyes, jug ears, close-cropped hair, almost the ideal Mounted Police height – and the Indian in his blanket and leggings – long hair, Roman nose, fox face, six feet tall in his moccasins.

Both were captives of history. Behind Almighty Voice hovered the ghosts of those who had bested the regulars in the coulées of

Fish Creek and Cut Knife Hill and who had died in the rifle pits at Batoche. He had been raised on stories of the rebellion and of the old days when his people freely roamed the plains, took as many wives as they wished, shot the buffalo without a by-your-leave, and needed not the white man's pass to leave the village on a mission of romance or adventure. Now authority hemmed him in, and the man in the navy blue cloak symbolized that authority.

Also, there was the girl. The girl was crying. Could a man of Almighty Voice's temperament lay down his weapon and meekly surrender while the girl was watching?

Back of Colebrook were the examples of Steele, who had stared down Crowfoot, and Walsh, who had seized Sitting Bull by the breech clout, and all the other policemen who by the magic of the scarlet uniform had worked their will on armed braves and sullen medicine men. Colebrook's right hand held the reins of his horse; his left gripped a small pistol in his pocket – a personal weapon; he had lent his service revolver to Dumont. He did not draw his gun; the Force's tradition was inviolable, and Colebrook knew only too well the penalty for "unnecessary violence." As Herchmer was to explain, Colebrook was following tradition; the Force would "always cause our men to risk their lives in making an arrest even in the case of notorious criminals rather than run the risk of being tried for manslaughter." This was not Tombstone or Dodge City, and Colebrook was determined to go by the book.

His horse reared, almost throwing him, then balked. The sergeant forced it forward at a slow walk. "Come on, old boy," he coaxed again. Almighty Voice had backed into the shelter of the poplars. Dumont, some distance back, could see only the double barrel of the gun emerging from the underbrush. Suddenly there was a flash and a report. Colebrook, shot through the neck, an artery severed, died instantly, his body tumbling to the ground. Dumont rode immediately to the nearest house and dispatched a man for the closest police constable. Small Face dug her heels into her pony and picked up Almighty Voice. "Now, indeed, they won't leave me alone for what I have done," he said. He took the pony, leaving his bride to walk back to her reservation, and vanished into the prairie.

Colebrook's corpse, accompanied by his grieving wife, was taken to Prince Albert. The body looked so natural, frozen in its coffin, that "the poor creature broke down completely and spoke to it." The prisoners in the Prince Albert jail were detailed to hack a grave out of the frosted turf; one of them, by bitter coincidence, was the unfortunate Constable Dickson, now serving his two months at hard labour. He protested vigorously that this was "a piece of refined cruelty worthy of Russia," but it did no good.

As soon as the news of Colebrook's murder was released the press began to hint at widespread native insurrection. The Regina *Standard*'s headline took up more column inches than its one-paragraph account of the killing. "ARE WE ON THE VERGE OF ANOTHER INDIAN OUTBREAK?" it cried.

The Mounted Police were concerned but for a different reason. It was unthinkable that anyone, Indian or white, should get away with the murder of one of their own. "Keep every available man out and give the murderer no chance to rest," the assistant commissioner, John McIllree, wired Inspector George Moffat at Prince Albert. That was an order more easily given than obeyed. For a man of Almighty Voice's skills, the prairie was a boundless hiding place. To seek him was like searching for a small ketch in the infinity of the ocean. In spite of the coming of the railway, the prairie remained virtually empty of settlers; in all the North West there were fewer than sixty-five thousand whites. Roads did not exist. Bridges across the ice-choked rivers were few. Deep coulées, wooded valleys, marshes, and those thick copses of poplars and tangled willows that the prairie people called bluffs provided cover.

All this would change within a decade. The North West was about to experience one of history's phenomenal mass movements. A million settlers would invade the prairies, on the heels of Clifford Sifton's astonishing publicity campaign, to transform the lifestyle and change the scenery. But that was still in the future. In 1895 the prairie was silent, as a heath is silent just before a thunderstorm.

The Indians were silent, too. The reservations acted as sanctuaries for the fugitive. Almighty Voice's enemies might give him away on a minor offence but not on a hanging charge. The native community closed ranks; Almighty Voice became invisible.

Although in this instance the police and the Indians were adversaries, there was a bond between them; they were all creatures of the frontier, and they shared a common plight: the federal government treated them as expensive nuisances. During the nineteen months when Almighty Voice was on the run, the Force was being reduced. From a strength of one thousand men in 1885 it was cut back in 1896 to seven hundred and fifty. The following year it was cut again, to five hundred, and its budget was slashed from $530,000 to $385,000. The Indians faced a similar circumstance. That same year, the budget for Indian affairs was again reduced, even though the treaty Indians were existing just above starvation level. In 1897, when Almighty Voice was still at large, the Saskatchewan *Herald*, editorializing on the newest economy scheme of the Indian department, reported that "the Indians have been notified that this is the last winter in which rations will be issued to them. The amount being given to them at present has been scientifically gauged as the least that will keep body and soul together and it will go hard with the Indians if these are further reduced." In short, both police and natives were seen by Ottawa as part of the past; the future belonged to the settlers. Implicit in the reports of Almighty Voice's trackers is the frequent shortage of sound horses and men. "We have traced our man up to this place but are terribly handicapped," Inspector John B. Allan wrote to his superior, Moffat, from Fort La Corne, early in the search. "Our horses are poor stuff with three exceptions . . . it seems everything has been against us." A year later, with the search still on, Corporal J.W. Bowdridge complained from Salt Lake that he could find work for four men and still not have too many.

Travel conditions were as bad as any the police had encountered in the North West. "Terrible country," in Allan's phrase. Allan, who liked to refer to himself as "Bronco Jack," described it in detail: "We started with flat sleds to search the hills North of Basin Lake, this being the range of heavily timbered hills where Almighty Voice could be hidden without fear of approach from any white man . . . and after 3 days of hard travelling, encountered such difficulties as must be looked for in crossing a range of thickly wooded hills, and in some instances very precipitous descents into the valleys, where the overflowings from numerous springs and some beaver dams, with dense brush to be cut through, we reached the valley of the Carrot River. . . ." Bowdridge was not quite so matter-of-fact: "This is the most difficult country I have ever been over," he wrote in his report of October 21, 1896, near the head of the Howder Valley. "It is impossible to get a horse off a walk and in a great many places we had to dismount and lead our horses through the slash and brush." In March, 1897, another discouraged searcher, Constable Hildyard, reported that he had travelled four weeks without encountering a single human, native or white: "The country I have worked over is extremely rough and apparently inaccessible in places and no doubt more likely spots have been unobserved by me; indeed it would require many months of very hard work before I could truthfully say the district has been thoroughly searched. I am not easily discouraged, but having devoted the whole winter to this work, without gaining the slightest clue, I consider it utterly useless to continue the search. . . ."

Meanwhile, a nervous public, haunted by the memory of Riel and his Cree allies, had been demanding action. The North West

Mounted Police came under criticism for failing to apprehend the murderer. McKenzie, the Indian agent, wrote to the Indian commissioner in Regina in February, 1896, that "since Colebrook's murder there is a different manner to be noticed in many of the Indians, one of independence and defiance, which was not noticeable formerly, and the half-breeds are not backward in pointing out to them that for all the trouble the Government takes to try to capture a murderer, there would not appear to be much risk in shooting a white man." The following day, the Prince Albert *Advocate* fanned the embers of panic:

"We do not wish to pose as alarmist, but simply by observation, and from various reliable sources gather the fact that the Indians are in an ugly mood, and . . . are now openly boasting that an Indian can shoot a white man and nothing is done or said by the government to bring him to justice. They are just awaiting the advent of spring . . . to sally forth and avenge supposed wrongs on a few white settlers who live nearest them. . . . "

There is no evidence that any such uprising was contemplated. The only suggestion of revenge was a remark attributed to Almighty Voice's father, now nearing the end of his six-month sentence, to the effect that he would get even with the Couture family, whose evidence had sent him to jail for theft. The Coutures were reported to have fled from their farm, but that story turned out to be false. The only man to decamp was François Dumont, the interpreter, who had been present at Colebrook's murder, and who felt himself safer in another district.

Both the Indian affairs commissioner in Regina and the police themselves did their best to prod Ottawa into posting a reward for Almighty Voice. McKenzie, the Indian agent, told his superior in Regina that if a reward were not posted "I have not the slightest doubt you will hear of other murders being committed. . . . " But Ottawa was reluctant and Ottawa was slow. At last a bounty of five hundred dollars was offered for anyone who could provide the police with information leading to the capture of the wanted man. After that there was no dearth of reports. Indians and half-breeds came forward to say that they had seen him, but none could or would lead the police to his hiding place.

In fact, while his pursuers were fanning out from the Canadian border to the edges of Lesser Slave Lake, Almighty Voice had never strayed far from his own reserve. He had spent the first winter trapping with a band of Wood Crees from the north and had headed home for the summer. From the root cellar under the floor of his father's house, he tunnelled a dugout where he hid while the Mounted Police searched the reserve. His mother, Spotted Calf, moved her bed over the trap door to the root cellar and sat on it, her ample skirt covering the opening, whenever the house was searched. On one occasion, the fugitive even visited his father at the Prince Albert barracks. Twice a day, John Sounding Sky had the job of driving the manure wagon from the stables to the dump; there the two met. The young man asked his father what he should do. Stay in hiding, the old man advised; later on you must make your own decisions; you are a man now.

The break in the case did not come until the afternoon of May 26, 1897, when two half-breed farmers, Napoleon and David Venne, spotted three Indians who seemed to be trying to run off some of their cattle near the Jungle Lake Hills, some ten miles east of Batoche. The Vennes cut them off and managed to accost one of them, whose horse had caught a foot in a gopher hole and thrown him. He was a thirteen-year-old Salteaux named Standing-in-the-Sky. Under the Vennes' questioning he identified one of his comrades as "Tupean" or "Dublin," a corruption of the baptismal name, Jean Pierre, the Crees being unable to pronounce the letters *r* and *j*. The Salteaux stubbornly refused to identify the third man, but since Standing-in-the-Sky was Almighty Voice's cousin and Tupean was the son of The Rump, and therefore a brother-in-law, the Vennes were suspicious. The third man must be either Almighty Voice or his father, and if the latter, could the wanted man be far away? Spurred on by hope of a five-hundred-dollar windfall, David Venne rode to the police post at Batoche, arriving half an hour before midnight. Corporal Bowdridge, a thirty-nine-year-old Irishman and militia veteran, wasted no time. He phoned Inspector James Wilson at Duck Lake, asking for reinforcements; then he and his constable, Ferris, headed for the Venne ranch. There they swore in Napoleon Venne as a special constable. His job was to guide them to the camp of One Arrow's band, who were only a few miles away gathering seneca roots to sell to traders.

The three men located the camp at eight the next morning. The atmosphere was distinctly odd. The fugitive's father trotted into the camp just ahead of them and then moved off to the far end. Venne was able to identify him as one of the trio he had seen the previous day. A friend revealed that the young Salteaux boy had been camped with Old John the previous night and had left after trading his horse for a rifle. Bowdridge moved with caution, talking casually to the Indians, making notes, counting the men and the carts, and trying not to excite mistrust. He had, at the outset, sent Ferris back up the trail to guide in the reinforcements from Duck Lake. Three hours passed, but the extra men did not arrive.

Bowdridge grew worried. The Indians were breaking camp, drifting away. Suddenly the atmosphere changed. Venne, from the vantage point of a cart, whispered that he had just seen some Indians in a poplar bluff not far away and that when they spotted him, they had dropped quickly out of sight.

"Take things quietly," said Bowdridge. "Do as I do." He had already unsaddled his horse to allay suspicion. Now, pretending that he was going to water the animal, he put the saddle back and moved off down the trail, circling to the top of a small hill where he could command the bluff. He told Venne to make his way to a second hill on the far side to cut off escape and to wait for the reinforcements. But as Venne rounded the poplars, he heard a rustle behind him, then a shot, and his right arm went numb. He tried to return the fire, but the bone of his arm had been shattered. He urged his horse to run, the Indians in pursuit. A second bullet passed through the brim of his Stetson. He spurred the horse toward Bowdridge, who took him into the camp and dressed his wound with flour and water. Bowdridge left Venne in the care of an Indian friend and galloped off to find the reinforcements and send a message through to Wilson at Duck Lake. There was no doubt now that one of the Indians on the bluff was Almighty Voice.

At that point – noon on May 27 – events were at a standstill. Almighty Voice was still at large; nobody was on his trail. Nine hours would elapse before news of the shooting would reach Duck Lake. Though distances were short by modern standards, all travel was by horseback, foot, or cart. Bowdridge lost his bearings and did not reach the Venne ranch until after one o'clock. Nor had he located the extra men, and by this time his horse was exhausted. David Venne was dispatched to the nearest telephone at Batoche with orders to call Wilson and order a doctor for his brother. Bowdridge, on a fresh horse, galloped back to the site of the Indian camp, where he caught up with Ferris and the extra constables. He took two men with him and set off after the fugitive Indians. Late that afternoon he ran into John Sounding Sky and arrested him as an accessory before the fact in the shooting of Venne. Old John was placed in irons, under guard. Bowdridge insisted on relieving the sentries during the night "as it was pretty hard work on the men to keep awake after being in the saddle all night." Bowdridge himself had gone without sleep for thirty-six hours and for most of that time had also been in the saddle.

At nine that night, Wilson at Duck Lake learned of the shooting. He alerted his superiors at Prince Albert and set off at once with a sergeant and two constables to rendezvous with Bowdridge.

At Prince Albert, the news interrupted a police smoker and concert, which had followed an afternoon cricket match between the police and townspeople. Within an hour Bronco Jack Allan left the post with a sergeant, C.C. Raven, a corporal, C.H.S. Hockin, and ten men. His orders were to ride through the night and rendezvous with Wilson in the Minichinas Hills, the "beautiful bare hills," not far from the One Arrow reserve. Allan was a tough, competent policeman with a remarkable history: he had served in the Fenian raids and in the American Civil War; he had taken part in the Gordon relief expedition to the Sudan and the Saskatchewan rebellion. As did many of his colleagues, he came of military stock; his father had been at Waterloo.

Shortly before nine the following morning, one of Allan's men spotted three figures running through the underbrush toward a poplar bluff in the lee of one of the beautiful bare hills. He thought at first they were Indians but decided they were deer. Bronco Jack thought otherwise: deer would have stayed in the open. The bluff, misty green with the new leaves of spring, lay in a hollow. It was cucumber-shaped, one hundred and fifty yards long and fifty yards thick, a dense cluster of skinny aspens surmounting a braided tangle of willows, so thickly massed and intertwined that it was not possible to see into their depths for more than a few feet.

Bronco Jack moved with a soldier's dispatch. He ordered his men to dismount and enter the bluff from the northern and western sides while he rode to the eastern end to prevent the fugitives from escaping when the others flushed them.

Sergeant Raven, carbine at the ready, entered the thicket with one constable. The others ringed the edges. Raven had penetrated fifty yards when, through a narrow opening in the underbrush, he saw two Indians armed with rifles crouched not twenty yards away. They fired at once, and the police returned their fire. The Indians, unhurt, melted deeper into the underbrush, but Raven could not follow; he had a bullet in the thigh and another in the groin. He called out to Allan, to warn him that the Indians were heading his way. Bronco Jack drew his revolver, flourished it, and galloped as close as he could to the edge of the woods. Suddenly, an Indian broke cover and fired. Bronco Jack fired back. By this time he had galloped past his quarry. Now, turning his horse about, he saw the three Indians in a small patch of willows directly in front of him – Almighty Voice standing upright in the centre, Winchester raised, the other two crouched on either side, a prairie triptych frozen for an instant in time. Bronco Jack spurred his horse forward to ride them down; Almighty Voice fired on the

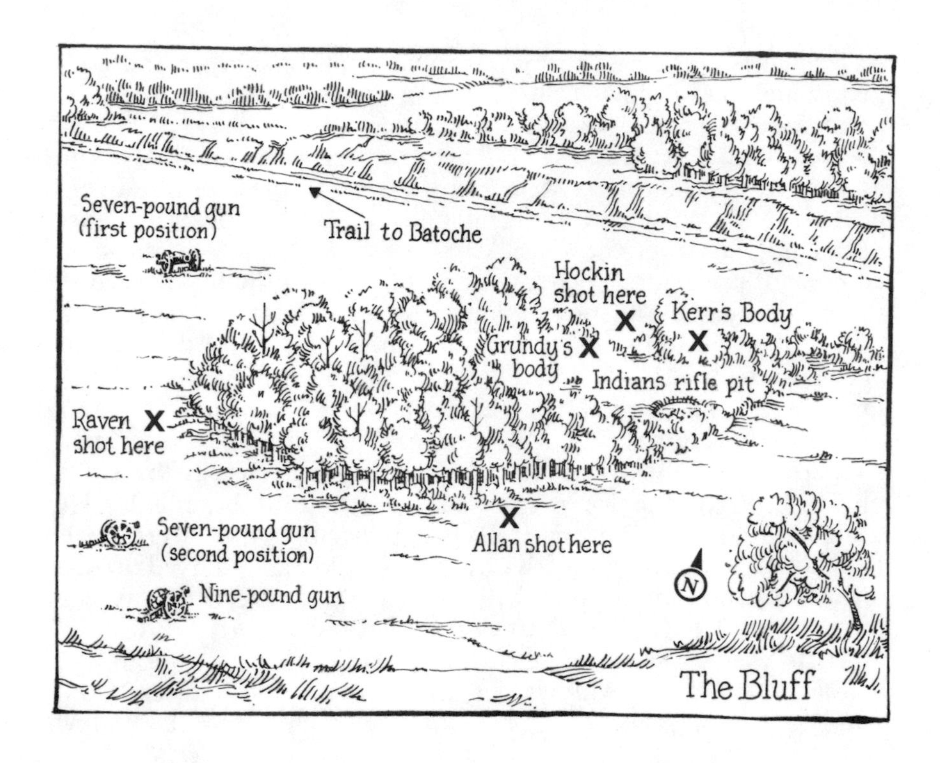

instant; the triptych dissolved as the policeman, his right arm shattered, tumbled from his horse, his revolver clattering to the ground. He dragged himself toward the shelter of a nearby tree stump and tried, unsuccessfully, to stand. Almighty Voice, not ten feet away, raised his Winchester. Bronco Jack, helpless, waited for the shot. It did not come. Instead, the Indian pointed to the policeman's gun belt: he wanted the ammunition. But now the wounded Sergeant Raven arrived with another policeman and opened fire. Almighty Voice vanished into the murk of the bluff.

Raven was certain that Bronco Jack Allan was dead. He ordered some of the men to carry the body to a wagon and then turned his attention to the bluff. "To capture Almighty Voice," he later recalled, "had become an obsession. . . . "

From within the bluff there emanated a succession of "the most blood curdling shrieks." The Indians were engaged in a war dance to keep up their spirits. The police fired into the trees; the shrieking stopped.

Bronco Jack was not dead. In fact, Bronco Jack would live to be ninety. Half conscious and in pain, he put Corporal Hockin in charge of the detachment with orders to set fire to the copse to drive the Indians into the open. At the same time he sent another man to Batoche to wire news of the gun fight to Superintendent

Sévère Gagnon at Prince Albert. Only then did he allow himself to be conveyed to Norman McKenzie's farmhouse at the crossing of the South Saskatchewan River.

At this point, twenty-one Mounted Policemen and one scout were engaged in the attempt to bring Almighty Voice to justice. It would not be enough. When Gagnon received the news of the most recent gun battle, he set off from Prince Albert with eight more men, including a police surgeon and a hospital steward. They reached McKenzie's Crossing late in the afternoon, bringing to twenty-nine the complement of men detailed to capture the Indians. But even that would not be enough. At the farmhouse the surgeon attended to Bronco Jack's mangled arm, digging out a saucerful of bone splinters. There was no anaesthetic; the surgeon suggested brandy. Bronco Jack waved it away and gritted his teeth. The operation took an hour. When it was done Bronco Jack allowed that he might smoke a pipeful of tobacco.

In the meantime, Corporal Hockin and his men, stationed at the bluff, were becoming edgy. Hockin had tried to fire the underbrush and failed, because the wood was too green. The weather was overcast; there would be no moon that night. The reinforcements had not yet arrived and Hockin did not have enough men to surround the bluff in a sufficiently tight ring to prevent the fugitives from slipping away in the dark. Shortly after 6:00 p.m. he made a rash decision: he would lead a force of nine men to storm the bluff while stationing the remainder on the perimeter to apprehend or shoot the fugitives if they tried to break out.

Hockin, too, came of military stock. An ex-British Army officer, he was the son of an admiral. At thirty-seven he was a seasoned veteran. The Indians had proved themselves to be crack shots. Their position in that labyrinth of willows and thick grasses was virtually impregnable. Casualties were inevitable. Hockin knew all this, knew that he and several of his men would probably be corpses before the hour was out; yet he could not face the alternative – that the Indians would escape again, that the Force, which had been under so much criticism for its failure to round them up, would be held in contempt. A more senior man might have been more cautious, but Allan was out of action and so was Raven, who had joined him at the makeshift infirmary at McKenzie's Crossing.

Five civilians had arrived from Duck Lake, including the Crown timber agent, a man named Cook, and Ernest Grundy, a former Mounted Policeman, now postmaster and an old friend of Colebrook's, anxious to avenge his murder. Grundy and Cook volunteered to join the storming party. Bowdridge, who had now arrived, was stationed with Ferris at the south. At 6:30 Hockin gave the order, and his men, walking in line at intervals of eight yards, entered the bluff from the west.

The line, with Hockin at its centre, moved through the bluff without seeing any sign of the Indians. The men wheeled about and slowly worked their way through a second time – nothing. They had now swept two-thirds of the woods; the densest section lay to the south. Once again the line wheeled and moved into the underbrush.

The Indians were waiting for them. In the tradition of Gabriel Dumont, Riel's great general at Fish Creek, they had scratched a rifle pit out of a depression in the ground, using an old butcher's knife blade tied to a stick and their bare hands. They could hear the rustling in the willows as the line of policemen approached, but they could not see them until their attackers were almost upon them.

The police were tense, revolvers and carbines at the ready. They knew now that their prey must be close ahead; they had searched the entire bluff save for this braided mass in the southwest corner. Suddenly there was a shot and a cry. Grundy, the postmaster, staggered back, screaming with pain, and fell to the ground dead, shot through the abdomen. The police line dropped. Constable Andrew O'Kelly spotted an Indian creeping through the brush directly ahead of the dead man. He fired. The Indian lay still, only his toes twitching. O'Kelly thought – wrongly, it turned out – that he had killed him. Fifteen yards farther on, he spotted the pit with the head of another Indian poking above it. He shouted a warning, but as he did another shot rang out, and Hockin dropped his carbine, clutched his chest and cried: "Oh, God, I'm shot!" Three of his men crawled forward and dragged him out of the bluff.

The others continued to fire in the direction of the pit. The Indians fired back. A bullet cut through the left shoulder of Cook's coat. Bits of poplar bark and splinters of willow flew about as bullets thudded through the trees. O'Kelly, flat on his stomach, urged his neighbour, Constable J. R. Kerr, to keep his head down; but Kerr, his pistol emptied, raised himself up and asked O'Kelly to pass him some more ammunition. As he reached for it a bullet struck him in the heart. The situation was hopeless. All the police were out of ammunition. Slowly and with great caution the survivors eased themselves backward out of the bluff, leaving two corpses behind.

Meanwhile, Bowdridge and the others were trying to carry the mortally wounded Hockin to the safety of a buckboard. They did so under heavy fire. One bullet struck the wheel of the cart, another slightly wounded one of the civilians in the heel. Hockin died the following morning, the sixth and last Mounted Policeman to be killed by an Indian. Almighty Voice had the dubious distinction of being responsible for three of these deaths.

Gagnon and his eight reinforcements arrived just as O'Kelly and the remaining members of the storming party eased their way out of the bluff under covering fire. The rest of Inspector Wilson's party arrived at midnight. There were now twenty-six policemen and several civilians on the scene. There would be no sleep. It was imperative that the Indians be kept imprisoned within their poplar fortress until more reinforcements arrived. A cordon was thrown around the bluff, the men staying in as close as possible during the night and moving out of rifle shot at dawn. At midnight, there came a curious call from within the poplars. It was Almighty Voice: "Brothers, we have fought a good fight. Send me food. I am starving. Tomorrow we will fight again!" The answer was gunfire.

At Regina, earlier that evening, a gala ball was in progress at the headquarters of the North West Mounted Police. In a flag-draped setting, women in long satin dresses with puffed sleeves swirled about with officers in blue and gold and NCOs in scarlet. The occasion was the departure, the following day, of the Mounted Police contingent to attend the Jubilee celebration in London of Queen Victoria. One is reminded of the eve of Waterloo. Just before midnight, as the band was playing "Tommy Atkins," Sergeant J.W. Heffernan, in charge of the town section, his face grave, entered the ballroom and handed a telegram to Herchmer. The commissioner, a stocky figure with a square face and a grizzled beard, walked to the centre of the dance floor, held up his hand to stop the music, and spoke: "I have here a telegram stating that Captain Allan, whom you all know, has been shot and seriously wounded and some others have been killed by the Indians near Duck Lake. The Police have other things to do besides dancing. The rigs will be at the door to take you to your homes."

Herchmer and his men worked through the night. At six the following morning, a Canadian Pacific special puffed out of the Regina station for Duck Lake, carrying Assistant Commissioner John McIllree, twenty-five men, thirteen horses, and a nine-pound Maxim gun.

Herchmer was taking no chances on another Indian uprising. He shot off telegrams to the commanders of the Police posts at Maple Creek, Lethbridge, Calgary, Edmonton, Macleod, and Battleford:

"In attempting to arrest Almighty Voice, three men are killed and Insp. Allan and two men are wounded and one Indian killed. They are surrounded but Duck Lake Indians excited. Explain matters to Indians and get ready in case of further trouble."

Herchmer ordered the Prince Albert division to ship half a ton of bully beef to the bluff plus a half ton of hard tack from Winnipeg. From Duck Lake he ordered half a ton of oats for the horses, fifty pounds of bread, and forty pounds of fresh beef for the men. He placed an order for an additional one hundred shells for the Maxim gun and ordered Gagnon at Prince Albert to swear in as many special constables as needed. And he asked permission of the Indian department in Ottawa to swear in fifty Blackfoot and Blood Indian scouts as well, for service in the north. The Blackfoot and the Bloods had taken no part in the Rebellion of '85.

In Prince Albert, Gagnon swore in thirty special constables from the ranks of the Prince Albert Volunteers, a unit formed during the Riel uprising. He also commandeered an old brass seven-pounder, which had long since been condemned, and dispatched it to the scene. By the time the Prince Albert Volunteers (their number increased to thirty-four) arrived at 7:30 that Saturday evening, the gun was in position. The low hill above the bluff was dotted with Indians from One Arrow's reserve, watching silently. Among them was Almighty Voice's mother, Spotted Calf, who, it is said, sang the plaintive notes of the Cree death song to her son in the bluff.

The Volunteers were under the command of a local lawyer, James McKay, who had been a Police scout in 1885 and was now something of a politician, having been narrowly defeated for the federal parliament the previous year by none other than the Prime Minister, Sir Wilfrid Laurier. Soon after McKay and his men arrived, the seven-pounder went into action, firing seven shells. When the first shell exploded, in the vicinity of the rifle pit, one of the Indians rushed to the edge of the brush and then retreated. There was desultory fire from the bluff, then silence.

Two hours later, Assistant Commissioner McIllree, a fierce-looking man with a monstrous cavalry moustache, arrived with the reinforcements from Regina. Fifty-two Mounted Policemen, thirty-four Prince Albert Volunteers, and a dozen or so additional whites and Métis now surrounded the bluff. This was overkill, and it was to reflect badly on the police – one hundred armed men and two cannons directed against three starving Indians, two of them mere youths. Yet the police had no choice; they might be condemned for the unequal odds, but this was not a football game. The Crees in the copse might be young, but they were killers and crack shots; if they were allowed to escape, the condemnation of the Force would be widespread; and, finally, lurking in the back of each man's mind, was the memory of Riel, Dumont, Poundmaker, and Big Bear.

The night was bitterly cold. A circle of bonfires ringed the bluff. Within, the Indians stripped the bodies of their victims to cover their own. They made several attempts to escape, but the cordon was too tight. They fired at the sentries; the sentries fired back. In the dark the watchers on the outside could hear branches being split and hacked.

Morning dawned, a bright, beautiful spring day, with just a smear of frost on the ground and the iridescent green of new growth tinting the countryside. At six, when the call to surrender went unanswered, the cannonade began. The nine-pound gun was placed seven hundred yards from the western end of the bluff, firing eastward. The smaller gun was six hundred yards to the north. Both guns fired for an hour, the shells ripping through the poplars and exploding in the willow tangle. At seven the seven pounder was moved up beside the Maxim. The silence within the trees was eerie. At nine, firing was resumed. The seven-pound gun lobbed twenty-five shells into the woods before it broke down. Altogether some fifty shells, most of them high-explosive shrapnel, tore into the bluff.

Shortly before ten, the firing ceased. The seven-pounder was out of action, its carriage demolished. Thirteen Maxim shells remained; McIllree decided to keep these for an emergency.

His orders were not to risk further lives by rushing the bluff. He proposed to dig a series of rifle pits through the poplars and to leapfrog his men from pit to pit under covering fire until the Indians were flushed out. For this purpose, he sent to Prince Albert for shovels and picks.

Now he was faced with the growing impatience of the undisciplined civilians, who were determined on a final act of machismo. Two men actually rushed the bluff, firing wildly, but retreated when they thought they heard return fire. McKenzie, the Indian agent, began to jeer at the police, saying that he and the other volunteers would send for women to do the job. The civilians grew more excited. A delegation informed McIllree that they intended to storm the bluff. He ordered them to desist, pointing out that they were special constables under police discipline and could be punished for disobeying orders. One man replied that he would be willing to serve a year in jail for the privilege of rushing the Indians. Others asked to be discharged on the spot. McIllree refused. Yet he realized he was losing control of the situation. More and more men were muttering that it was a farce that one hundred armed men could be held off by two or three natives. Somebody said that the Indians, who had been without food or water for three days, were cannibalizing the bodies of the men they had killed. This increased the tension. The volunteer force was rapidly degenerating into a mob.

McIllree was in a dilemma. He was a consummate policeman, a member of the original Force. He had been one of the first to join in 1873 and had led the first Mounted Police patrol in the North West. He knew that if any of the Indians was alive, some of these men would surely die. Yet what if all three were dead? Could any living thing have withstood that bombardment? He doubted it. And if they *were* dead and the police sat around for another night, cowed by three corpses, it would be in his words "a ghastly joke"; the Force would become a laughing stock.

At 2:30 that afternoon he gave in. He announced that they would rush the bluff and "there was pandemonium for a moment or two." Everyone wanted to go, and so the entire company was formed into a line and on the signal "Go!" raced to the poplars and, having gained the protection of the woods, began to fire. It was comic opera that came perilously close to tragedy. The line grew ragged. "It is a great wonder some one was not shot," McIllree reported. Some, indeed, thought the Indians were firing at them, but it was their own comrades, for all three Indians were dead. It took some time to inform the men, who were in such "a high pitch of excitement" that having rushed right through the bluff, they wanted to rush back again, firing as they went. McIllree managed to calm them down, then went himself to the rifle pit to identify the bodies.

All three had been dead for some time. The corpse of Standing-in-the-Sky, the thirteen-year-old Salteaux, dressed in Grundy's clothes, lay in a pit on top of that of Almighty Voice. A fragment of exploding shell had struck him in the head, killing him instantly. Almighty Voice had obviously been wounded the previous night from case shot, which had mangled his leg, the ball entering the front part of the thigh and tearing downward, smashing the kneecap. He had tied the wound up with a blanket, using the dead Kerr's revolver lanyard, and then made himself a crude crutch on which he had apparently tried to escape, for the crutch was found at the edge of the bluff. The following morning the top of his head was blown off by shellfire, probably by the same shrapnel that had killed his cousin. The corpse of Tupean, his nineteen-year-old brother-in-law, was found some distance away, clad in Constable Kerr's breeches and shot through the head. He had apparently been killed by a sentry during the night while trying to escape. In their thirst the three had attempted to dig for water in the pit, using a rifle butt, and then had stripped the green bark off some thirty aspens, to suck on the sap.

The end of Almighty Voice was pathetically unromantic. Yet his brief saga was such that it could scarcely fail, like that of Jesse James or William Bonney, to inspire legend. As the Toronto *Globe*, hardly a sympathetic newspaper, put it, "Almighty Voice was a bad Indian but he had the stuff in him of which heroes are made."

The reputation of the North West Mounted Police was not enhanced by the incident. They had got their man, but only at terrible sacrifice and only after the longest manhunt in their history – a manhunt that had used up more men, covered more miles, and cost more money than any other. Its dénouement was dark comedy. The Mountie image was that of the lone policeman riding fearlessly into an armed camp of restless braves to capture his man single-handed without bloodshed. But in the beautiful bare hills of the South Saskatchewan on that bright May Sunday, that image became a caricature.

No Indian was brought to book for shielding Almighty Voice from the law. John Sounding Sky was released for lack of evidence. Small Face, the Cree's last love, was delivered of a male child some time after his death. Bronco Jack Allan was invalided out of the Force. The two Venne brothers applied for, and eventually received, the five-hundred-dollar reward. The Indians on One Arrow's reserve were, according to the observations of both Inspector Wilson and agent McKenzie, relieved that the battle was over; they asked only to be left in peace, and so they were – to fend for themselves or starve on the reservation. As for the bluff – the bloody, battered bluff – it was eventually cut down and the earth ploughed into farmland.

Almighty Voice was the last of his kind. Sunday, May 30, 1897 stands as a watershed day in the history of the frontier for it marked the end of open warfare between whites and natives. The days were over when police or Indians could gallop freely over unfenced prairie, across empty, echoing valleys, and down trails that had not yet become roadways, fording wild rivers still unbridged, cantering in the lee of poplar bluffs, and mounting the ridges of beautiful bare hills that had never felt the bite of a cold steel plough. An era was ending, a new one dawning. On the steppes of Eastern Europe and along the muddy Danube, men in sheepskin coats were marching to the beat of Sifton's insistent drum. The human tide was on its way; the wild frontier was gone forever.

SOURCES AND ACKNOWLEDGMENTS

These seven stories were originally narrated by me on television in considerably simpler form. Six appeared on the half-hour *My Country* program, seen on the Global Television network and various independent stations. The seventh, the story of Wilfred Grenfell, was the subject of a one-hour CBC filmed documentary. For this book, however, a much greater depth of research was needed; my assistant, Barbara Sears, and I began again, using primary sources wherever possible. Five of these stories now contain information that has not been published before; in several instances, in fact, the new material has altered the thrust of the narrative. The other two narratives – those of Isaac Jogues and John Jewitt – are told from a viewpoint that differs from the conventional. This is especially true of my view of Jogues; new research into the Huron Indians has changed our attitude towards the Jesuit martyrs. In the Jewitt story, I have again tried to place more emphasis on the Indians and most especially on Maquinna, by far the most fascinating character in the tale.

I am indebted, as always, to Miss Sears, whose work has been invaluable. My relationship with Terence Macartney-Filgate, who produced and directed the Grenfell story on television, has been one of personal friendship, and I am grateful for all his help. A special word of thanks must go to Stan Horrall, the RCMP historian, whose dedication to and enthusiasm for the Force's history is legendary, and also to Carl Betke and Glen Gordon, both of the Force's historical section. A television credit roll would also include the names of my editor, Janet Craig; my secretary, Ennis Armstrong, and her assistant, Heather Lane; the producer of the *My Country* series, Elsa Franklin; its story editor, Janice Tyrwhitt; and Grace Campbell and David Smith of the Public Archives of

Canada. Charles Templeton was kind enough to read the manuscript and I benefited greatly from his advice. The comments of my wife, Janet, were pertinent as always, and her proofreading has been as impeccable as the unspeakable computers will allow.

The slavery of John Jewitt

The two primary sources for Jewitt's personal story are his *A Journal Kept at Nootka Sound*, originally published in 1807 and reprinted in Boston in 1931, and *The Adventures and Sufferings of John R. Jewitt, Captive Among the Nootka, 1803-1805* written in 1815 and republished in McClelland and Stewart's Carleton Library series in 1974. Primary background sources include John Meares's *Voyages Made in the Years 1788 and 1789 from China to the North West Coast of America . . .*, published in 1790; Captain George Vancouver's three-volume *A Voyage of Discovery to the North Pacific Ocean and Round the World . . .* (London, 1798); José Mariano Mozino's *Noticias de Nutka: An Account of Nootka Sound in 1792*, translated and edited by Iris Wilson (Seattle, 1970); Vol. 3, Part 2 of *The Journals of Captain James Cook . . .*, edited by J. C. Beaglehole (Cambridge, 1967); *James Strange's Journal and Narrative of the Commercial Expedition from Bombay to the North-West Coast of America . . .* (Madras, 1928); and Cecil Jane's translation of *A Spanish Voyage to Vancouver and the North-West Coast of America* by José Espinasa y Tello (London, 1930). My major secondary sources have been "The Later Life of John R. Jewitt," by Edmund S. Meany, Jr. (*British Columbia Historical Quarterly*, July, 1940); *The Northern and Central Nootkan Tribes*, by Philip Drucker (Washington, 1951); *Flood Tide of Empire: Spain and the Pacific Northwest, 1543-1819*, by Warren L. Cook (New Haven, 1973); *Peoples of the Coast: The Indians of the Pacific Northwest*, by George Woodcock, (Edmonton, 1977); and several articles by F. W. Howay, notably "The Spanish Settlement at Nootka" (*Washington Historical Quarterly*, July, 1917); "Early Days of the Maritime Fur-Trade on the Northwest Coast" (*Canadian Historical Review* 4, 1923); "Indian Attacks Upon Maritime Traders of the North-West Coast, 1785-1805" (*Canadian Historical Review,* 1925); and "An Outline Sketch of the Maritime Fur Trade" (Canadian Historical Association *Report*, 1932).

The adventures of Wilfred Grenfell

The major primary source for any study of Sir Wilfred Grenfell must be the Grenfell Papers, a fascinating and voluminous grab-bag of letters, documents, and clippings now at Yale University.

These documents, transcripts of which I have obtained through the kindness of Terence Macartney-Filgate and Catherine Orr of the Arts and Science Department of the Canadian Broadcasting Corporation, form the underpinning for the present essay. I am also grateful to Mr. Macartney-Filgate, who produced the CBC's documentary on Grenfell, for making available to me his transcripts of interviews with Wilfred Grenfell, Jr., and Dr. Theodore Badger. I wish also to thank Dr. Gordon W. Thomas for his many kindnesses to me during my stay in St. Anthony and the International Grenfell Association, which made it possible for me to fly up the Labrador coast to Indian Harbour and Hopedale. Of the published sources, the most valuable have been Grenfell's own *A Labrador Doctor* (Boston, 1919) and J. Lennox Kerr's *Wilfred Grenfell: His Life and Work* (Toronto, 1959), the official biography but also the best of several.

The saga of Sam Steele

Steele's own autobiography *Forty Years in Canada*, written shortly before his death, is a major source for anything written about the famous policeman. But the archives of the Royal Canadian Mounted Police and the Public Archives of Canada contain a wealth of information, never before published, which casts new light on Steele's ambitions, his frustrations with police politics, and his final downfall at the hands of Clifford Sifton. In addition to the police files, the papers of Sifton, Wilfrid Laurier, and John A. Macdonald have all proved useful, as have the files of the Dawson *News* and Klondike *Nugget*. My earlier researches into the Klondike stampede 1897-99 and the construction period of the Canadian Pacific Railway were invaluable. Much of the anecdotal material, which Steele was too modest to include in his own story, comes from the various sources I consulted when preparing the earlier works.

The martyrdom of Isaac Jogues

The major source for anyone writing about Father Jogues is "The Jogues Papers," published in the *Collections of the New York Historical Society*, Second Series, Vol. 3, Part 1 (New York, 1857) and also *The Jesuit Relations*, Vol. 28, edited by R. G. Thwaites (Cleveland, 1898). The best of several biographies is that of Francis X. Talbot, S.J., *Saint among Savages: the Life of Isaac Jogues* (New York, 1935). Francis Parkman's *The Jesuits in North America in the Seventeenth Century* (Boston, 1867) and John A. O'Brien's *The American Martyrs: the Story of the Eight Jesuit Martyrs of North*

America (New York, 1953) are leading secondary sources. I owe a very special debt to Bruce Trigger's brilliant two-volume history of the Huron people, *The Children of Aataentsic* (Montreal, 1976), a fascinating piece of anthropological and sociological detective work that helps to redress a long-standing historical imbalance. Also useful was Cornelius J. Jaenen's *Friend and Foe: Aspects of French-Amerindian Cultural Contact in the Sixteenth and Seventeenth Centuries* (Toronto, 1976) and Paul Le Blanc's "Indian Missionary Contact in Huronia, 1615-1649," published in *Ontario History*, June, 1968.

The odyssey of Cariboo Cameron

The major source for the story of John Alexander Cameron is his old friend Robert Stevenson, who told the story twice, in W. W. Walkem's *Stories of Early British Columbia* (Vancouver, 1914) and again in a long memoir in the Vancouver *Saturday Sunset* of April 3, 1909. Stevenson's diary of 1863 is in the Public Archives of British Columbia, together with a family history by Sandy Stevenson of Sardis, B.C.; two family memoirs, one by Cameron's nephew, Duncan Cameron, and the other by his grand-nephew, C. A. Cameron; another memoir by James Cummings; and an analysis of the Cameron holdings on Williams Creek. The files of both the *British Colonist*, Victoria, B.C., and the Cornwall *Freeholder* for the relevant years have been of inestimable value, providing material heretofore unpublished. I should also like to thank Mrs. Beatrice Elder, Ewan Ross, Doug Cameron, Jean Cameron, and Sister Mary Clair Macdonald for their assistance in piecing the story together, and Leigh Turner of the Barkerville Historic Site and Leonard C. DeLozier of the Public Archives of B.C. for their help.

The revenge of Mina Hubbard

There are six main sources for this tangled tale: three diaries in the Public Archives of Canada, those of Leonidas Hubbard Jr., his widow, Mina Hubbard, and their guide, George Elson, and three books: *The Lure of the Labrador Wild*, by Dillon Wallace (New York, 1905), *The Long Labrador Trail*, also by Wallace (New York, 1907), and Mrs. Hubbard's *A Woman's Way Through Unknown Labrador* (New York, 1908). Also useful were the files of *Outing* magazine for the period, especially Caspar Whitney's article in the March, 1905, issue, "The Leonidas Hubbard, Jun., Expedition into Labrador" and two articles in the *Beaver*: "A Woman's Way," by Alan Cooke (Summer, 1960) and "Dillon Wallace of Labrador," by R. G. Mauro (Summer, 1975). I would like to thank Mr. Mauro for allowing me the use of several of the Wallace papers and also Edgar Benson, Elizabeth Goudie, W. G. Brittain and Sheila Grover for their contributions to the tale.

The legend of Almighty Voice

There is an enormous volume of secondary material on the story of the renegade Cree, but, for reasons indicated in my text, I have preferred to ignore it in favour of archival sources that have rarely, and in some instances never, been consulted. Yet few incidents in Canadian frontier history have been more heavily documented. The files of the Indian department and of the North West Mounted Police in the Public Archives of Canada are voluminous and are supported by further documentation in the RCMP's own archives. Post letterbooks, patrol reports, inquest affidavits, telegrams, letters, diaries, biographical material, and eyewitness accounts are all available. In addition, we have consulted the contemporary newspapers: the Regina *Standard*, the Qu'Appelle *Vidette*, the Saskatchewan *Herald*, and two Toronto newspapers that sent reporters to the final scene, the *Globe* and the *Evening Telegram*. I have also made some use of three later memoirs: those of John B. Allan in *Scarlet and Gold* for 1922 and 1924, of C. C. Raven in *Scarlet and Gold* for 1940, and of Prosper John, Almighty Voice's younger brother, interviewed by H. S. M. Kemp in the RCMP quarterly of July, 1957. Ronald Atkin's history of the force, *Maintain the Right* (Toronto, 1973), was the most useful of several similar works consulted.

INDEX

INDEX

Mina Hubbard
George Elson
Leonidas Hubbard Jr.
Dillon Wallace